THE UNITED STATES AND MEXICO

Patterns of Influence

George W. Grayson

PRAEGER SPECIAL STUDIES • PRAEGER SCIENTIFIC

New York • Philadelphia • Eastbourne, UK
Toronto • Hong Kong • Tokyo • Sydney

Library of Congress Cataloging in Publication Data

Grayson, George W., 1938-
    Patterns of influence.

    (Studies of influence in international relations)
    Bibliography: p.
    Includes index.
    1. United States—Foreign relations—Mexico.   2. Mexico
—Foreign relations—United States.   I. Title.
II. Series.
El83.8.M6G78   1984   327.73072   83-24514
ISBN 0-03-061584-4 (alk. paper)
ISBN 0-03-061586-0 (pbk.)

Published in 1984 by Praeger Publishers
CBS Educational and Professional Publishing,
a Division of CBS Inc.
521 Fifth Avenue, New York, NY 10175 USA

456789 052 987654321

Printed in the United States of America
on acid-free paper

THE UNITED STATES
AND MEXICO

STUDIES OF INFLUENCE IN INTERNATIONAL RELATIONS

Alvin Z. Rubinstein, *General Editor*

To Kathleen Green Burruss
In appreciation of her loving kindness
to me and our family

Relations between the United States and Mexico have come of age. In the interests of friendship and a constructive approach to difficult problems, the relationship must be very different from that of the past, when the United States was often a covetous neighbor, rather than a good one. The realization in both countries of a need for basic changes in attitude and approach is a welcome first step. But, as this sensible and comprehensive analysis emphasizes, old suspicions, divergent national policies and perceptions, disparities in power and wealth, and dissimilar cultural values will put official professions of goodwill to severe tests in the years ahead.

This book is both assessment and agenda. Its special value derives from the analysis of the key issues in the Mexican-U.S. relationship: trade and investment, oil and natural gas, immigration, and Central America. Economically, the United States is Mexico's principal partner; Mexico is the United States' third most important trading partner, and its enormous untapped reservoirs of oil and natural gas foreshadow ever-increasing interdependence. The problems become especially politically explosive when considered in conjunction with awesome demographic projections: Mexico's population, which has grown from 20 million in 1945 to 75 million in 1983, is expected to exceed 120 million by the turn of the century. Already beset by large-scale unemployment and underemployment and poorly endowed with natural resources other than oil and natural gas, Mexico's safety valve lies in massive illegal immigration to the United States, whose uneasiness over such an influx may well make the immigration issue the litmus test of Mexican-U.S. relations in the future.

In foreign affairs, Mexico's policy toward Cuba, Central America, and the entire spectrum of North-South issues, differs markedly from that of the United States. Recent Mexican presidents, spurred by high expectations arising from petropower and ambitions to play a leading role on the international scene, staked out independent positions, which served also to nurture a deep sense of Mexican nationalism.

Apart from the specifics of any issue, be it Cuba, Nicaragua, El Salvador, or Granada, every Mexican government has been determined not to be an echo of the United States in world affairs. In spite of Washington's erratic oscillations from inducements to indifference, Mexico has maintained close relations with Castro's Cuba (it was the only Latin American country not to rupture diplomatic ties in the 1960s), upheld the Sandinista regime, mounted initiatives for a solution that goes contrary to U.S. preferences on El Salvador, and enthusiastically supported proposals for hemispheric cooperation that were not always welcomed by Washington. So sensitive is the Mexican leadership to any hint of U.S. influence that it refused to permit the Peace Corps to operate in the country.

As Professor George Grayson explains, though Mexico speaks defiantly in public to emphasize its independence of the United States, when confronted with an issue that a U.S. president considers nonnegotiable, it will usually accommodate out of regard for the overall relationship. But Mexico's penchant for independence also determined its unique reluctance among third world countries to affiliate with the Nonaligned Movement.

The frustrations inherent in assessing influence in various sectors of the U.S.-Mexican relationship are understandable once we have read Professor Grayson's informative, insightful study. He writes eloquently and forthrightly, with compassion and dispassion, of the many links that bind and sometimes pain Mexico and the United States. He identifies the formal components of issues and illumines the informal patterns that define Mexico's distinctive political and decision-making system. His revealing vignettes of Mexican leaders and their meetings with U.S. counterparts are capsule commentaries on an eristic relationship.

The policy-oriented character of Professor Grayson's book gives it particular importance at this time. It probes more deeply than other works on the subject into the realm of high politics and diplomacy, deftly balancing personalities, bureaucratic and domestic considerations, and regional developments, and shedding new light on critical issues. This major contribution to our understanding of Mexican-U.S. relations should prove of great value to those concerned with the future of our two countries. *The United States and Mexico* is a distinguished addition to the Praeger series Studies of Influence in International Relations.

Alvin Z. Rubinstein
University of Pennsylvania

ACKNOWLEDGMENTS

The United States' relationship to Mexico is more crucial to its vital interests than any of its other bilateral ties, with the possible exception of those with the Soviet Union. Although Mexico has attempted to diversify its international contacts in recent years, the United States remains paramount in its foreign affairs. Oil and natural gas production, trade, migration, and civil strife in Central America are the most important of scores of issues in which the two countries, which share the second longest undefended border in the world, are continuously concerned. The interests of the two nations often diverge, leading each to attempt to influence the other's behavior. This book focuses on past, present, and prospective patterns of influence between the United States and Mexico.

The idea for analyzing these patterns of influence sprang from Professor A. Z. Rubinstein of the University of Pennsylvania, who serves as General Editor for Praeger's Studies of Influence in International Relations. Not only did he fashion the theoretical foundation on which this volume is constructed, but his painstaking reading of the manuscript also enriched the style of the edifice, while improving the quality of its substance. Throughout the project, he consistently provided the author with unobtrusive encouragement, intellectual stimulation, and creative patience. For this extraordinary assistance, I am in his debt.

For invaluable comments on portions of the manuscript, I also want to thank Judith Ewell, Alan J. Ward, and John Peterson, colleagues at the College of William and Mary; Marvin Alisky of Arizona State University; David Scott Palmer of the Foreign Service Institute and the School of Advanced International Studies of the Johns Hopkins University; Ing. Walter Friedeberg M., formerly production manager for Petróleos Mexicanos and now a member of the engineering faculty of the National Autonomous University of Mexico; Stephen Lande, formerly the chief negotiator with Mexico in the U.S. Office of Special Trade Representative and now vice-president of Manchester Associates, Ltd.; and Robert A. Pastor, formerly a specialist on Latin America for the National Security Council and now associated with the University of Maryland's School of Public Affairs.

Moreover, I am indebted to approximately three dozen British, Canadian, French, Mexican, and U.S. officials whose lengthy, off-the-record interviews contributed greatly to my understanding of the subject at hand. I only regret that the sensitivity of their positions prevents my individually naming these outstanding public servants. Discussions with 20 U.S. trade unionists, who also wish to remain anonymous, further benefited this study.

A number of the ideas found in the concluding chapter were first expressed in a paper, "Mexico: The Politics of Petrolization and Devaluation," presented on October 13, 1982, as a part of the International Energy Seminar Series of the Johns Hopkins Foreign Policy Institute. I appreciate Wilfrid Kohl, the series' moderator, having invited me to take part in the proceedings.

Years consumed in preparing a manuscript also create obligations of a financial nature. The College of William and Mary, through its Faculty Research Committee and Department of Government, awarded funds that facilitated two of the four research trips made to Mexico while writing this volume.

My thanks go to Robert L. Quinan, Jr., and Marsha Pearcy, William and Mary students, who diligently assisted with research and proofreading; and to Brenda Wrightington, Vicki Sprigg, Teresa McCoy, Wanda Carter, and Laura Terrell, who with cheerfulness and forbearance typed the manuscript.

Dr. Carmen Brissette Grayson, a superb historian whose intelligence, curiosity, erudition, good humor, and sensitivity have made her an exceptional marital and intellectual companion for 20 years, furnished trenchant insights, suggestions, and criticisms that sharpened my thinking about the subject matter. Our children, Gisèle and Keller, generously permitted their dad evenings at the office to complete "that book," while making his breaks from the typewriter an unalloyed joy.

With all of the assistance received, it goes without saying that the shortcomings of this study are my own.

George W. Grayson
Williamsburg, Virginia

CONTENTS

LIST OF TABLES

Table

THE UNITED STATES AND MEXICO

1

THE MEANING AND
ASSESSMENT OF INFLUENCE

Even before his inauguration, Ronald Reagan made history with respect to U.S.-Mexican relations. Although several prospective Mexican chief executives had visited the United States, Reagan became the first U.S. president-elect to journey to Mexico. On January 5, 1981, he crossed the Bridge of Friendship spanning the Rio Grande to meet José López Portillo. Warm *abrazos* opened a 70-minute session highlighted by a luncheon in Ciudad Juárez's mushroom-shaped Museum of Art and History.

Leaders of the two countries have come face to face 25 times since Porfirio Díaz and William Howard Taft met in 1909. Yet North American affirmations of good neighborliness have often sounded like vapid rhetoric to Mexicans who have gained the impression that they were really considered poor and distant relations. Thus, the symbolism of Reagan's initiative encouraged many Mexicans to believe that, at last, their country was being accorded the treatment they deemed proper to its status in the hierarchy of nations. After all, the president-elect had admitted a historical tendency on the part of his nation's leaders "to talk too much and listen too little." He expressed his readiness "to listen more carefully" to what the Mexicans had to say. ¡Magnífico! was López Portillo's response to such sentiments, while Mexico's foreign minister characterized the meeting as a "complete success." They were also heartened by a joint communiqué, acknowledging that the bilateral "relationship is based on mutual respect and reciprocal understanding." Such language recognizes Mexico's insistence on "a worthy place standing erect in the world and not a seat in a sphere of influence."[1] A writer for the *Washington Post* succinctly, if romantically, described the factors that underlie such aspirations:

> Although its leaders refrain from calling Mexico a "power," its size, its population, its location and now its oil have made it just that in the region—a new major power, at least in local terms, capable of challenging and in some cases already competing directly with the United States.[2]

It is clear, therefore, that many Mexicans and North Americans believe that the U.S.-Mexican relationship has been transformed in recent years.

This book examines the changing influence and power relations between the United States and Mexico, with emphasis on the twentieth century. As a working definition, influence is demonstrated when either country affects through nonmilitary means, directly or indirectly, the behavior of the other in a manner designed to achieve a policy advantage. Essential to diplomacy and the interactions of sovereign states is the attempt by some nations to induce others to follow or turn away from certain courses of action, to enter into accords, make concessions, or otherwise subordinate their policies. Of course, no influence is involved when the two countries have coincidental interests or when the policy reached is one that the supposedly influenced country would have taken on its own.

A semantic problem arises because the phenomenon of influence is both a process and a product. As defined above, influence is a process; on the other hand, what is actually observed and assessed is the net result of this process, and that is also termed influence.[3] Both process and product shall be the subject of inquiry in succeeding chapters.

Influence may be considered a derivative of power, with power defined as a nation's relative capability in terms of human, geographic, economic, technological, military, cultural, and ideological resources complemented by the will to use these resources in a specific way. But the two concepts should not be confused: influence is situational, manifest, and short-lived; power is general, latent, continuing, and relative. With respect to the last point, it could be argued that the military resources of France remained virtually unchanged between 1929 and 1939; however, Germany grew increasingly stronger. As one scholar has observed: "Influence is the successful use of power, and power is to international relations what energy is to physics, or money to the economy—the mediator of in-teractions."[4] In broad terms, it may be stated that the opportunity to exert influence stems from the inequality of power between two states. President Jimmy Carter learned to his dismay that the posses-sion of power does not assure the exertion of influence. Influence also depends on the issue involved, its importance to one or both parties, and the willingness to absorb necessary costs in pursuing or resisting the application of power. That the United States is a giant and Iran a dwarf in almost every power category did not enable the former to secure the release of 52 hostages until 444 days had elapsed. Simi-larly, Presidents Carter and Reagan have had limited success in influ-encing the Sandinista regime in Nicaragua, a country that the United States once easily manipulated with threats, money, and the Ma-rines. Alvin Z. Rubinstein has termed the limited ability of super-powers to exercise influence at a time when they possess awesome military and economic power "the great paradox of the second half of the twentieth century."[5]

Even amid frequent disagreements, Mexicans and North Ameri-cans recognize the discrepancy in power between their two coun-tries. The United States boasts a land mass (3,615,123 square miles) over four times greater than Mexico's (761,601), a population (226.5 million) that is significantly larger (75 million), and a gross domestic product ($3,012 billion) that far eclipses that of its southern neighbor ($239 billion). United States-Mexican commerce is only 4 or 5 per-cent of total U.S. foreign trade, but approximately two-thirds of that of Mexico. Mexican investment in the United States is trivial; in con-trast, U.S. firms, often dominant in leading economic sectors, have invested $6.4 billion in Mexico, a figure that represents only 4 per-cent of overall national investment but 72 percent of total foreign investment in the Mexican economy.[6] The United States also sur-passes Mexico with respect to average number of school years com-pleted by its citizens, the mean quantity of calories consumed, life-expectancy rates, the size and equipment of its armed forces, and the richness and diversity of its technology. Like Premier Pierre Elliott Trudeau of Canada, a Mexican chief executive might candidly speak of his country's uneasiness as the position of a mouse in bed with an elephant.

Throughout most of the nineteenth and twentieth centuries, the difference in power capabilities gave rise to enormous U.S. influence over Mexican behavior. Arrogance and contempt often attended this domination. As once explained by Philander C. Knox, President Taft's secretary of state, U.S. naval vessels patrolled the Gulf Coast to keep the Mexicans "in a salutary equilibrium, between a dangerous and exaggerated apprehension and a proper degree of wholesome fear."[7] Early in the revolution that exploded in Mexico in 1910, U.S. Ambassador Henry Lane Wilson openly meddled in Mexican affairs to secure the kind of government that he perceived would advance the interests of his country and, specifically, the financial barons whom he revered. In the face of rising unemployment following the Korean War, the U.S. Immigration and Naturalization Service (INS) launched the paramilitary "Operation Wetback" to capture and return to Mexico illegal workers. The United States would never have tolerated draconian searches and large-scale expulsions by the Mexican government to return U.S. citizens unlawfully living in Mexico. As late as 1975, senior officials of the U.S. Environmental Protection Agency approved a plan to use Mexican rather than U.S. citizens as guinea pigs in evaluating the effects on the human thyroid of massive doses of fungicides known to cause cancer in animals. The experiment, to be undertaken in a Mexico City hospital, was cancelled at the last minute due to what newspapers called an "administrative fluke."[8] The asymmetry in influence and power makes unthinkable the use of Americans as subjects of medical tests conceived by Mexican scientists and carried out in the United States.

The gap in power capacities notwithstanding, it is erroneous to assume that the United States can still readily influence Mexican behavior on any issue of importance to Mexican leaders. While conspicuously less industrialized than the United States, Mexico has averaged a 6 percent growth in GNP since the end of World War II, as its economy, which currently ranks tenth on the United Nations' index of industrial production, has become more diversified and sophisticated. Despite awesome problems in the early 1980s, this "economic miracle" has vaulted Mexico to the forefront of the so-called developing countries, making it a prime candidate for regional and even international leadership.

Meanwhile, a confluence of factors has attenuated the hegemonic position once enjoyed by the United States in the western hemisphere.[9] Traditional elites friendly to Washington have been replaced in many countries of the region by modern technocrats, whose nationalism leads them to seek independence from—and, sometimes, confrontation with—the United States. Such elites have often joined with their counterparts in other areas of the third world to oppose U.S. initiatives in the United Nations, the United Nations Conference on Trade and Development, UNCTAD, the Organization of American States, commodity cartels, and other international bodies. In security terms, Cuba's existence as a communist nation just 90 miles from Florida has given Soviet vessels ready access to the Caribbean Sea—once considered a "U.S. lake." In the economic sphere, the resurgence of Western Europe and Japan following World War II has enabled their trade with Latin American countries to multiply at the expense of the latter's commerce with the United States. Meanwhile, East European and selected developing states are also expanding their commercial activities within the region. On the U.S. domestic front, the post-Vietnam growth of opposition to high-handed or interventionist policies toward Mexico and other poorer countries has limited the options available to Washington policy-makers, particularly in the freewheeling deployment of the Central Intelligence Agency (CIA). Additional debilitating problems at home arising from the 1973 and 1979 energy crises, chronic unemployment, and economic stagnation have further circumscribed U.S. action in foreign affairs. Finally, the emergence of Hispanics as the second-fastest growing minority in the United States has provided Latin America in general and Mexico in particular with lobbying groups that endorse fairness, generosity, and compassion in U.S. dealings with countries south of the Rio Grande. Mexican-Americans or Chicanos have focused their attention on immigration, civil rights, and the *maquiladora* program, whereby U.S. companies operate plants on both sides of the border.[10]

Above all, the discovery of new oil and gas deposits has lofted Mexico's standing among nations. With the prices of petroleum, natural gas, uranium, and coal having shot up dramatically in recent years, it is obvious that the possession of energy reserves enhances a country's power, influence, and independence. Such was not the case early in this century, when entrepreneurs first discovered commercial quantities of oil in Mexico. The vital holdings served as a magnet, attracting ruthless profit seekers, avaricious transnational firms, and the diplomats and soldiers of industrialized countries. Once these foreigners had wheedled, bribed, intimidated, and coerced local politicians and their praetorian guards, the resources fell under the sway of outsiders, offending the dignity and attenuating the sovereignty of the possessing state.

That kind of control is a thing of the past. The hydrocarbon deposits enjoyed by Mexico during its current oil boom are identified, lifted, priced, and marketed by Mexicans in accordance with their country's stated goals.

Mexico's announcement of Mideast-sized oil holdings coincided with increasing energy imports by the United States and soaring oil prices. The upshot has been an intense interest in Mexico on the part of U.S. policymakers, which has prompted attempts by the Carter and Reagan administrations to ingratiate themselves with their oil-endowed neighbor.

This new attentiveness toward Mexico has not always produced agreement on major policy matters. Following an overview of U.S.-Mexican relations and an analysis of foreign policy demarches by President Luis Echeverría Alvarez, chapters will be presented on issues where the two countries have exhibited notable differences: the marketing of oil and gas, policy toward Central America and Cuba, Mexico's proposed entry into the General Agreement on Tariffs and Trade (GATT), the illegal immigration of Mexicans to the United States, and the forging of a stabilization program for Mexico, supervised by the International Monetary Fund. No Rosetta stone exists for deciphering influence, a concept that is easier to discuss than measure. While admitting the impossibility of avoiding hollow, unsubstantiated generalities, an effort will be made in these chapters to determine factors that have led one country either to modify its behavior in a manner congenial to the other, or to resist the entreaties of its supplicating neighbor. In attempting to determine why a given policy outcome occurred, special attention will be paid to the following questions:

- Did the sovereignty of one or both countries appear to be undermined?
- Was the president's honor or reputation at stake?
- What was the position of the United States at the beginning of negotiations? This is an important consideration in light of the defensive and reactive character of Mexican foreign policy.
- Was there cohesion among key constituencies affected by the decision?
- Was either country attempting to project its influence in the region?
- Was either country's economic viability in question?

A number of problems arise in attempting to analyze influence patterns between the United States and Mexico. First, the theory of the third world's dependency on industrialized nations suffuses academic and journalistic writing in Mexico, with the result that one Mexican group or another sees a U.S. hand in nearly every action affecting their country. In a biography of Louis XI, Paul Kendall described the political and diplomatic machinations among the medieval states of the Italian peninsula in language that invites comparisons with contemporary U.S.-Mexican relations:

> The smallest gesture, subjected to elaborate analysis, became a menace; the slightest fortuity, studied with unrelenting minuteness, was turned into a dangerous portent. The face of Italian politics was scrutinized at claustrophobically close range: the twitch of a cheek, tremor of a lip, a slide of eyeball assumed significance, probably sinister. . . . Within this closed space, statecraft had become capable of everything but statesmanship; subtlety of calculation able to master all political mathematics except harmony.[11]

Indeed, U.S. actions and inactions are scrutinized "at claustrophobically close range" by politicians, parties, professors, newspapers, and others in Mexico who then continually assign significance to "the twitch of a cheek, tremor of a lip, [or] a slide of eyeball." Publicity often focuses on government agencies such as the CIA or U.S.-based multinational corporations as the presumed agents of intervention whose actions are ubiquitous and omnipotent. Seldom is evidence considered a necessary prerequisite to leveling such charges. For instance, in mid-1980 Mexican officials and newspapers had a field day accusing the United States of stealing rain by diverting hurricanes from Mexico's shores. The villain was the U.S. National Oceanographic and Atmospheric Administration, whose hurricane-hunter aircraft had allegedly intercepted a storm named "Ignacio" off Mexico's Pacific coast in October 1979, thereby contributing to the country's worst drought in 20 years. Mexican observers, including the director of the country's National Meteorological Service, apparently believed that Yankee ingenuity was so great that Uncle Sam could bend Mother Nature to his will.[12]

The United States also represents a convenient scapegoat. Amid the 1982 economic crisis that was largely of his own making, President José López Portillo appealed to his country not to stand with open arms and allow Mexico to be bled dry, gutted, and eaten away. He said that "their nation cannot work and be organized only to have its life blood drained off by the gravitational pull of the colossus of the north."[13]

Second, there is the problem of the great number of private, highly specific, day-to-day contacts and exchanges by state and local governments, as well as by corporations, trade unions, churches, and other private parties. That the majority of these interactions fall outside the purview of the respective national governments greatly impedes the monitoring of influence. Indeed, some voluntary organizations appear committed to undermining the role of the respective national governments. A case in point is the Organization of United States Border Cities and Counties, a key objective of which is "to inveigle both countries' Federal governments into granting limited treatymaking power to local administrations in the border area, to enable them to function more effectively."[14] This situation has prompted the comment that "relations between the Soviet Union and the United States are easier to manage than those between Mexico and the United States."[15]

Third, such monitoring is further complicated by the large cast of public actors who participate in the drama of bilateral relations. For example, with respect to the U.S. government alone, energy questions involve the departments of State, Energy, Defense, Treasury, Commerce, and Health and Human Resources, as well as the Office of Management and Budget, the CIA, the Export-Import Bank, and the Office of the Special Trade Representative. Moreover, federal agencies have different, often competing objectives. Undoubtedly, the Pentagon has among its many contingency options a plan for invading Mexico. Yet, dispatching troops south of the Rio Grande is as alien a thought to the State Department as a Mayan temple would be in Foggy Bottom.

Fourth, influence is often difficult to identify because it would be political suicide for a Mexican leader to admit he had acted in response to pressure from the United States. As will be seen, Washington's advocacy of Mexico's affiliation with GATT led Mexicans to infer that such a move would be beneficial to the United States and, hence, adverse to the well-being of their country. This sensitivity toward U.S. interference was epitomized by the recent opening in Mexico City of a National Museum of Interventions, which highlights indignities suffered by Mexico at the hands of its North American neighbors.[16]

Fifth, the Mexican government's preferred negotiating and diplomatic style works against the discovery of successful efforts to exert influence. Generally speaking, the State Department and other U.S.

agencies charged with fashioning policy prefer to deal with issues individually, reducing them to their technical aspects. Even though blurred lines of authority and bureaucratic rivalries may require creation of intra-agency task forces to coordinate policymaking, it is normally possible to fathom this process within the U.S. government. However, centralized decisionmaking in Mexico contributes to what has been called "closet diplomacy."[17] In the foreign-policy field, Mexicans prefer to establish personal contacts with high-level U.S. officials. Their goals are to nurture a mutual confidence, engage in unpublicized, informal discussion, and seek solutions to a number of issues affecting bilateral relations. In so doing, they make it difficult for observers to comprehend what is going on. A major problem in assessing influence is that the less conspicuous both pressure and moral suasion are, the more likely they are to be truly influential.

Sixth, even though enjoying more freedom than is found in most third world countries, Mexico's press is beset by corruption—with many reporters and columnists for allegedly objective publications in the pay of individual politicians, government agencies, or special interests. Until 1968, when Julio Scherer García became executive publisher of *Excelsior*, the nation's most influential newspaper, a prominent politician could buy a front-page story lauding himself for $8,000.[18] Scherer subsequently lost his post after crossing swords with confidants of President Luis Echeverría Alvarez, a master at manipulating the media. Government entities possess special funds to pay reporters assigned to cover their activities. Such covert payments, known as *igualas*, should not be confused with *gacetillas*, stipends given to editors or reporters to carry specific stories in the news columns of their publications.[19] The government's ability to shape what appears in print prompted political scientist Evelyn P. Stevens to comment:

> To read a Mexican newspaper is to venture onto a factual desert in the midst of an ideological hailstorm. Headlines scream, news stories below, and columnists and cartoonists belabor "enemies of the revolution" with sledgehammer sarcasm.[20]

While attention to bilateral affairs by the U.S. and Mexican press is growing, the limited nature of such coverage serves as an obstacle to understanding who is influencing whom on key questions. The United Press International, the Associated Press, Reuters, and the Knight-Ridder and Cox chains serve as sources of information, as do *Time, Newsweek*, and the three major television networks. Yet, of the 1,745 daily newspapers in the United States, only seven have Mexican bureaus, and these often serve countries of Central America and the Caribbean as well.[21] Only three Mexican newspapers—*Excelsior, El Día*, and *Unomásuno*—have full-time reporters in the United States, although *El Heraldo* employs a stringer and Televisa, the Spanish-language television network, also provides coverage.

Finally, one of the indicators of influence most salient to Professor Rubinstein and other theorists of the subject is foreign aid.[22] Nationalistic pride prevents Mexico's receiving Peace Corps volunteers or overtly seeking loans and grants from the U.S. Agency for International Development, even though AID does respond effectively to largely unpublicized Mexican requests for technical and material assistance, particularly in the area of family planning. Moreover, the 1982 economic crisis gave rise to the shipment to Mexico of $1.7 billion in farm products, payment for which was guaranteed by the U.S. Department of Agriculture. The reluctance to admit, much less publicize, the receipt of U.S. assistance, makes it difficult for analysts of Mexican affairs to study one of the more visible means by which one nation attempts to influence another.

Scholars and journalists have evinced fascination for the "Iran analogy," that is, the belief that Mexico may be buffeted by the same forces that overturned the shah's regime in Iran, including mobilization of the masses, militant anti-Americanism, and social revolution. In view of the growing popularity of such comparisons, a judgment will be made in the final chapter as to the validity of the analogy.

A brief history of U.S.-Mexican relations introduces this book.

NOTES

1. For the text of this communiqué, see the *New York Times*, January 6, 1981, p. A-8.

2. *Washington Post*, January 6, 1981, p. A-13.

3. The theoretical discussion in this chapter profits greatly from Alvin Z. Rubinstein (ed.), *Soviet and Chinese Influence in the Third World* (New York: Praeger, 1975), pp. 1–18.

4. Robert Wesson, *The United States and Brazil: Limits of Influence* (New York: Praeger, 1981), p. 1.

5. Alvin Z. Rubinstein in Wesson, *The United States and Brazil*, p. v.

6. These figures, provided by the American Chamber of Commerce in Mexico, were published in *Excelsior*, February 16, 1980.

7. Howard F. Cline, *The United States and Mexico* (New York: Atheneum, 1965), p. 155.

8. *Washington Post*, May 11, 1977, pp. A-1, A-7.

9. The following material benefits from A. F. Lowenthal and A. Fishlow, *Latin America's Emergence: Toward a U.S. Response* (New York: Foreign Policy Association, Headline Series, 243, 1979), pp. 22–26, and Bruce Bagley, "Mexico in the 1980's: A New Regional Power," *Current History* 80, No. 469 (November 1981): 353–54.

10. Peter T. Flawn, "A Regional Perspective," in Richard D. Erb and Stanley R. Ross (eds.), *U.S. Policies toward Mexico: Perceptions and Perspectives* (Washington, D.C.: American Enterprise Institute for Public Policy Research, 1979), p. 33.

11. *Louis XI: The Universal Spider* (New York: Norton, 1970), pp. 333–34.

12. The U.S. embassy claimed that flights into the storm, which had been authorized by the Mexican government, were made only to record Ignacio's temperature and other vital signs. Without contradicting this explanation, Foreign Minister Castañeda barred U.S. hurricane-hunters from Mexican airstrips during the summer until a thorough investigation of the matter was completed. See the *Washington Post*, July 7, 1980, pp. A-1, A-12.

13. *Daily Report (Latin America)*, November 2, 1982, p. V-1.

14. "A Tepid 'Abrazo': A Review of U.S.-Mexican Relations," *Latin American Times*, No. 54 (October 1983): 7.

15. Susan Kaufman Purcell, "Mexico-U.S. Relations: Big Initiative Can Cause Big Problems," *Foreign Affairs* 60, No. 2 (Winter 1981–82): 380.

16. *Washington Post*, December 28, 1981, p. A-28.

17. David Ronfeldt and Caesar Sereseres, "Immigration Issues Affecting U.S.-Mexican Relations," paper presented to the Brookings Institution-El Colegio de México Symposium on Structural Factors Contributing to Current Patterns of Migration in Mexico and the Caribbean Basin, Washington, D.C., June 28–30, 1978, p. 9.

18. Marvin Alisky, *Latin American Media: Guidance and Censorship* (Ames: Iowa State University Press, 1981), pp. 40–41.

19. Alisky, *Latin American Media*, p. 35.

20. *Protest and Response in Mexico* (Cambridge, Mass.: MIT Press, 1974), p. 30.

21. These are the *New York Times, Washington Post, Wall Street Journal, Los Angeles Times, Dallas Times Herald, Dallas Morning News,* and the *Miami Herald*.

22. Rubinstein, *Soviet and Chinese Influence in the Third World*, p. 14.

2

HISTORY OF
U.S.-MEXICAN RELATIONS

POST-INDEPENDENCE PERIOD

At the time of its independence from Spain in 1821, Mexico was similar to the United States in several power capabilities. Thanks to the Louisiana Purchase of 1803 and the Transcontinental Treaty of 1819, the United States had doubled its area from 890,000 square miles at the time of its own independence to 1.788 million square miles. For its part, Mexico boasted 1.710 million square miles, not counting the disputed Oregon territory. The advantage of the United States was only slightly more pronounced in population size. In 1810 it had 7.2 million people compared to Mexico's 6.1 million. Moreover, during the 1820s both nations earmarked about half of their budgeted expenditures for the military.[1]

These superficial comparisons mask profound social, economic, and cultural differences between the neighboring countries. Mexico emerged from a Hispano-Arabic and Indian heritage that emphasized religious orthodoxy, militarism, personalism, fatalism, centralism, hierarchical control, a manipulative attitude toward law, and the importance of leisure over work. In contrast, the United States inherited English traditions—nourished by the Reformation and the Enlightenment that had barely affected Spain—that stressed religious tolerance, civilian control of the military, aggressive competition, the importance of work, exaltation of technology and capitalism, respect for law, and an orientation toward the future.[2] Distinct outlooks preordained distinct development paths. Further, the

United States separated itself from England with governmental machinery and political rules of the game embraced by the majority of influential citizens. The question of institution-building resolved, its people's energies could be focused on economic development and territorial expansion. In contrast, Mexico's 11-year struggle for independence (1810 to 1821) left the country politically rent, economically debilitated, and burdened by the political domination of churchmen, landowners, and militarists. The armies and revolutionaries who had mauled each other during this conflict devastated the agricultural and mining sectors, which were crucial to the colonial economy. Mexico resembled the newly independent nations of the mid-twentieth century inasmuch as it was beset by instability, low productivity, capital flight, budget deficits, and foreign indebtedness. Economic distress and foreign invasions contributed to Mexico's victimization by predatory ex-generals from the wars of independence. During its first half-century of independence, over 50 governments rose and fell as 30 different men served as president. Sixteen men headed 22 governments during one 15-year period alone.[3] The most contemptible of these men was Antonio López de Santa Anna, "a cryptic, mercurial, domineering military chieftain," who captured the presidency nine times between 1833 and 1855.[4] During this time, his name became synonymous with treachery, intrigue, and betrayal.

Mexico's dilemma was that of a politically divided, economically hobbled, and territorially defensive nation suffused by values that impeded unification and development, living cheek by jowl with a unified, productive, and expansionist neighbor. Some U.S. leaders viewed with hope the independence of Mexico and other Latin American nations. Here were prospective allies, optimists believed, joined to the United States by the ideals of the Enlightenment, in confronting Old World monarchies. Such idealism may have been more rhetorical than real; the U.S. government discouraged a plan in 1825 by Mexico and Venezuela to free Cuba, because Washington self-interestedly preferred that the island be held by Spain, not Great Britain, into whose hands it might have fallen. Moreover, the enunciation of the Monroe Doctrine demonstrated that the United States would be the dominant party in any partnership with Latin American nations. In addition, Washington's failure to act when Spain (1829) and France (1838) invaded Mexico indicated that the doctrine's lofty principles would be applied selectively, if at all. By the early 1830s, any optimism in the United States had

faded as noble constitutions were denigrated by the actions of unscrupulous generals-turned-politicians. "Dictators like Antonio López de Santa Anna seemed to be at best slight improvements over the
Bourbon kings or Iturbide I. Ignorance, fanaticism, and military
despotism still prevailed over political freedom, civil rights, and general toleration."[5] Obtaining independence from Spain had changed
little in Mexico's social, economic, and political order.

The two countries collided over Texas, originally a northeast
province linked to the Mexican state of Coahuila into which colonists, most of whom were enterprising and aggressive slave-owning
cotton planters from the United States, had been invited to settle.
Despite having sworn allegiance to Mexico, both English-speaking
and Mexican settlers resented interference in their affairs from Mexico City as they spurred the economic development of what had once
seemed a remote and unproductive wasteland. In 1819 the United
States had renounced its questionable claims to Texas in exchange for
Florida. Mexico rejected subsequent efforts by U.S. presidents to
purchase the province. Nonetheless, Washington waited only a few
months before acceding to the colonists' request to recognize Texas as
a sovereign country. This action was taken in 1837, the year after the
Lone Star Republic had wrested its independence from Mexico with
the benefit of supplies and manpower from the United States. A series of complex diplomatic maneuvers led to the annexation of Texas
eight years later. This move ignited a two-year war between the
neighbors that was concluded by a peace treaty signed at Guadalupe
Hidalgo on the outskirts of Mexico City on February 2, 1848. By its
provisions, Mexico surrendered a crescent of territory from Colorado
and New Mexico to California, embracing over one million square
miles. In return, the United States paid a $15 million cash indemnity,
while assuming claims of its citizens against Mexico that would not
exceed $3.25 million.

Vehemently criticized by Illinois Congressman Abraham Lincoln, South Carolina's John C. Calhoun, and Virginia's Robert E.
Lee, the conflict cost the United States about $100 million and ap-
proximately 13,000 lives. These figures paled in comparison to the
war's impact on Mexico, which lost upwards of 50,000 lives, significant amounts of foodstuffs and livestock, and one-half of its national
territory.[6]

The war exacerbated national disunity and political fragmenta-
tion. In addition to the areas ceded under the treaty, Santa Anna,
through the Gadsden Purchase of 1853, consented to sell the Mesilla

Valley in what is today southern New Mexico and Arizona. The disparities between the two countries were sharply delineated and permanently set as Mexico shrunk in size to about 760,000 square miles while the United States expanded to over 3 million square miles as it settled the boundary to its own satisfaction. Further, the one advantage that Mexico enjoyed over the United States before the war—a standing army several times larger and presumably more powerful—had disappeared.[7]

The physical devastation of the war was secondary to its psychological effects. Mexico was humiliated in what is deemed by careful scholars in the United States and Mexico as a U.S. war of aggression.[8] The Mexican army failed to win a single major battle; U.S. forces easily and rapidly moved from Veracruz to Mexico City; the United States navy maneuvered at will, virtually lacking opposition; and some commanders refused to obey direct orders of Santa Anna. So thoroughly had the venal general alienated Benito Juárez and the liberal opposition that they ousted him in the Revolution of Ayutla, which gave birth to a new kind of movement based on ideology instead of personalism.

The war has long receded in the memory of North Americans, whose attention is riveted on the present and future. For Mexicans, an indelible scar of "virulent, almost pathological Yankeephobia"[9] remains from the wound of defeat and humiliation produced by what is officially known as "the war of the North American invasion."[10] Resentment in the Deep South toward the military phase of Reconstruction provides the closest North American analogy to a bitterness so deeply etched on a people's psyche. For Mexicans, however, occupation was followed by the permanent loss of land to a foreign country that had helped provoke hostilities. To add insult to injury, the lost territory encompassed Sutter's Fort in California where, one year after the war's conclusion, prospectors discovered the gold that would help finance the United States' industrial revolution.

Juárez, who as the Liberal candidate won the presidential elections held in March 1861, desperately needed a period of normalcy to heal his war-scarred country and get it back on its feet. The desolation left in the aftermath of the civil conflict showed on the landscape dotted with burned haciendas and mills, potted roads, barren fields, destroyed bridges, and decimated villages. A disciple of democracy, Juárez proved tolerant of those opponents inside and out of his party who excoriated his leadership in Congress and in the press. But economic problems overshadowed political ones, as a near-empty treasury forced the liberal chief executive to declare a two-year moratorium on paying his country's foreign debt. This move led to the invasion of Mexico by Spanish, British, and French troops, whose monarchs were emboldened by the United States' preoccupation with the Civil War.

Emperor Napoleon III, nephew of Napoleon I, longed to reestablish a French empire in North America. Although suffering a resounding defeat at Puebla on May 5, 1862, his blue-caped troops, cheered on by conservative monarchists and church officials, overthrew Juárez and installed an Austrian archduke, Ferdinand Maximilian of Hapsburg, as Mexico's "emperor." After the conclusion of the U.S. Civil War, Washington turned a scornful eye to this European presence on its southern flank, and the French units were withdrawn. The exodus left Maximilian at the mercy of Juárez, who was determined to show that foreign nations could not compromise with impunity his nation's sovereignty. Despite pleas for clemency from European monarchs, the archduke was court-martialed and executed. Like other forms of government attempted before it, a monarchy proved anything but a panacea for the disarray, disillusionment, and disorder afflicting the country. While an authoritarian hand might be needed to mold the nation into a cohesive productive unit, the attempt to destroy Mexico's independence had failed dismally, and, as a result, "Mexican nationalism and self-esteem began to grow perceptibly for the first time."[11]

THE PORFIRIAN ERA: 1876 TO 1911

After a brief liberal interlude following the emperor's demise, Porfirio Díaz seized power in November 1876. At first blush, this hero of the war against the French appeared as simply the latest in a long line of ambitious but politically inept generals. Yet, through the imposition of law and order he "managed to amputate the cancerous political instability that had been eating away at the country since 1810."[12] The crude but cunning dictator pursued a policy of *pan o palo* (bread or club) in bringing peace to a country that he ruled for 35 years. Lucrative rewards awaited allies of Díaz, who used to say that a dog with a bone in his mouth cannot steal or kill. Enemies could expect repression or extermination, often at the hands of a hated national constabulary known as the *rurales*, threateningly visible in their broad felt hats, silver-buttoned uniforms, and silver-embellished saddles. They broke strikes, suppressed labor unions, and cowed peasants, assuring an inexpensive supply of workers to factory owners, mine operators, and large farmers. These officially sanctioned brigands made the ancient Aztec nation one of the safest countries in the world—for all except Mexicans.

Díaz's brain trust, known as *científicos* (scientists), embraced the Social Darwinism of Herbert Spencer and the positivism of August Comte; that is, they believed in their country's progress through investment in mines, railroads, factories, and harbors; the incomparable value of technology; and the cultural superiority of white men over Indians and mixed breeds. Democratic institutions and the sharing of political and economic power with the aboriginal population were luxuries that could be contemplated only after the country had advanced economically and passed through a period of "administrative power," a euphemism for dictatorship employed by Justo Sierra, a *científico* spokesman.[13]

Foreign investment was essential to the success of this "scientific" development strategy. First, Díaz had to obtain the imprimatur of the United States government, which delayed recognizing him until Mexico made a substantial payment on claims of private citizens. It was also feared that Díaz might be too nationalistic, an ironic judgment in light of subsequent relations between his government and the United States. The Grant administration was favorably disposed toward the new regime; however, the War Department insisted on an accord permitting reciprocal troop crossings of the Rio Grande so that U.S. authorities could pursue and track down bandits who attacked settlements north of the frontier and then fled into Mexico. Such a treaty was finally signed in 1882 when the problem had significantly abated because of the increasing number of permanent settlements along the borders, giving rise to almost three decades of tranquility between the two nations.

During the Porfirian era, North American direct investment and trade climbed dramatically. Steel rails shot across the country as U.S. businessmen built flourishing railroad and mining empires. Such magnates as E. H. Harriman, Jay Gould, and Collis P. Huntington helped expand Mexico's rail network from 417 miles in 1877 to 9,600 in 1901 to 15,325 in 1911, with virtually all lines running to the United States.[14] While the French lavished capital on industrial activities, Americans gained dominance over extractive ventures, as Mexico became the world's leading silver producer and second in copper output. United States firms, spearheaded by Guggenheim interests, controlled 840 of the approximately 1,000 foreign mining companies operating in Mexico in 1908.[15] Nationalists viewed with alarm a repetition of the colonial period. "Few of the profits from investment were being redirected into the Mexican economy. The Spanish treasure ships, the famous galleons, were again departing Mexican shores laden with the country's wealth and leaving behind an impoverished populace."[16]

Díaz's policies also spurred land acquisition by foreigners. The *rurales* cruelly evicted Indians and others who did not possess clear title to their holdings, leaving 90 percent of the peasants landless by 1910; the courts enforced *mortmain* ("dead hand") laws restricting the inalienable tenure of lands by the Roman Catholic Church and Indian communities, known as *ejidos*; and the government granted and sold at concessional prices large tracts of land, often in defiance of a prohibition on settlements in frontier areas by natives of a bordering country. By 1910 foreigners owned nearly 25 percent of Mexico's land area; about one-half of this total rested in North American hands, thanks in part to acquisitions made by U.S. surveying companies, which frequently received payment in property in lieu of cash.[17]

Edward L. Doheny, a millionaire from the freebooting California oil industry, organized a company that developed the first commercial petroleum deposits in Mexico. Also active in the hydrocarbon sector were St. Louis entrepreneur Henry Clay Pierce, who set up the Water-Pierce Oil Company, and Weetman Dickinson Pearson, a Yorkshire contractor who won fame in construction projects before forming the El Aguila firm, which became the nation's largest oil producer. As a result of these efforts, output soared from 10,000 barrels in 1901 to 12.5 million barrels in 1911.[18]

Increased bilateral trade complemented investment. Exports outstripped imports as Mexican trade multiplied sevenfold between 1877 and 1911. While gold and silver dominated exports, such products as henequen, rubber, coffee, chicle, sugar, chick-peas, zinc, copper, graphite, and lead lengthened the list of items sold abroad. Díaz's economic advisers sought to balance their country's commercial relations between the United States and Europe. Nevertheless, the former, benefiting from a rapidly expanding population and industry as well as improved rail ties, became Mexico's predominant trading partner. United States purchases of Mexican goods rose from 42 percent of total exports when Díaz took office to 67 percent in the early 1890s to 75 percent in 1911.[19] By 1910, the centennial year of Mexican independence, it was tempting to conclude that the country had become an economic satellite of the United States, which was just then emerging as a world power. Inevitably, U.S. diplomats and politicians treated Mexico with arrogance, condescension, and paternalism. As one perceptive scholar observed, Mexico had become the "father of foreigners and stepfather of Mexicans."[20]

Still, José Ives Limantour, Díaz's extraordinarily talented treasury secretary, implemented a bureaucratic reform, cut government waste, increased tariff collections, paid off Mexico's debt to the United States, and gave the country its first budget surplus in modern memory. The upshot was enhanced international respect for Mexico, which not only opened diplomatic relations with most European states, but for the first time began participating actively in international conferences.[21]

Although Mexico's dependence on the United States increased under President Díaz, his policies promoted the country's economic unification. He reduced taxes that had impeded free trade, and the railroads that carried primary products north to U.S. consumers drew some previously isolated areas into an ever more extensive transportation network. This system lowered the freight costs of Mexican goods, many of which became competitive in international markets. The expanded demand for exports had a multiplier effect on the Mexican economy. The economic unification and growth promoted during the *Porfiriado* were essential to Mexico's subsequent attempts to gain control over its external affairs.

Still, embedded in the regime's development strategy were the elements of its own political destruction. Mexico's rapid growth, powered by foreign capital, enhanced the wealth of an elite who dominated and manipulated a destitute mass of Indians. No sizable, propertied middle class bridged the chasm to imbue the system with stability and persuade those at the base of a squat social pyramid that opportunities for upward mobility existed. A phalanx of military governors and local *caciques* harshly enforced the inequalities of a society that gave the back of its hand to peasants, workers, and a small middle class. The favoritism enjoyed by foreigners and the af-

fluent also extended to Mexico City and Veracruz, whose development was encouraged at the expense of other cities and regions, especially those in the north and west. Hence, beneath an icy surface of
apparent calm churned the deep waters of discontent. This discontent, intensified by declining real wages and reduced food consumption by the masses during the last decade of the Porfirian era, became
evident in a growing number of strikes.[22]

Díaz's remarkable interview with U.S. journalist James
Creelman, published on February 17, 1908, in *Pearson's Magazine*,
channeled the antipathy toward the dictatorship into organized political opposition. In this interview, the 78-year-old despot expressed
his determination to "retire when my presidential term of office ends
[1910], and I shall not serve again." The appearance in Mexico of this
article, which may have been intended exclusively for a foreign audience, emboldened critics of the regime to speak out and even offer
themselves as candidates for the country's highest office. Ultimately,
Francisco I. Madero, a well-to-do landowner and spiritualist from
the northern state of Coahuila, captured the attention of reformers
by opposing continued military dictatorship and absolutist rule. His
opposition party, dedicated to the precepts of effective suffrage and
no-reelection, helped unleash an armed uprising that swept Madero
into power after Díaz, who was re-elected in 1910, resigned the presidency and fled to Europe.

THE REVOLUTION AND ITS AFTERMATH

The fall of Díaz in 1911 proved to be one of the first in a series of
events that lasted six years and represented the military phase of the
Mexican revolution. During this period, the United States intervened
shamelessly in its neighbor's affairs. Ambassador Henry Lane
Wilson, a quintessential supporter of dollar diplomacy, actively plot-
ted Madero's ouster from the presidency and may have even given
"tacit approval" to the brutal assassination of the so-called apostle of
Mexico's revolution.[23] President Woodrow Wilson, who had once expressed a determination "to teach South American republics to elect
good men," used as pretext the temporary arrest of North American
sailors in dispatching U.S. troops to occupy the port city of Veracruz
in April 1914. Intervention also took the form of a punitive expedi-
tion when General John J. "Black Jack" Pershing led 6,000 troops

onto Mexican soil against Pancho Villa who had, on March 9, 1916, looted and burned the border town of Columbus, New Mexico, killing 18 Americans.

General Pershing failed to capture his quarry. Yet, skirmishes with Mexican forces pushed the two countries to the brink of warfare as Republican jingoists such as Senator Albert Bacon Fall of New Mexico cried for blood. Despite the crusading moralism that guided many of his actions, President Wilson understood the dangers inherent in a major military conflict with his southern neighbor at the very time that his country was increasingly at odds with Germany. Indeed, the kaiser's foreign secretary, Arthur Zimmerman, later sought an alliance with Mexico, offering as bait the recovery of Texas, New Mexico, and Arizona. Negotiations in mid-1916 dragged on past the November presidential election in which Wilson recaptured the White House, thereby reducing pressures for bold action. Early in 1917, the United States—increasingly preoccupied with events in Europe—withdrew the last of Pershing's troops. Meanwhile, Mexico's acting president Venustiano Carranza, former governor of Coahuila who became the first chief of the Constitutionalist Army, tightened his grip on the reins of government, began to quiet the unrest that had plagued his nation, and secured election under the provisions of a new constitution promulgated on February 5, 1917. The Wilson administration ultimately recognized the new government, but not without attempting to alter several objectionable clauses in the new Fundamental Law—notably article 27 that reaffirmed national ownership of subsoil rights, a provision that would permit the expropriation of such foreign firms as those heavily involved in the petroleum industry.

These U.S. and European companies had escaped most of the turmoil associated with the revolution as they continued to increase oil production. After all, the fields were located on the Gulf Coast, far removed from the central combat theaters; the companies employed bribery and their own brutal "white guards" to protect their hydrocarbon fiefdom; and the occupation of Veracruz served as proof that U.S. forces would intervene if the sanctity of the petroleum zone were violated. At the height of the civil war, the oil companies paid General Manuel Peláez, who had rebelled against the Carranza regime to seize an important portion of the oil-producing region, $15,000 per month to safeguard their properties.[24] Other commanders also received danegeld from the companies.

Thanks to the relative tranquility of the oil zone, output reached 193.4 million barrels in 1921, when Mexico could claim the second highest production level in the world. Ironically, yields began declining the next year after Carranza's elected successor, Alvaro Obregón, moved effectively to professionalize the army and secure the peace. The companies became concerned that their privileged status might change under a viable government that could enforce tax collections and listen sympathetically to labor demands. In addition, ruinous exploitation had diminished the productivity of the wells, and operating costs had begun to rise.

The oilmen began to look with interest at Venezuela where President Juan Vicente Gómez, who seemed almost as pliant and cooperative as Díaz, promised huge reserves, immediate profits, and investor security. Some medium-sized firms left Mexico, while others shut down refineries, dismantled pipelines, and closed terminals. Yet, the rate of well-drilling increased two and one-half times between 1921 and 1926, and the number of wells drilled in the 1924 to 1927 period was five times greater than the number completed before the production peak in 1921. But the majority of the wells opened at this time were dry, compared with less than 38 percent of the wells abandoned at the termination of drilling before 1921.[25]

A score of foreign corporations continued to dominate the petroleum industry. They were encouraged by a ruling of the Mexican Supreme Court that companies holding concessions before 1917 enjoyed perpetual rights over their holdings. Nonetheless, the question of resource ownership continually agitated relations between the trusts and Mexico's "revolutionary" government.

Article 123 proved another source of controversy between foreign firms and the government. This measure embraced guarantees for workers, including the right to organize unions, bargain collectively, and strike in support of their demands. It further stipulated that workers should enjoy an eight-hour day, one day of rest each week, full compensation for overtime, cash payment for their labor, social benefits, and safe and healthy working conditions.

Ambassador Dwight Morrow worked informally but sensitively to assure President Plutarco Elías Calles (1924 to 1929), a tough-minded general from Sonora, that questions related to oil rights should be resolved in Mexican courts. Morrow also impressed his hosts by taking a keen interest in myriad aspects of Mexican life, inviting his future son-in-law Charles Lindbergh to make a goodwill tour of Mexico, and arranging meetings between government and Roman Catholic leaders that helped end the bloody, three-year Cristero Rebellion.

Bilateral tensions mounted after the 1934 election of President Lázaro Cárdenas, who encouraged the formation of strong national labor unions. He urged the 10,000 oil workers, then members of 19 labor organizations linked to separate petroleum corporations, to forge a single national union. On August 15, 1935, the Union of Oil Workers of the Mexican Republic sprang to life. Soon after its founding, the union began to press the companies for 26.3 million pesos in wage and welfare benefits. This demand set off a chain of events that led directly to the expropriation of the private component of the oil industry. The dispute between the workers and the oil trusts culminated at 10:00 P.M. on March 18, 1938, when the husky voiced Cárdenas announced by radio the expropriation of the property of 17 U.S. and European corporations. He did not, however, seize the holdings of several large companies—Mexican Gulf and Ohio-Mex, for example—that cultivated amicable relations with their employees and which had not been the object of strikes.

As he said in the speech, later christened "the Declaration of Mexico's Economic Independence":

> It is evident that the problem which the oil companies have placed before the executive power of the nation by their refusal to obey the decree of the highest judicial tribunal is not the simple one of executing the judgment of a court, but rather it is an acute situation which drastically demands a solution. The social interests of the laboring classes of all the industries of the country demand it. It is to the public interest of Mexicans and even of those aliens who live in the Republic and who need peace first and afterwards petroleum with which to continue their productive activities. It is the sovereignty of the nation which is thwarted through the maneuvers of foreign capitalists who, forgetting that they have formed themselves into Mexican companies, now attempt to elude the mandates and avoid the obligations placed upon them by the authorities of their country.[26]

This reclaiming of the nation's patrimony set off a massive display of public support. The call for public collections to support Cárdenas's pledge that "Mexico will honor her foreign debt" brought an overwhelming response. "State governors, high Church officials, patriotic grand dames, peasants, students—all the numberless and picturesque types of Mexicans—pitched in what they had, including money, jewels, even homely domestic objects, chickens, turkeys, and pigs."27

The expropriation is one of the most significant dates in Mexican history. To begin with, in taking over the industry, Mexico asserted its sovereignty vis-à-vis a country that had often treated it and its citizens with contempt. Oil represented not only the richness of this cornucopia-shaped nation, but also its potential of becoming a significantly more developed state. In addition, Cárdenas's bold act is a common symbol of liberation for a revolutionary process in which rhetoric has often transcended accomplishments. Indeed, the oil industry ranks with the president and the Virgin of Guadalupe as a unifying symbol in a nation riven by differences in language, geography, and social class. Finally, the establishment of Petróleos Mexicanos (PEMEX) to run the industry—a challenge the state monopoly slowly but successfully met—demonstrated that Mexicans could be masters of their own ship; that they could successfully manage and operate a technologically complex industry, even when confronted with political, economic, and legal obstacles.

WORLD WAR II

Accustomed to wielding enormous influence, the nationalized oil companies brought pressure to bear on their governments to retaliate against Mexico. For example, U.S. firms argued that the oil sold abroad by PEMEX had been unlawfully confiscated and was still their property. They slapped liens on Mexican oil cargoes in Europe; they undertook primary and secondary boycotts against Mexican shipments; they used their financial leverage to prevent the transport of PEMEX crude on non-Mexican tankers, while keeping U.S. companies from supplying equipment to Petróleos Mexicanos; and they refused to sell the monopoly the tetraethyl required to make high-octane fuels. Meanwhile, they launched an abusive, racist propaganda campaign against Mexico, which they denounced as a nation of communist thieves.

Ambassador Josephus Daniels urged restraint on the State Department. Still, Secretary of State Cordell Hull dispatched a strong letter of protest to the Mexican government. He also persuaded the Treasury Department to halt the purchase of Mexican silver, a move supported by the oil lobby to intimidate Cárdenas and lower the price of an important Mexican export. This proved a largely symbolic act because, while cancelling a special purchase agreement, the United States continued to buy Mexican silver on the open market. A possible reason for this was that most of the silver producers in Mexico were, in fact, U.S. companies and their Washington lobby was almost as powerful as that of the oil industry.[28] These companies feared that retaliation would precipitate their expropriation and that of other North American firms in Mexico.

President Franklin D. Roosevelt did not enter the maelstrom of controversy. He publicly accepted Cárdenas's promise to pay U.S. firms for the dollars invested minus depreciation, but warned the oilmen not to expect compensation for the anticipated earnings they insisted were owed them. Such a moderate position reflected Roosevelt's lack of sympathy for the grossly inflated claims of the U.S. firms. More important, it demonstrated a desire for good relations with Mexico in view of the polarization of forces in Europe that preceded Hitler's blitzkrieg assault on Poland in 1939. Just as King Charles I identified the hangman's noose as a powerful force in focusing the mind, Roosevelt found in Germany's courting of Mexico a strong inducement for cooperation with his southern neighbor. The U.S. chief executive viewed with misgivings Germany's readiness to purchase PEMEX crude. Far from intimidated by the United States, Cárdenas successfully sought a constitutional amendment in 1940 that not only reaffirmed that oil belonged exclusively to the state, but stipulated that only the state could engage in the exploitation of the black gold.

The United States sought to strengthen ties with the Mexican government. Beginning on April 1, 1941, several important treaties were signed, including mutual landing rights for the aircraft of each other's country and a U.S. agreement to purchase Mexico's output of strategic raw materials, which were destined for war-related industries in the United States. Mexican officials worked with their U.S. counterparts to curb German activities in Mexico, and President Manuel Avila Camacho, who had succeeded Cárdenas in 1940, implied that his country would enter the war on the Allied side if the United States were attacked.[29]

The oil trusts, still hoping to negotiate management contracts to operate their former holdings, held up a settlement on the oil expropriation. By late 1941, Secretary Hull lost his patience with the companies and decided to conclude an agreement without their consent. The two countries exchanged instruments of ratification on April 2, 1942, for a convention that provided that two experts would determine the value of the oil properties; settled for $40 million outstanding general and agrarian claims by U.S. citizens against Mexico; and stipulated that the United States should purchase up to $25 million worth of Mexican silver each year, furnish $40 million in credits to stabilize the peso, lend Mexico $30 million through the Export-Import Bank for road construction, and negotiate a commercial treaty with its neighbor.

Military cooperation took the form of a joint United States-Mexican Defense Commission created in January 1942 to coordinate military action and assure the training of Mexican officers in the United States. Credits and discounts facilitated Mexican purchases of military equipment to upgrade its armed forces, even though shortages arising from the war prevented the filling of many orders. The settlement of outstanding grievances led to the resumption of Mexican oil sales to the United States. The sinking of Mexican tankers by the Germans persuaded President Avila Camacho, who was less of a strident nationalist than his predecessor, to secure a declaration of war on May 30, 1942. This declaration did not generate noticeable enthusiasm, but there was little opposition.[30]

Closer military cooperation followed Mexico's entry into the war. The two countries agreed upon the mutual conscription of resident aliens into the armed forces of the other. While Mexican authorities drafted few Americans, Uncle Sam took approximately 250,000 Mexicans into the U.S. armed forces: 14,000 of these men participated in combat; 1,000 died in battle.[31] Three squadrons of Mexican air force officers and recruits were trained in the United States and, in March 1945, Squadron 201 flew to the Philippines where it saw action during the last summer of the war.[32]

An additional contribution to the war effort was a contract labor program whereby Mexican field hands replaced U.S. workers from the Southwest who had been mobilized into the armed forces. Begun in 1942, this initiative brought as many as 400,000 braceros per year into the United States before it was discontinued in 1964. The supply of Mexican workers exceeded the demand, and many applicants who failed to secure entry under this program entered the United States as illegal migrants.[33] As one astute observer has noted, during World War II "Mexico entered into closer economic, political, and military relations with its northern neighbor than at any time before or since."[34]

President Roosevelt's meeting with Avila Camacho on April 20, 1943, symbolized this closeness. Although Coolidge and Calles had talked by telephone and Ortiz Rubio had paid a preinaugural visit to Herbert Hoover, this was only the second encounter between U.S. and Mexican heads of state and the first since 1909. This was also the first time that both the U.S. president and vice president had been out of the country at the same time (Henry Wallace was in South America).

Roosevelt slipped secretly across the border to Monterrey, drove in a caravan with Avila Camacho through 20 triumphal arches bedecked with U.S. and Mexican colors, and exchanged heartening words about "mutual esteem," "brotherhood," "mutual confidence," and the Good Neighbor Policy, which the Mexican president—ready to cast aside "negative memories"—suggested should be extended to "all the peoples of the earth." Most encouraging to Mexico was Roosevelt's assertion that "the day of the exploitation of the resources of the people of one country for the benefit of any group in another country is definitely over."[35]

THE POSTWAR YEARS

Mexico emerged from the war with a sense of confidence in its ability to determine its future. The United States still loomed large as an economic and military power. Yet, an official "revolutionary" party established by Calles in 1929 indisputably controlled the machinery of government; Washington had toned down its dollar and gunboat diplomacy; and foreign investment had fallen to less than 25 percent of what it had been in 1911 as Mexicans dominated their own country's economy.[36]

Miguel Alemán, who became president in 1946, gave impetus to economic development, and for the next 25 years Mexico registered an average annual growth rate of 6 percent. Import substitution formed the core of his strategy as the Mexican government employed tariffs, quotas, and import licenses to shelter domestic producers from the bracing winds of foreign competition. The payoff came in the impressive increase in the output of consumer goods.

After intensive debate among Mexicans, the decision was reached to aggressively seek foreign capital. United States investment, followed by loans, flowed across the border, expanding fivefold between 1950 ($566 million) and 1970 ($2,822 million). In contrast to the Porfirian era, such investment was modest or negligible in railroads, mining, electricity, and communications. Instead, postwar funds were overwhelmingly concentrated in the industrial sector, where its proportion rose from 25 percent in 1950 to 74 percent in 1970. The prime target was newer industrial activities, where modern technology and product innovation are important. These also proved to be the most dynamic and lucrative industries.[37]

President Alemán had largely ignored the "Mexicanization" efforts of Cárdenas. However, he used jawboning and fiscal policy to encourage foreign investors to seek out Mexican partners, thereby promoting equity ownership by nationals. Such an approach became "very self-conscious" in the 1960s as the government employed tariff preferences, tax exemptions, import licenses, and its own purchasing power to reward companies with Mexican stockholders. By the end of the decade, Mexican ownership was preponderant in areas considered of paramount national interest, such as electricity, banking, fishing, insurance, transportation, and communications. Mexican interests also dominated the steel, textile, mining, and construction sectors, while the state controlled the production of oil and petrochemicals.[38]

The indefatigable Alemán and his successors enlarged the government's role in the economy so that by 1962 public investment outstripped that of the private sector. The Nacional Financiera, a central development bank, facilitated the state's participation in many nominally private enterprises, while helping to attract foreign loans. The postwar presidents also spurred the construction of highways, harbors, dams, airports, and storage facilities. Sustained growth elevated Mexico to eighteenth in ranking among the world's economies. During the same period, industrial output expanded tremendously, as did its population, which grew from 25.8 million (1950) to 48.2 million (1970).

A "climate of cordiality" pervaded U.S.-Mexican relations after World War II, a period referred to as the "longest crisis-free era in their history."[39] A testimony to this harmony was the number of presidential summits: no fewer than 12 took place in the period 1945 to 1970. The most active U.S. participant in such high-level sessions was President Dwight D. Eisenhower, who met twice with Ruiz

Cortines (Falcon Dam on the Texas-Mexican border, October 19, 1953; White Sulfur Springs, West Virginia, March 26–28, 1956) and three times with López Mateos (Acapulco, February 19–20, 1959; Washington, October 9–14, 1959; and Ciudad Acuña, Coahuila, October 24, 1959).

Of all the official visits, that of President and Mrs. John F. Kennedy attracted the greatest fanfare. Growing coolness between the countries over policy toward Cuba prompted López Mateos to invite his young counterpart to Mexico City for a three-day visit, beginning on June 29, 1962. So tumultuous was the reception accorded the Kennedys that the *New York Times* likened it more to a "giant United States-Mexican fiesta" than a state visit. The youth, Catholicism, and attractiveness of the couple captured the romantic imagination of the Mexican people. Cries of "¡Viva Kennedy!" filled the air whenever they appeared in public; hordes of well-wishers frustrated the Secret Service as they sought to touch and be touched by the foreign guests; and 200,000 men, women, and children crowded into the area of the Basilica of Guadalupe where the couple attended Sunday mass.

The correct handshake with which López Mateos had greeted his visitor turned to a warm *abrazo* at the conclusion of the trip. The U.S. president had approved the guiding principles of Mexican foreign policy: national sovereignty, juridical equality of nations, self-determination, and nonintervention. He had pledged $20 million in agricultural credits as part of Mexico's involvement in the Alliance for Progress, Kennedy's program to speed social and economic development in the Americas. In addition, he expressed a readiness to use his energy and authority to resolve the question of ownership of El Chamizal, 437 acres of tamale shops, rundown houses, and stockyards near downtown El Paso (the United States' long-disputed claim to the strip sprang from a change in the channel of the Rio Grande that had occurred in the mid-nineteenth century). Finally, Kennedy promised to work to clean up the Colorado River, whose salinity was contaminating cotton and wheat crops in Mexico's Mexicali Valley, causing a loss of more than $16 million in crops in 1961.[40]

Presidential visits could not disguise the tendency of the United States either to ignore problems in the region or to see them through a cold war prism. Following the conclusion of World War II, Mexico had ratified both the Inter-American Treaty of Reciprocal Assistance, known as the Río Treaty (1947), and the Bogotá Treaty (1948).

The former reaffirmed the wartime principles of hemispheric defense; the latter created the Organization of American States (OAS) as successor to the Pan American Union. To many Latin Americans, the Río Treaty and the OAS appeared to be handmaidens of U.S. foreign policy as Washington attempted to immunize the Americas from the virus of communism that had afflicted Eastern Europe.

Mexico's resistance to being swept into the East-West conflict on the U.S. side grew as its national wealth, industrial production, and population expanded. This resistance became apparent both in Mexico's refusal to sign a military pact with the United States and in positions taken at a series of inter-American conferences held in Washington (1951), Caracas (1954), Santiago (1959), San José (1960), and Punta del Este (1962). For instance, its foreign minister joined Argentina's at the Washington meeting in opposing a resolution that called "the strengthening of their defenses" the most urgent task of all American states. Three years later at Caracas, the Mexican representative abstained from voting for a U.S.-backed anticommunist resolution aimed at the reformist government of Jacobo Arbenz Gúzman in Guatemala on the grounds that it violated the cardinal principle of nonintervention. Mexico also opposed both the creation of an inter-American military organization that could threaten the sovereignty of hemispheric nations as well as occupation of the Dominican Republic by U.S. forces in 1965. An even greater divergence of views between Mexico and the United States appeared at subsequent inter-American meetings dealing with Cuba.

The United States reacted with equanimity to Mexico's independence in inter-American affairs. Several factors help explain this forbearance. To begin with, bilateral economic ties were growing stronger even as Mexico played a lone hand in hemispheric councils. Moreover, Mexico's stances in the OAS were "essentially solitary ones"; that is, the country's leaders neither attempted to recruit supporters for their positions nor did they go so far as to challenge vital U.S. interests. For instance, Mexico supported the blockade during the Cuban missile crisis and, following that event, was slow to expand trade with the Castro regime. United States decisionmakers also recognized the contribution that a pro-Cuban foreign policy made to Mexico's internal stability by placating leftists who were critical of domestic social and economic conditions.[41] Finally, the essential anticommunism of the Mexican government was evident when President Alemán endorsed the United Nations' action in Korea and López Mateos threw world-renowned painter David Alfaro Siqueiros and 130 other veteran communists and agitators into Mexico City's Lecumberri Prison.

Nevertheless, even after receiving a slice of Cuba's cancelled sugar quota for the U.S. market, Mexico sedulously refused to support ousting Fidel Castro's regime from the OAS, endorse sanctions, or sever diplomatic ties with Cuba's Marxist-Leninist government. Devotion to nonintervention and the recognition of de facto governments (the Estrada Doctrine bears the name of Mexican diplomat Génaro Estrada) explain this posture. It sprang also from a strategy of the official party, now known as the Institutional Revolutionary Party (PRI), to court left-wing groups and politicians, one of the most prominent of whom was Lázaro Cárdenas, a saint to millions of Mexicans and, until his death in 1970, an unabashed admirer of Castro. Irrespective of ideology, many Mexicans sympathized with their struggling Cuban brothers, whom they perceived as victims of Yankee exploitation. As one Mexican economist expressed it: "Like the drunk at a party, Fidel has been yelling all the things about you Americans we'd like to but didn't dare."[42] Students at the National Autonomous University expressed a similar viewpoint when they marched in large numbers into the Zócalo, Mexico City's grandest square, to protest the United States' invasion of Cuba in 1961. "Americans! Pick on Someone Your Own Size!" proclaimed their banners.[43]

This overview of U.S.-Mexican relations reveals several strands in the bilateral pattern of influence and power. First, Mexico's cultural heritage is so distinct from that of the United States that different values, institutions, and styles of leadership assure misunderstandings, distrust, and conflicts. Second, although in many respects a third world state, Mexico differs in various ways: the post-World War II economic miracle produced a broad industrial base and one of the highest per-capita incomes among developing countries; in PEMEX, it boasts the most sophisticated oil company outside of the United States, Western Europe, and the Soviet Union; and it is largely free of the militarism so conspicuous in the rest of Latin America and the third world. Third, national cohesion, industrial development, strong leadership, and the diplomatic and political backing of other developing nations are associated with greater Mexican assertiveness vis-à-vis the United States in foreign affairs; yet, through the 1960s, discretion tempered this independence. Fourth, Mexico has increasingly relied on lofty principles—such as sovereignty, juridical equality, self-determination, and nonintervention—in seeking international support as it resists U.S. influence. Fifth, the revolution sharpened Mexico's nationalism and increased sensitivity toward foreigners trying to exert hegemony over the country's natural resources such as oil, which enjoys a special status in the country's political culture. Finally, the history of binational affairs, which includes U.S. military, economic, and diplomatic interventions and a war that halved the size of Mexico's territory, makes Mexico apprehensive about the intentions of its giant neighbor, to which virtually unlimited power is imputed.

NOTES

1. Karl M. Schmitt, *Mexico and the United States, 1821–1973: Conflict and Coexistence* (New York: Wiley, 1974), pp. 44, 45, 48.

2. Octavio Paz, "Mexico and the United States: Positions and Counterpositions," in Tommie Sue Montgomery (ed.), *Mexico Today* (Philadelphia: Institute for Human Study, 1982), pp. 1–21.

3. Roger D. Hansen, *The Politics of Mexican Development* (Baltimore: Johns Hopkins University Press, 1971), pp. 11–12.

4. Peter H. Smith, *Mexico: The Quest for a U.S. Policy* (New York: Foreign Policy Association, n. d.), pp. 6–7.

5. Schmitt, *Mexico and the United States*, pp. 42–43.

6. Justin H. Smith, *The War with Mexico*, 2 vols. (Gloucester, Mass.: Peter Smith, 1963), pp. 253–67, 318–19; see Schmitt, *Mexico and the United States*, p. 67.

7. Schmitt, *Mexico and the United States*, pp. 67–68.

8. Michael C. Meyer, "Roots and Realities of Mexican Attitudes toward the United States: A Background Paper," in Richard D. Erb and Stanley R. Ross (eds.), *United States Relations with Mexico: Context and Content* (Washington: American Enterprise Institute, 1981), p. 30.

9. Michael C. Meyer and William L. Sherman, *The Course of Mexican History* (New York: Oxford University Press, 1979), p. 352.

10. Smith, *Mexico: The Quest for a U.S. Policy*, p. 8.

11. Meyer and Sherman, *The Course of Mexican History*, p. 401.

12. Frank Brandenburg, *The Making of Modern Mexico* (Englewood Cliffs, N.J.: Prentice Hall, 1964), p. 37.

13. Meyer and Sherman, *The Course of Mexican History*, p. 457.

14. Carleton Beals, *Porfirio Díaz: Dictator of Mexico* (Westport, Conn.: Greenwood Press, 1971), p. 29.

15. Mira Wilkins, *The Emergence of Multinational Enterprise: American Business Abroad from the Colonial Era to 1914* (Cambridge, Mass.: Harvard University Press, 1970), pp. 116–20.

16. Meyer, "Roots and Realities of Mexican Attitudes," p. 31.

17. Schmitt, *Mexico and the United States*, p. 104.

18. J. Richard Powell, *The Mexican Petroleum Industry, 1938–1950* (New York: Russell & Russell, 1972), p. 208.

19. Schmitt, *Mexico and the United States*, pp. 99–100.

20. Brandenburg, *The Making of Modern Mexico*, p. 40.

21. Meyer and Sherman, *The Course of Mexican History,* p. 442.

22. Hansen, *The Politics of Mexican Development*, pp. 21, 23, 28.

23. Smith, *Mexico: The Quest for a U.S. Policy,* p. 8.

24. Lorenzo Meyer, *Mexico and the United States in the Oil Controversy, 1917–1942* (Austin: University of Texas Press, 1977), p. 50.

25. Powell, *The Mexican Petroleum Industry,* p. 15.

26. William Cameron Townsend, *Lázaro Cárdenas, Mexican Diplomat* (Ann Arbor: George Wahr, 1952), p. 257.

27. Howard F. Cline, *The United States and Mexico* (New York: Atheneum, 1965), p. 242.

28. Schmitt, *Mexico and the United States*, p. 181.

29. Schmitt, *Mexico and the United States*, p. 186.

30. Schmitt, *Mexico and the United States*, p. 190.

31. Johnny M. McCain, "Contract Labor as a Factor in United States-Mexican Relations, 1942–47" (Ph.D. dissertation, University of Texas, 1970), p. 10; cited in Schmitt, *Mexico and the United States*, p. 190.

32. Schmitt, *Mexico and the United States*, pp. 190–91.

33. Wayne A. Cornelius, *Mexican Migration to the United States: Causes, Consequences and U.S. Responses* (Cambridge, Mass.: MIT, Migration and Development Study Group; Center for International Studies, 1978), p. 17.

34. Schmitt, *Mexico and the United States*, pp. 187–89.

35. *New York Times*, April 21, 1943, pp. 1, 10, 11.

36. Schmitt, *Mexico and the United States*, pp. 191–92.

37. Richard S. Weinert, "Foreign Capital in Mexico," in Susan Kaufman Purcell (ed.), *Mexico-United States Relations* (New York: Academy of Political Science, 1981), p. 117.

38. Weinert, "Foreign Capital in Mexico," p. 119.

39. Olga Pellicer de Brody, "A Mexican Perspective," in Susan Kaufman Purcell (ed.), *Mexico-United States Relations* (New York: Academy of Political Science, 1981), p. 7.

40. A joint presidential communiqué was published in the *New York Times*, July 1, 1962, p. 2.

41. Olga Pellicer de Brody, "Mexico in the 1970s and Its Relations with the United States," in Julio Cotler and Richard R. Fagen (eds.), *Latin America and the United States: The Changing Political Realities* (Stanford: Stanford University Press, 1974), p. 319, footnote 16.

42. Quoted in Laura Bergquist, "Mexico: Friendly or Unfriendly Neighbor," *Look*, July 18, 1961, pp. 22, 25.

43. Bergquist, "Mexico: Friendly or Unfriendly Neighbor," p. 22.

3

THE ECHEVERRÍA YEARS

INTRODUCTION

Mexico's growth in wealth and population has emboldened its chief executives to stand their ground against the United States on international questions. At the same time, they have opened their arms to North American investment, trade, and loans—a posture that enhanced their northern neighbor's economic influence. These foreign resources poured into an economy evincing signs of stress. Domestic manufacturers, who had taken advantage of import substitution in consumer goods, relied on protectionism to produce items of uneven quality, with profits based on high markups on a limited output. Failure to promote import substitution in capital goods led to a quickening stream of imports accompanied by growing balance-of-payments deficits. Annual population growth reached 3.4 percent in the 1960s, and the economy failed to generate sufficient jobs for this population. By 1970 nearly half the able-bodied labor force either lacked employment or worked only a few weeks each year, generally during the harvest season. The populist momentum of the Cárdenas years had long since abated, and the income spread between "haves" and "have-nots," as well as between regions, widened.[1]

THE SELECTION OF ECHEVERRÍA

A new elite composed of industrialists, state managers, bankers, large landowners, labor chieftains, well-placed bureaucrats, and foreign investors championed growth with stability. Despite the problems mentioned above, economic expansion continued during the regime of Gustavo Díaz Ordaz (1964 to 1970); however, repressive action became the instrument used to preserve order threatened by worker, peasant, and student activists. The most egregious example of repression in recent memory occurred on October 2, 1968, when soldiers and police opened fire on student-led demonstrators in Mexico City's Plaza of the Three Cultures, killing as many as 400 people.

The PRI's decision to nominate Luis Echeverría Alvarez, Díaz Ordaz's handpicked choice, appeared an act of *continuismo* rather than change. In 1945, as a studious, intense 23-year-old law student, Echeverría seemed like "one more bright young Mexico Cityian on the make. . . ."[2] He then married the daughter of José Guadalupe Zuno Hernández, a party strongman from Jalisco who presided over a large political family that was eminently provincial and nationalistic in the old revolutionary tradition. A year later, the young lawyer was recruited into the PRI and trained for a career of national service. Although never holding elective office, Echeverría climbed through the ranks of the party secretariat and the Ministry of Education until, in 1954, he was awarded the third-ranking post. In 1956 he graduated to undersecretary of the Ministry of Interior; seven years later he replaced Díaz Ordaz as minister when the latter became president. Throughout his bureaucratic ascent, he appeared anything but a left-winger. In fact, one highly respected observer of Mexican politics called him "a perfect paladin of the established regime."[3]

Such a characterization was understandable because Echeverría had a hand in arranging the army's occupation of the National Polytechnic Institute following "communist-inspired riots" in 1956. Later, he helped crush a "communist-inspired" strike among railroad workers; gathered evidence on *fidelista* organizations; destroyed several radical publications; imposed official scripts on television and radio newscasters; smashed two big "communist cells"; assisted the PRI in capturing two bungled gubernatorial elections; and—after the president himself—was the civilian most identified with the brutal handling of the October 1968 demonstrations. "Indeed Echeverría was widely *believed* to have taken—in the face of an indecisive Díaz Ordaz—the fatal decision to move on the unarmed crowd at the Plaza of the Three Cultures and to put a rapid end to the movement with a public bloodbath of unprecedented proportions."[4]

ECONOMIC POPULISM

It was anticipated that Echeverría would act to defuse the popular frustrations that built up during the last years of Díaz Ordaz. After all, it was customary for a new chief executive to grant amnesty to prisoners, loosen muzzles on the press, and speak in an idiom of conciliation. For that reason, foreign financial interests did not regard with alarm candidate Echeverría's promise to uplift the land-hungry peasants and "reduce the gap between the powerful and the unprotected." He articulated variations on this theme as he traveled more than 35,000 miles and visited over 9,000 cities, towns, and villages during a seven-month presidential campaign that took him from the dusty plains of Sonora to the steamy jungles of Chiapas and Quintana Roo.

The distinct glow of economic nationalism, a leitmotif that characterized his *sexenio*, appeared in the 48-year-old president's inaugural address. While recognizing a continued need for infusions of foreign capital, he stressed that Mexico (and by implication the rest of Latin America) could not afford to welcome external capital unless investments boosted export earnings in order to pay dividends, foreign remittances, and interest on loans contracted abroad. He also emphasized the need for foreign investors to associate their funds with domestic capital and to shift from import substitution toward producing internationally competitive exports.[5]

What explains this turnabout by a man who had exuded orthodoxy and conservatism as a party apparatchik? To begin with, despite his right-wing behavior as interior minister, Echeverría fancied himself the legatee of Cárdenas, with whom he invited comparisons. The self-proclaimed "peasants' president" often made unannounced weekend trips to remote areas of the country. Local political leaders soon learned that he thrived on face-to-face contacts with peasants and workers instead of spending time feasting with industrialists, ranchers, bankers, and other notables of the region. Meanwhile, in Mexico City, he demanded that government officials arrive at their desks at 9 A.M., pause only for a brief lunch, and continue their work until late in the evening. Otherwise, his administration's shift from the previous policy of "stabilizing development" to one of "shared development"—namely, redistributing income toward peasants and workers, speeding up the last stages of the agrarian reform, earmarking more credit for small farmers, creating jobs, decentralizing industry, and improving the balance of payments—could not be accomplished. In addition, a special advisory committee was charged with exploring and suggesting fiscal reforms.

Echeverría's economic reformism coincided with an austerity program. This plan entailed government restriction of outlays (including a 10 percent reduction in capital expenditures), increased public savings through new taxes, and improved external accounts through introduction of a 10 percent export subsidy and a curbing of foreign borrowing. The upshot was a closing of the current account deficit in the balance of payments and lowering the inflation rate to only 5 percent. The cost of these gains was a sharp recession—with the rise in gross domestic product (3.7 percent) barely exceeding population growth in 1971.[6]

Stung by the dismal performance of the economy, Echeverría turned heaven and earth to promote recovery in 1972. But private entrepreneurs, uneasy about the direction of policy, looked askance at a president who cultivated the landless and advocated higher taxes on capital to reduce inequities in the highly regressive fiscal system. Echeverría used the alleged failings of the private sector to justify a huge increase in public spending. Between 1971 and 1976, federal government expenditures shot up from $4.5 billion to $19 billion as the share of GDP generated by the public sector rose from 26.8 to 39.6 percent. Concurrently, over 250 economically specialized federal agencies called *Fideicomisos* and approximately 30 major government institutions sprang up, often in competition with existing entities. Airports, railways, and 70,000 miles of roads and highways were constructed; spending on education increased sixfold, public investment in industry fivefold, and agriculture sevenfold. Furthermore, the Echeverría administration sought to enhance its popular support through expensive wage, price, housing, and rural investment activities. Especially noteworthy was the enlarged role of CONASUPO, a state agency that pays a guaranteed price to farmers for foodstuffs that are sold at relatively low prices in poorer areas, thereby undercutting the profits of middlemen. During the first five years of his *sexenio*, the number of retail outlets operated by CONASUPO mushroomed fivefold to 6,000. Mexico's real GDP expanded by 7.3 percent in 1972 and 7.6 percent in 1973 before OPEC price increases slowed economic activity in 1974. Rhetoric notwithstanding, taxes failed to keep pace with expenditures. Thus, the printing of crisp new pesos to finance ever larger government deficits fueled an inflation that marred the rest of Echeverría's administration.

The state's increased intervention in the economy combined with the peso's deterioration in value vis-à-vis the dollar further chilled relations between Echeverría and domestic capitalists. He launched a verbal onslaught against these "emissaries of the past"; they retaliated by refusing to invest. Relations were especially strained between the president and the "Monterrey Group" of industrialists, some of whom descended from Basques, Sephardic Jews, and the poor who settled the barren scrubland of New Spain a century after the conquest. Tough, self-reliant, and nationalistic, these northern entrepreneurs are joined by kinship or business activity to the immensely wealthy Garza Sada clan.[7] The simmering feud boiled over in September 1973 when Eugenio Garza Sada, patriarch of the group and father of Monterrey's industrialization, fell under a hail of assassin's bullets. Arriving at the airport to attend the funeral, Echeverría learned that the victim's widow adamantly refused to receive him; the bishop who delivered the funeral mass deliberately talked at great length while the president waited impatiently in his limousine outside the cathedral (Mexican presidents do not enter churches); and one graveside orator, a spokesman for local industrialists, stated bluntly in Echeverría's presence that the government was responsible for terrorist activities because officials were trying "to foment hate and division within social classes." Rarely has a chief executive in any country been subjected to a more studied insult.[8] A logical corollary of the government's effort to gain control over the economy was to regulate the behavior of foreign capitalists who often worked in an "alliance for profits" with the Monterrey Group and other Mexican interests.

Also important in understanding Echeverría's economic nationalism is his attachment to the "dependency" theory in explaining the plight of Mexico and other third world countries. The body of literature on this subject is far from homogeneous; however, certain elements of agreement exist. For instance, Raúl Prebisch, a pioneer of the dependency approach, portrayed the world as divided between a developed center and an underdeveloped periphery, with a confluence of factors—the periphery's deteriorating terms of trade, the

competitive disadvantage of developing states in producing manufactures, the center's tight grip on technology and finance—continuing if not accentuating the unbalanced relationship. During the mid-
1960s, a group of Latin American scholars went beyond Prebisch's
perspective and "interpreted the phenomenon of *dependencia* in a
holistic fashion and in terms of the capitalist mode of production."
These theorists point to large business conglomerates or multinational corporations as providing a structural link between internal
and external factors of dependency. They argue that transnational
firms expanded into the economies of weaker countries, conditioning
their economic, social, and political behavior. They despoil them of
primary products, control capital movements, limit technology
transfers, employ undemocratic methods to manipulate local politics, and place on their payrolls energetic members of the middle
class, thereby "denationalizing" them, for their loyalties shift from
national priorities to accomplishing the objectives of Citibank, General Motors, Gulf Oil, or some other foreign enterprise.[9]

The idea of dependence strongly influenced Mexican foreign
policy between 1970 and 1976. Echeverría, who until his inauguration had dedicated his life to domestic matters, decided—according
to his aides—"that Mexico could not achieve true development while
it remained politically identified with and economically dependent
on the United States."[10] Several factors reinforced this outlook.
When Echeverría took office, Mexico shipped 60 percent of its exports to the United States, from which it received 64 percent of its
imports. In addition, the United States accounted for $1.7 billion of
the $2.2 billion foreign investment in his country. These funds were
concentrated in the production of capital goods, the most dynamic,
profitable, and strategically important sector of the economy. The
annual burden of payments abroad in dividends, royalties, and other
obligations to foreign private capital was more than $300 million.[11]
Additionally, the economic problems faced by the U.S. economy led
the Nixon administration to impose a 10 percent surcharge on imports in 1971. This move, which caught Mexico by surprise, provided further evidence of the vulnerability of peripheral countries to
the center of the capitalist world.

To strengthen national influence over foreign economic activities in his country, Echeverría's administration in 1971 bought 51
percent of the stock in the Cananea Mining Company, an Anaconda
copper subsidiary, thereby completely "Mexicanizing" the mining

sector; took over the Pan-American Sulfur Company in May 1972; and, also in 1972, purchased a majority of shares in Teléfonos de México. After Nacional Financiera, a state-run development agency, revealed that in the first quarter of 1972 remittances by foreign interests ($105 million) exceeded their investments ($62.4 million), the government announced that subsidiaries had to generate export earnings or import savings equivalent to their profits dispatched abroad.[12]

The Mexican Congress approved another nationalistic measure on February 16, 1973, by enacting the Law to Promote Mexican Investment and Regulate Foreign Investment. This statute, which reaffirmed and formalized existing decrees and regulations on the subject, established a special commission with broad authority to approve and supervise foreign investment in Mexico. Seventeen criteria were to be considered in evaluating requests from foreigners to assure that their investment neither monopolized a market nor displaced local capital, but rather complemented Mexican capital, thereby brightening the country's balance-of-payments picture. Such investment was to be encouraged where it would create jobs, train Mexican technicians, or help improve conditions in impoverished regions.

The law identified those areas of economic activity—for example, oil and other hydrocarbons, basic petrochemicals, electricity, railroads, communications, and nuclear energy—that should be set aside exclusively for the state. Reserved for Mexican citizens and corporations were endeavors such as air and maritime transport and radio and television broadcasting. In other areas of the economy, foreigners could not as a rule own more than 49 percent of the equity in any new company, although the commission could grant exceptions based on the type of industry and geographic area. The foreign investment law provided for careful supervision and regulation of the acquisition of fixed assets or stock and capital in a Mexican company by foreigners, who were then required to list their investment in Mexico with the newly created National Registry of Foreign Investment.[13]

The president also championed the Law on the Transfer of Technology and the Use and Exploitation of Patents and Trademarks. This legislation sprang from Echeverría's concern that many foreign corporations were charging their Mexican clients, associates, or subsidiaries excessive amounts for trademarks, patents, licenses, royalties, and technology in general. Such technical information, it was alleged, often proved to be outdated, inappropriate to Mexico, and—above all—excessively dear. Some subsidiaries of multinational firms purportedly preferred to make payments to their parent companies and deduct 23 percent from their federal taxes, rather than keep the funds at home where they would be subjected to the corporate income tax, compulsory profit sharing, and other levies. An added refinement, the indictment goes on, is that "some subsidiaries pay for know-how to 'ghost' companies in Liechtenstein or Panama, so enabling the parent concerns to evade taxes at home."[14] "Scientific colonialism deepens the differences between countries and maintains systems of international domination," the president asserted.[15]

The statute was designed to halt such fraudulent practices. It required that any contract involving the payment by a Mexican firm for foreign technology must be registered with the ministry of trade and commerce. Refusal to comply with this provision invalidated the agreement. Approval for the transfer of know-how would depend upon the proven inaccessibility of such technology in Mexico, the reasonableness of the price, and the compatibility of the product to be manufactured with the country's development needs.

Following the introduction of this legislation, Ambassador Robert H. McBride complained that U.S. investors, unsure whether they were welcome in Mexico, found it difficult to play the investment game amid unexpected rule changes. Foreign Minister Emilio Rabasa replied drily that the ambassador's own country had itself precipitously changed the rules of the game by decreeing a 10 percent import surcharge during the 1971 dollar crisis.[16]

FOREIGN POLICY DEMARCHES

The "peasant's president" at home, Echeverría embarked on an assertive foreign policy to enhance his standing among disaffected groups on the left, a need accentuated by the failure of his domestic reforms. He also aspired to the role of "leader of the third world" to reduce his country's reliance on the United States. He sought neither an active role in the U.N. Security Council nor in the OAS, but selected or created forums where the United States was not the dominant actor or where the interests of major nations were balanced.[17]

He perceived correctly that the emergence of new power centers offered the possibility—if not the immediate establishment—of new structures and affiliations in a more complex and interdependent world.[18] An example of this new approach appeared in the Charter of the Economic Rights and Duties of States, whose approval he secured from the United Nations' General Assembly. Offered as an "alternative to war" between industrialized and less-developed nations, the document affirmed the sovereignty of all states over their wealth, resources, and economic activity, while stipulating their right to control foreign investment and supervise multinational firms in accordance with their laws. Another provision, strenuously resisted by most advanced countries, recognized every nation's right to expropriate foreign property without observing traditional compensation guarantees. The charter also specified that trade should be guided by the principles of mutual advantage, fair benefits for all parties concerned, and cooperation in adjusting the export prices of primary products to those received by manufacturing centers for their finished goods. Echeverría's program called for the right to organize commodity cartels.

Although the nonbinding charter precipitated nearly three years of controversy and debate, it finally gained approval in late 1974 by a margin of 120 to six (with ten abstentions) in the U.N. General Assembly. The highly industrialized nations, whose support was crucial to achieving the document's goals, either abstained or voted nay. Still, for Echeverría and his country, "it was a declaration of redistributive justice which bestowed a patina of prestige to Mexican Foreign Policy."[19]

Echeverría sought to inculcate the principles of the United Nations-approved charter in an organization designed to establish a "system of economic consultation and cooperation" in Latin America. First mentioned by the Mexican leader in a July 15, 1974, speech in Lima, the Latin American Economic System (SELA) enjoyed the wholehearted backing of Venezuela's President Carlos Andrés Pérez. The two chief executives then proceeded to convince their regional neighbors that "the countries of the third world and those of Latin America, in particular, must unite in defense of their common principles and interests or resign themselves to remaining underdeveloped indefinitely."[20] Divided by "North American expansionism," Latin America would remain the poor cat's paw of the North unless the countries of the hemisphere banded together, argued Echeverría.

Their joint effort bore fruit on October 17, 1975, when 25 nations signed SELA's charter. Included among the signatories was Cuba; excluded was the United States, against which the system was implicitly aimed.

The organization was intended to promote national development projects and create Latin American transnational firms, defend the prices of manufactured goods and raw materials, establish cartels in primary products, provide information about the prices of these goods, stimulate food production and encourage multinational ventures for the production of fertilizers, facilitate the acquisition of capital goods for the region, and foster technical cooperation among Latin American and third world nations.[21]

SELA's most ambitious venture, yet to be achieved, was the creation of a multinational fleet of passenger and cargo ships to serve the Caribbean countries, thereby expanding intraregional trade. Reality brought instead erratic schedules and freight rates so exorbitant that they constituted a brake on those nations' export industries.[22] Echeverría fathered the idea of this intrazonal fleet, NAMUR, to be composed of vessels leased from Norway, West Germany, Great Britain, and other countries until the region had shipyards of its own in which to build freighters.

On questions like shoring up the prices of raw materials through OPEC-type accords (Mexico, for example, helped organize an international sugar agreement and actively participates in a coffee cartel), SELA, which Fidel Castro termed Echeverría's "greatest initiative," proved equally ineffective. OPEC's initial success as a cartel owed much to a conflux of particularly favorable elements: elastic demand for oil, limited possibility of substitution, production flexibility (Saudi Arabia regularly adjusts its output to advance mutual interests), convenient storage, a limited number of suppliers, and political bonds among Arab members based on anti-Zionism. The absence of such factors, especially the lack of a country like Saudi Arabia that can perform a balancing function, militates against the success of commodity accords in sugar, bananas, coffee, cotton, and other important Latin American exports. In addition, despite a mutual concern about United States economic and political influence and a commitment to common goals, it was questionable whether oil-rich, semi-industrialized countries like Mexico and Venezuela shared basic interests with Bolivia, Haiti, and Paraguay.

U.S. Secretary of State Henry A. Kissinger, a close friend of Mexican foreign minister Rabasa, responded to the efforts of Echeverría and others by offering to participate in discussions with developing nations on: standards to govern the treatment of multinational corporations and the transfer of technology; intergovernmental mechanisms to prevent and resolve investment disputes; and the encouragement of private enterprise to foster economic advances in developing countries in a manner compatible with the political and economic needs of the host states.

The conciliatory attitude of the United States converged with a growing belief among the world's nations that the best hope for combating global poverty and dependence lay in establishing a New International Economic Order. To this end, the first North-South dialogue between developed and developing nations began in Paris in 1975. These discussions collapsed without agreement after 18 months of diatribe and deadlock.

Echeverría further attempted to diminish Mexico's longstanding dependence on the "colossus of the North" by developing ties with dozens of other countries, most of which belonged to the third world and seemed receptive to his ideas on revamping international economic relations. Even though its traditional economic ties were with the United States and Europe, Mexico joined the Latin American Free Trade Association and, through the mechanisms of this organization, increased its commerce with South American nations.[23] In contrast to his predecessors, who rarely left Mexico during their administration except perhaps to visit the United States, Echeverría appeared as a perpetual motion machine.[24] All told, he visited 36 nations and held meetings with 64 monarchs, presidents, or prime ministers in all major regions of the world.[25] His most publicized jaunt began in mid-1975 as a two-week, five-nation tour—hastily expanded to 44 days and 14 countries on three continents. The improvised, frenetic nature of the trip inspired analysts to characterize Echeverría as a combination of "Superman and Speedy González," as he glad-handed his way across India, the Middle East, Africa, and nations of the Caribbean region.

Although justified as a search for new markets for Mexican exports, the tour provoked stinging criticism in Mexico. Detractors charged that Echeverría was seeking to divert public attention from worsening economic conditions, that he was ignoring pressing problems at home, and that he was merely politicking abroad for election as U.N. secretary-general, to replace incumbent Kurt Waldheim whose term would end in December 1976.

With Echeverría's constant travels and the steady stream of foreign dignitaries to Mexico City, diplomatic relations were forged with many other nations. In all, Mexico exchanged diplomats with 31 additional countries during Echeverría's six-year term.

The majority of the countries Echeverría visited were nonaligned in the East-West ideological struggle, and the trips seemed calculated to establish Mexico's independent position as a third world country. Nonetheless, early in his administration Echeverría moved to bolster ties with China and the USSR by paying a visit to both Peking and Moscow—an historic first, in both instances, for a Mexican chief executive in office. His political preference clearly lay with the Chinese, who "are trying to find new ways of life in a process worthy of close attention." In contrast, he linked the Soviet Union, seat of "big Communism," to imperialism and warned that such superpower interventions as the 1968 invasion of Czechoslovakia must be ended. It should be remembered that he had expelled five Soviet diplomats from Mexico in 1971 on the grounds that they had arranged the training of Mexican urban guerrillas in North Korea.[26] With his five-day trip to Cuba in August 1975, the Mexican leader became the first non-Marxist president to visit Havana since Castro seized power in 1959. Relations had been stengthened when Mexico led the successful effort in July 1975 to lift sanctions imposed against the island by the OAS. In Havana, Echeverría exchanged words of praise with his host and asserted that the Cuban revolution provides "unquestionable evidence that our time is one of social change, that our era is one of reaffirmation of the Third World, and that our task is to build a more just and humane society."[27]

President Salvador Allende Gossens was one of the first foreign leaders to travel to Mexico, spending four days there in late 1972. Echeverría declared three days of official mourning at the time of the September 1973 coup d'état that took Allende's life; more than 800 leftists, including Allende's widow Hortensia, accepted Echeverría's offer of diplomatic asylum in Mexico to any Chilean seeking refuge after the upheaval; and Mexico severed diplomatic relations with Chile's military junta in late 1974.[28] This action added to the country's nonintervention doctrine an "Echeverría corollary," whereby diplomatic pressure would be placed on regimes that violated human rights.

North Korea and Spain remained the only other states of importance left unrecognized by Echeverría: the former because it had fomented guerrilla activities in Mexico; the latter because of Mexico's fervent support for the losing Republican side in the Spanish civil war, refugees from which poured into the country.

Echeverría did not confine his diplomatic efforts to individual countries. In December 1974 he signed an agreement for commercial cooperation between Mexico and the European Community (EC), the fourth such compact between the EC and a Latin American republic. The Mexican government hoped the accord would help curb the country's growing trade deficit with the EC, as well as reduce Mexico's economic dependence on the United States. Echeverría also negotiated an agreement for economic, scientific, and technical cooperation between his country and the Council for Mutual Economic Assistance, the Communist bloc's economic alliance. Additionally, Mexico served as host for a number of international conclaves, including one that highlighted the International Women's Year in 1975.

In toto, Echeverría's efforts produced 160 international pacts and agreements; half of these concerned economic or commercial questions, while one-third focused on cultural, technical, or scientific matters.[29]

In another display of independence, Mexico announced on August 5, 1975, the establishment of "an exclusive economic zone" extending 200 miles from its coastline. In so doing, it claimed sole authority over fishing and exploitation of any other natural resource in the rich Gulf of California, which averages 100 miles in width and is bounded on one side by the Mexican peninsula of Baja California and on the other by the states of Sinaloa and Sonora. Vessels from the United States, the Soviet Union, Great Britain, and Japan regularly fished in this area along with Mexican boats. While closing off the area to foreigners for fishing, the Mexican government did not assert territorial rights over the area. Hence, the free passage of ships, submarines, airplanes, or underwater cables would not be impaired.

Foreign Minister Rabasa called the measure one of the most important events in his country's history and "a vindication of the large loss of Mexican territory in the past." With this move, he said, Mexico acquired an economic zone larger than the national territory. Despite his affinity for international codes of conduct and his designation of the economic zone, Echeverría stopped short of challenging the vital interests of his powerful neighbor. For instance, even though Rabasa explored the possibility of seeking observer status in OPEC, the chief executive declared that Mexico would not enter the cartel itself.[30]

CONFRONTATION WITH NORTH AMERICAN JEWS

Intonations about sovereignty and independence notwithstanding, the susceptibility of the Mexican economy to influence from U.S.-based interest groups became evident in 1975. In that year, Echeverría met with Yasser Arafat and immediately announced that the Palestinian Liberation Organization (PLO) would open an information office in Mexico City. This tacit recognition of the PLO, which struck many observers as odd because Mexico had recently regained self-sufficiency in oil and had no reason to ingratiate itself with the Arab world, preceded the country's support in the United Nations of a resolution declaring that "Zionism is a form of racism and racial discrimination." On November 10, 1975, the General Assembly passed this initiative by a vote of 71 to 24, with 26 abstentions.[31]

The Jewish community in the United States responded to this anti-Zionist vote by urging Jews and others sympathetic to Israel to boycott Mexico. Advertisements filled the pages of U.S. newspapers urging "good people of all faiths" to shun Mexico as it had become a "less desirable place to visit or do business with." B'nai B'rith and the American Jewish Congress, which excoriated the Echeverría regime for having "allied itself with a Soviet-Arab bloc engaged in a program of political anti-Semitism and anti-Americanism," cancelled its group tours to Mexico. Conventions were shifted to U.S. cities or Caribbean islands. This publicity campaign produced the cancellation of 30,000 hotel reservations within a week, according to the president of the Mexican hotel association.[32] It was estimated that Mexico derived more money from U.S. tourists than from those of all the 70 other countries voting for the U.N. resolution combined and that the boycott cost the Mexican treasury an estimated $200 million.[33] The blow was especially hard inasmuch as tourism generated about 13 percent of the country's earnings on current account, which had recorded a deficit of $1.7 billion during the first half of 1975.[34]

Mexico did its best to mollify the outraged American Jewish community. In late November, former president Miguel Alemán, head of the Mexican National Tourist Council, hosted dinners for Jewish travel officials and other community leaders in New York, Chicago, and Los Angeles. Alemán emphasized that Mexico had offered asylum to persecuted Jews, that his country's Jewish population had encountered no repression, and that the Mexican government had acted unilaterally—the people were not involved in the U.N. action. He also invited prominent Jews to attend an informal dinner with President Echeverría at Alemán's home in Mexico City.[35] There the chief executive rejected the equating of Zionism with racism and assured the visitors that his country's U.N. vote had not been intended to give that impression.

In December Foreign Minister Rabasa flew to Tel Aviv "at the invitation" of his Israeli counterpart "to clear up any misunderstanding" over Mexico's policy. The process of clarification turned into a repudiation of the U.N. vote. After laying a wreath at the tomb of Theodor Herzl, the founder of Zionism, the Mexican official declared: "There is no discrimination in Zion . . . and where there is no discrimination, there is no racism." These words drew a sharp rebuke from Mexico City's *Excelsior*. In an editorial, it stated that the principles of the nation's foreign policy should be "neither improvised nor respondent to pressures, but neither should they be impolitic nor injurious to the values of Mexican diplomatic tradition."[36]

Rabasa concluded his visit with an assertion that the misunderstanding had been "forgotten, pardoned and buried." But journalists back home took exception to this performance and words deemed offensive to national dignity. Samuel I. del Villar, an *Excelsior* columnist, labeled Rabasa's statement "intolerable" and asserted that "these acts are without parallel and degrade our foreign policy to the lowest levels in our history."[37] Another publication thundered against the government for "begging Israeli forgiveness on its knees." In view of this pressure, the foreign minister resigned on December 29, 1975.[38] A senior official of the Echeverría government also stated that it was an error for Rabasa to have used the word "pardon."[39] He was replaced by Alfonso García Robles, a veteran diplomat. Most observers viewed this move as Mexico's "admission of guilt" for its action at the United Nations. Mario Ojeda, a well-known Mexican scholar, insists that his country was "blackmailed" because of the "extreme vulnerability of the Mexican economy. . . ."[40]

Israeli leaders were believed to have exerted pressure on North American Jews to end the boycott, insisting that relations with Mexico soured over a series of misunderstandings. The government of Israel generally viewed Mexico as an important ally in the anti-Israeli third world. "We honestly want to end this affair," said one diplomat in Jerusalem. "It does no good for our relations with Mexico."[41]

ECONOMIC CRISIS AND U.S. ASSISTANCE

An even more notable example of Mexico's vulnerability to North American influence occurred during a financial crisis that reached its peak in mid-1976. Several problems produced the critical situation. A series of government deficits, financed by increases in the money supply that outpaced productivity, nourished an inflation rate that reached 11.6 percent during the first half of 1976. The spiraling prices made Mexican exports more costly and less attractive to customers, especially those in the United States where a recession diminished demand for foreign goods. To make matters worse, robust public spending contributed to a sharp upsurge in imports, giving rise to a current account deficit that grew from $1 billion in 1970 to $3.7 billion in 1975. Population growth and inefficiency in the agricultural sector necessitated growing food imports.

The differential between the inflation rates on opposite sides of the Rio Grande stimulated Mexicans to travel and spend in the United States. In the absence of expanded exports and healthy earnings from tourism, huge foreign borrowing was required to pay for goods purchased abroad, particularly those linked to the state's move into heavy industry. Consequently, nearly 25 percent of export earnings were needed simply to pay the interest and dividends on previously acquired debt that stood at $17.5 billion from international financial institutions, $12 billion of which was on the books of U.S. banks. To make matters worse, Mexican investors, who saw public investment exceed that of the private sector for the first time in history, seriously doubted the competence of the president to pull the country out of the quagmire. "Echeverría was a romantic intellectual who never understood finances," complained a U.S. banker.

"He tried to complete so many projects in a short time that he spent the Treasury silly."[42] Speculation against the peso, fed by the fear that its substantial overvaluation would precipitate a devaluation, gave impulse to capital flight of some $4 billion to U.S. and European banks. The government vowed to maintain the integrity of the peso, whose fixed parity to the dollar—unchanged from a 12.5-to-one ratio since 1954—had become a vital symbol of national pride and international confidence. With the dollar reserves of the Bank of Mexico nearly exhausted and officials unable to staunch the hemorrhage, Mexico had no option but to capitulate. On August 31, Finance Minister Mario Ramón Beteta stated that the peso would be allowed to float freely against the dollar. This announcement led to an effective devaluation of 37 percent when the selling rate of the dollar was fixed at 19.9 pesos on September 11. Speculation resumed as neither business nor the general public believed in the government's ability to manage the economy. Wage and price increases vitiated much of the effect of the August 31 devaluation, and Echeverría continued to rail against "pro-fascists" and "plutocrats" in the private sector. In particular, he denounced the Monterrey industrialists as "egoists" and "bad Christians" who put their own interests before the national good.[43] Even thousands of small depositors took their life savings out of pesos and converted them to dollars. To counteract this second exodus of capital, the Bank of Mexico stopped supporting the peso on October 27, producing a second devaluation. Thus, the peso's overall depreciation exceeded 50 percent.

The United States government and North American financial institutions came to the rescue of the besieged currency. As early as April 1976, Mexico received $360 million under a short-term lending arrangement, known as a "swap," with the U.S. Federal Reserve. The Federal Reserve and the Treasury Department made available additional support to counter "disorderly" conditions in the foreign exchange markets until the International Monetary Fund (IMF) provided $1.2 billion in further assistance in November. In addition, the Bank of America served as the agent for a consortium of 18 international banks that furnished an $800 million Eurodollar loan to help finance Mexico's "investment program of basic infra-structure and other capital intensive projects." Also participating in this venture were Bankers Trust International Ltd., Chase Manhattan Ltd., Chemical Bank, Citicorp International Ltd., and the Manufacturers Hanover Trust Company. The discovery of new oil deposits in 1973 sharpened the interest of these banks in lending to Mexico. Oil exports averaged only 105,000 barrels per day (bpd) in 1975, but the U.S. government predicted exports of as many as 1 million bpd by 1980. Indeed, the London *Economist* observed that foreign bankers "have an almost blind faith in the country's oil reserves."[44]

The foreign assistance was predicated on Mexico's putting its economic house in order. Under its constitution, the IMF must supervise the recovery plan of any member that undergoes a devaluation of more than 10 percent. The IMF's stabilization plan, projected for three years, emphasized improving the country's balance-of-payments picture by imposing a $3 billion cap on the net increase in government foreign indebtedness in 1977, with declining ceilings anticipated for 1978 and 1979. Also of concern were public sector accounts, savings ratios, and investment levels. The scheme stressed the need to control inflation by tightening credit, squeezing wages, reducing public spending, and limiting borrowing from abroad. While imposed by an international organization, the austerity package enjoyed the fulsome backing of the U.S. government, as well as the strong support of foreign banks, which demanded the IMF's guarantee as a condition of extending credits to Mexico.[45]

United States influence was also evident with respect to border crossings. Echeverría's many pronouncements about the poor and downtrodden may have raised expectations. Yet, despite the expansionist economic policies, at least 150,000 to 200,000 men and women joined the already bloated ranks of the unemployed and underemployed in each year of his administration.[46] Furthermore, a study published in early 1975 estimated that of Mexico's 58 million inhabitants, 14.5 million were illiterate and 10 to 11 million never ate meat or drank milk.[47] The failure to find sufficient opportunities at home impelled hundreds of thousands of workers to seek their fortunes in the United States. According to figures supplied by the U.S. Immigration and Naturalization Service, apprehensions of illegal aliens more than doubled during Echeverría's term, rising from 348,178 (1971) to 781,474 (1976). Echeverría's meetings with Presidents Nixon (June 1972) and Ford (October 1974) produced pledges to study the problem, but no support for a Mexican proposal to establish a quota system for Mexican workers. The accelerating flow of these workers gave the United States government important leverage to exert when and if it sought to curb the influx.

Echeverría's mercurial behavior, erratic pronouncements, and inept handling of economic problems alienated both the right and left: the former because of resentment toward the government's intrusion into the economy; the latter because the president's performance did not match his rhetoric of reform. The left's hostility became evident in March 1975 when Echeverría visited Mexico's National Autonomous University, UNAM. Traditionally, the president of Mexico, who has been compared to an Aztec emperor, a Spanish viceroy, and even the Pope, enjoys public respect that borders on reverence. But the students defied tradition to hurl epithets, stones, and bottles at the visitor, whom they drove from the campus. Echeverría tried to blame the incident on U.S. meddling in Mexican affairs. During the disturbance, he branded the increasingly abusive student audience as "young fascists, manipulated by the CIA." Later, he told a large political gathering that Mexico "will not tolerate the chain of events which produced the overthrow of President Salvador Allende." No proof was advanced to bolster the charges; however, Foreign Minister Rabasa declared, "We must assume that the CIA operates in all of Latin America, unless there is proof to the contrary."[48] Throughout his administration, Echeverría readily attributed acts of violence to social maladies as varied as drug abuse, casual sex, broken homes, television violence, and yellow journalism.

Echeverría sought to curry favor with the left by requiring thousands of PEMEX employees in professional and managerial positions to affiliate with the corrupt, pro-government Oil Workers Union. He raised industrial wages 17 percent in 1974, 22 percent in 1975, and 16 to 23 percent in 1976. On October 1, 1976, he also froze prices on 270 products, including staple consumer goods, whose prices had been allowed to increase slightly after the August devaluation. Finally, just 12 days before López Portillo's scheduled inauguration, the chief executive—in an attempt to polish his populist image—charged that affluent landowners in the North had broken the law by concealing their holdings under relatives' names. Thus, he ordered that 243,000 acres valued at approximately $80 million in Sonora's lush, irrigated Yaqui Valley be turned over as small parcels to landless campesinos. Government-sponsored unions quickly moved to accomplish an "invasion" by 8,000 farm families. The seizure stirred a hornet's nest of protest from large farmers and their allies. The Monterrey Group took the lead as businessmen throughout the country closed stores and plants in a 24-hour sympathy strike. Full-page newspaper ads flogged Echeverría for "attacking the productive men of Mexico and demanded that the expropriations be canceled." Spokesmen for business interests warned darkly of the president's attempt to impose a "socialist or Communist system."[49]

The publicity lavished on the Sonora occupations aroused peasants in neighboring Sinaloa who, on November 26, threatened to seize 100,000 acres if the government did not continue its expropriations. At that point Echeverría backed down. To prevent an armed battle between peasants and landlords, he announced that only a token 32,000 acres would be handed over to farmhands; additional distributions would await the pleasure of the next president. Peasants in Durango state also occupied large areas of land on November 29. The conflict precipitated widespread rumors for the first time in recent memory that the military would stage a coup d'état. The most prevalent version of this rumor suggested that the army would act to keep Echeverría in power—a ludicrous possibility in view of the president's unpopularity within the officer corps. Four bomb explosions on the eve of the new president's inauguration concluded a sexennium that seemed as absurd as it was tragic.

CONCLUSIONS

Despite abandonment of a defensive and isolationist foreign policy in favor of highly politicized activism that emphasized institution-building and widespread diplomatic relations, Mexico was more dependent on its northern neighbor when Echeverría left office than when he had donned the green, white, and red presidential sash six years earlier. Borrowing abroad, chiefly from U.S. financial institutions, had ballooned Mexico's public foreign debt from $4.5 billion in 1971 to $19.6 billion in 1976. During the same period, U.S. investment in Mexico had risen sharply even with the passage of new regulations. Imports from the United States, which accounted for 61 percent of Mexico's total in 1971, stood at 63 percent in 1976. Only in the category of Mexican exports to the United States was a slight decline registered from 62 to 57 percent.[50] But these statistics do not begin to describe the psychological dimensions of a hegemonic relationship painfully evident in the U.S.-backed rescue of Mexico from the brink of bankruptcy.

Even as Mexico became more beholden to the United States, its own masses found themselves increasingly dependent on the nation's elite because inflation had sharpened discrepancies in income distribution and insufficient job creation had swelled the ranks of the unemployed. To mask this growing external and internal dependency, Echeverría resorted to the highly demagogic acts described above. For many Mexicans, oil and natural gas seemed to provide the last best hope for realizing the long deferred goals of the country's revolution, while enabling the country to act independently in international affairs.

NOTES

1. Robert E. Looney, *Mexico's Economy: A Policy Analysis with Forecasts to 1990* (Boulder, Colo.: Westview Press, 1978) p. 61.

2. John Womack, Jr., "The Spoils of the Mexican Revolution," *Foreign Affairs* 48, No. 4 (July 1970): 684.

3. Womack, "Spoils of the Mexican Revolution," p. 684.

4. Judith Alder Hellman, *Mexico in Crisis* (New York: Holmes & Meier, 1978), p. 148.

5. *New York Times*, December 6, 1970, p. 23.

6. Looney, *Mexico's Economy,* p. 74.

7. David Gordon, "Mexico: A Survey," *Economist*, April 22, 1978, p. 18.

8. George W. Grayson, "The Making of a Mexican President, 1976," *Current History* 70, No. 413 (February 1976): 52, 83; and the *New York Times*, August 4, 1974, p. 10.

9. For a collection of essays on the dependency model, see Heraldo Muñoz (ed.), *From Dependency to Development: Strategies to Overcome Underdevelopment and Inequality* (Boulder, Colo.: Westview, 1981).

10. *Washington Post*, August 31, 1975, p. 31.

11. *New York Times*, December 6, 1970, p. 23.

12. *Latin America*, September 15, 1972, p. 293.

13. Al R. Wichtrich, "Mexican-American Commercial Relations," in Robert H. McBride (ed.), *Mexico and the United States* (Englewood Cliffs, N.J.: Prentice Hall, 1981), pp. 96–99; and Looney, *Mexico's Economy,* pp. 80–81.

14. *Latin America*, November 10, 1972, p. 358.

15. *New York Times*, December 6, 1970, p. 25.

16. *Latin America*, November 10, 1972, p. 358.

17. Guy Poitras, "Mexico's Foreign Policy in an Age of Interdependence," in Elizabeth G. Ferris and Jennie K. Lincoln (eds.), *Latin American Foreign Policies: Global and Regional Dimensions* (Boulder, Colo.: Westview, 1981), p. 107.

18. Poitras, "Mexico's Foreign Policy," p. 107.

19. Poitras, "Mexico's Foreign Policy," p. 107.

20. *Times of the Americas*, April 2, 1975, p. 1.

21. *Facts on File*, April 5, 1975, p. 210; and *Proceso*, November 20, 1976, pp. 11–12.

22. *Times of the Americas*, April 2, 1975, p. 1.

23. Edith B. Couturier, "Mexico," in Harold Eugene Davis, Larman C. Wilson et al. (eds.), *Latin American Foreign Policies: An Analysis* (Baltimore: Johns Hopkins University Press, 1975), p. 125.

24. According to *Facts on File* and the *New York Times Index*, the United States was the only foreign country visited by Presidents Cárdenas (1934–1940), Avila Camacho (1940–1946), Alemán Valdés (1946–1952), Ruiz Cortines (1952–1958), and Díaz Ordaz (1964–1970) during their terms. In addition to a trip to the United States, López Mateos (1958–1964) also spent three days in Canada.

25. Of the three dozen nations visited, the breakdown is as follows: Europe (9), Asia (4), Africa and the Mid-East (9), and the Americas (14); see Luis Echeverría Alvarez, *VI Informe de Gobierno* (Mexico City: Cultura y Ciencia Política, A. C., 1976), n. p.

26. *Latin America*, March 30, 1973, p. 98.

27. *Facts on File*, September 20, 1975, p. 691.

28. *Washington Post*, November 27, 1974, p. 4.

29. Echeverría, *VI Informe de Gobierno*.

30. Poitras, "Mexico's Foreign Policy," p. 108.

31. *New York Times*, December 17, 1975, p. 13.

32. *Latin America*, December 19, 1975, p. 393.

33. *Newsweek*, December 6, 1976, p. 37; *New York Times*, December 17, 1975, p. 13.

34. *Latin America*, December 19, 1975, p. 393.

35. *Washington Post*, November 28, 1975, p. C-4.

36. *Latin America*, December 19, 1975, p. 393.

37. *New York Times*, December 30, 1975, p. 2.

38. *Washington Post*, December 19, 1975, p. A-16.

39. *New York Times*, December 30, 1975, p. 2.

40. Mario Ojeda, "The Negotiating Power of Oil: The Mexican Case," in Jerry R. Ladman et al. (eds.), *U.S.-Mexican Energy Relationships* (Lexington, Mass.: Lexington Books, 1981), pp. 207–8.

41. *Washington Post*, December 19, 1975, p. 16.

42. *Newsweek*, December 6, 1976, p. 37.

43. *Latin America*, November 5, 1976, p. 341.

44. *Economist*, July 3, 1976, p. 100.

45. María del Rosario Green, "Mexico's Economic Dependence," in Susan Kaufman Purcell (ed.), *Mexico-United States Relations* (New York: American Academy of Political Science, 1981), p. 109.

46. Richard R. Fagen, "The Realities of U.S.-Mexican Relations," *Foreign Affairs* 55, No. 5 (July 1977): 694.

47. *Times of London*, February 24, 1975, p. 14-A.

48. *Washington Post*, March 18, 1975, p. 15.

49. *New York Times*, November 20, 1976, p. 8; November 23, 1976, p. 54; and November 26, 1976, pp. 1–10.

50. Wichtrich, "Mexican-American Commercial Relations," p. 80.

4

OIL AND GAS POLICY
UNDER LÓPEZ PORTILLO

INTRODUCTION

Energy policy loomed large in both the United States and Mexico during the 1970s. The former, which shifted from an exporter to an importer of oil, paid out billions of dollars to purchase supplies from Mexico and other countries. The latter, which shifted from an importer to an exporter, earned billions of dollars in sales to its northern neighbor and other nations.

Certain energy goals of the two countries differed. Mexico's president and the director-general of PEMEX wanted to receive the highest prices possible for ever larger shipments of oil and natural gas, diversify Mexico's exports to keep from relying too heavily on a single customer, and link sales to the acquisition of foreign loans, investment, and technology. For its part, the United States, while willing to pay the world price for oil, was loath to approve higher prices for foreign suppliers of natural gas than it paid domestic producers. It was also eager to see an expansion in overall oil output, both to restrain prices charged by OPEC and to reduce its dependence on the Arab members of that cartel. However, despite strong interest by private groups in significantly higher PEMEX output, U.S. policymakers viewed stability in Mexico as an objective that transcended increased exports. Rather than involve itself in package deals, the United States preferred to see private corporations carry out energy transactions on commercial terms, subject only to the domestic regulatory process. This chapter will explore the adjustment of these sometimes conflicting objectives during the presidency of José López Portillo. It will also evaluate Mexico's use of the vaunted oil weapon in exacting concessions from the United States in trade, investment, immigration, and other areas of concern.

LÓPEZ PORTILLO TO THE PRESIDENCY

López Portillo owed his selection as Mexico's sixtieth president to Echeverría.[1] Born into what he described as a "typical middle-class family," the new chief executive attended state-operated elementary and secondary schools in Mexico City before entering the National Autonomous University of Mexico in 1939. There he became acquainted with Echeverría, a fellow student, and the two young men won scholarships to study political science at the University of Chile. López Portillo practiced law before joining the faculty of UNAM in the early 1950s as a professor of law, political science, and public administration. In 1959 he accepted his first government post in the Ministry of National Patrimony; six years later, President Díaz Ordaz named him director general of legal affairs in the Ministry of the Presidency, the government agency then responsible for the public investment. In 1968 he was promoted to undersecretary in charge of planning. During the first year of Echeverría's administration, López Portillo served as an undersecretary in the Ministry of National Patrimony. Then Echeverría appointed him director of the Federal Electricity Commission, a post he held for only nine months before his elevation to minister of finance and public credit. In this position he attracted attention for his competent, if unimaginative, management of fiscal policy and the skillful handling of an unwieldy bureaucracy.

Although a member of the PRI, López Portillo had never held elective office until he captured the presidency on July 4, 1976. This victory followed nine months of dawn-to-dark campaigning that covered 50,000 miles and took him to some 924 communities. Describing himself as a man of "neither the left nor the right," the 56-year-old candidate enunciated only general goals under the slogan "La solución somos todos" (We are all the solution). While supporting such objectives dear to the left as "justice for all" and the liberation of Mexicans from "imperialism," he also appealed to the right by favoring expanded investment, improved governmental operations, and budgetary discipline. López Portillo's lack of either a political base within the revolutionary party or a well-developed ideology may have encouraged the power-hungry Echeverría to believe that, even after leaving office, he could influence the actions of his long-time friend.

Though Echeverría's handpicked candidate, López Portillo quickly showed that he would neither be manipulated by, nor follow the path of, his predecessor. Nowhere was the difference between the two men greater than in economic policy. As mentioned above, Herculean problems awaited the new chief executive. Whereas Echeverría practiced confrontation with the business community, López Portillo stressed conciliation and cooperation. He supported stern anti-inflation measures to shore up the peso; signed an agreement with 140 companies that received tax concessions in exchange for stable prices of basic consumer goods; struck a deal with organized labor to limit the size of wage increases; and announced an "Alliance for Production"—a ten-point investment program involving government, private industry, and labor to spur production and create some 300,000 new jobs. While endorsing "efficiency and justice" in agriculture, he publicly doubted whether reallocating the country's scarce arable land to propertyless peasants would further these objectives. He favored a "realistic" strategy; namely, the integration of small, inefficient parcels into larger, more productive units combined with the generation of more nonagricultural jobs. When asked about this approach, Alberto Santos, head of Nuevo Leon's industrialists, said: "In comparison with the previous president, we feel we are in heaven. His ministers not only listen to us—they pay attention."[2]

OIL TO THE RESCUE

Soothing rhetoric, official belt-tightening, administrative reform, and a cabinet dominated by middle-aged technocrats helped to restore the confidence of domestic and foreign economic interests. Nevertheless, the key element in securing their support was the new administration's oil policy.

In May 1972 PEMEX struck oil in the steamy marshes and lagoons of southeast Mexico near Villahermosa. The prolific Cactus and Sitio Grande fields revealed the presence of the Reforma trend, which arches across the states of Tabasco and Chiapas. The discovery attracted worldwide attention. For example, on October 12, 1974, the *Washington Post* reported that preliminary estimates indicated that these fields contained 20 billion barrels of high-grade oil and looked "exciting enough to be another Persian Gulf of petroleum."[3] Output from the trend, labeled "little Kuwait" by journalists because of the vast quantities of oil located in a relatively small area, rose from 27,400 bpd (1973) to over 1 million bpd (1979) before declining to 835,000 bpd (1982).

Even more impressive than the Tabasco and Chiapas fields were those discovered in Campeche Sound, 50 miles north of the shrimping port of Ciudad Carmen. The May 1972 Chiapas-Tabasco success led PEMEX to delineate a 3,000 square-mile adjacent offshore block to be studied for its potential. In 1976 a drilling ship, aided by a local fisherman's report of a natural leakage, struck commercial quantities of oil approximately 10,500 feet deep at a site called Chac (named for a Mayan god, as are all wells in this area). The following year, the Bacab exploratory well, 14 miles above Chac 1, also yielded oil, indicating a productive capacity of 2,000 bpd. But so productive was the Akal field, found in 1977, that "the pressure was barely controllable," according to one petroleum engineer.[4] The Campeche area is substantially larger than the Reforma zone and its first 27 production wells averaged 30,000 bpd, compared with a 7,000-barrel mean output for the region's onshore wells. Akal, the largest field in the prolific Cantarell complex, includes the Akal 3 and Akal 74 wells, which produce 60,000 and 50,000 bpd, respectively. The size and volumes of the offshore deposits prompted one PEMEX official to state: "We seem to be facing another startling development [after the Reforma discovery]. It's like the nurse coming out of the delivery room to tell the anxious man he's the proud father of a baby. . . only to come back a while later to tell him it's twins."[5] By 1982, the offshore twin was producing almost twice as much oil (1.6 million bpd) as its mainland sibling.

To achieve this greater output, López Portillo announced a six-year program that called for over-all production to climb from 894,219 bpd in 1976 to 2.25 million in 1982, when half of the output would be exported. The plan, which carried a $15.5 billion price tag, also contemplated an expanded refining capacity of 1.7 million bpd, a sharp increase in petrochemical output to 15.5 million tons, and a doubling of natural gas production to 3.6 billion cubic feet per day.

The men who held key positions in the monopoly in the early 1970s either worked in the oil industry during the 1938 expropriation or joined the state monopoly soon thereafter when it was attempting to become a self-sustaining enterprise. They were dedicated professionals who insisted on rigorous verification of new deposits before including them in the country's "proven" reserves. At that time, PE-MEX announced neither "possible" nor "probable" reserves as was the practice of some firms. Above all, the "generation of '38," as the men who had experienced the nationalization were known, resisted flamboyant disclosures of huge holdings to prevent the industry's once again becoming the target of foreign aspirations. Francisco Viniegra, PEMEX's former exploration manager, alleged that company officials kept the true reserve levels from the president lest he or corrupt politicians misuse the increased earnings. "We were afraid of Echeverría," he said. "Let's face it, he would have given the oil to Cuba and other Communist countries."[6] In fact, Cuba was the first country to which Mexico offered to sell its "new oil." Castro ultimately refused, deciding instead to continue receiving petroleum at approximately one-third the world price from the Soviet Union. Viniegra's superiors denied that scientifically verified holdings remained unreported. Nonetheless, despite the disclosure of impressively large deposits and a 25 percent increase in production that shifted Mexico from a net importer to a net exporter in September 1974, proven reserves only expanded from 5.4 billion barrels in 1971 to 6.3 billion barrels in 1976.

López Portillo wasted no time in revising this figure. During the presidential campaign, he had appointed Jorge Díaz Serrano to study the oil sector. A petroleum engineer, entrepreneur, millionaire oilman, and a close friend of the president-designate, Díaz Serrano claimed to use new techniques employed on Alaska's North Slope and in Iran to reevaluate PEMEX's geological logs of the Reforma. Upon assuming office, López Portillo named Díaz Serrano as director-general of the state agency. Within one month, they nearly doubled Mexico's proven holdings to 11.2 billion barrels, an amount derived from drilling with a pencil rather than drilling wildcat wells or completing new engineering studies of reservoirs. By mid-1977, the national company had raised its estimate of proven reserves to 14 billion barrels.

Thanks to successful exploration efforts onshore and in Campeche Sound, Mexico's announced oil wealth climbed at a spectacular rate. On December 31, 1982, PEMEX claimed 72 billion barrels of proven reserves, 90.3 billion barrels of probable deposits, and 250 billion barrels of possible holdings. These figures, which have inspired comparisons between Mexico and Saudi Arabia, vaulted Mexico from fourteenth to fourth in the ranks of oil-possessing nations during López Portillo's *sexenio*. Meanwhile, it shot up from fifteenth to fourth in terms of worldwide production.

Questions have surfaced regarding the magnitude of Mexico's holdings. With respect to the possible reserve figure, Viniegra told reporters for the *Los Angeles Times*: "It's impossible. I know the geology of Mexico and it's not there." A.A. Meyerhoff, a Tulsa-based geologist who has worked for the monopoly, termed the estimate of 200 billion possible barrels, a figure announced on December 31, 1978, "utter nonsense."[7]

No one doubts that Mexico has lots of petroleum. But industry experts point to practices that cast doubt on Mexico's claim to be the world's fourth largest repository. To begin with, PEMEX includes natural gas and associated liquids in its proven deposits, thereby inflating the figures by one-third. Also embraced within these proven reserves are some 17.6 billion barrels in the Chicontepec field between Tampico and Poza Rica on the Gulf coastal plain, whose development would require some 16,000 wells, more than the state firm has drilled since its inception in 1938.

Equally serious is PEMEX's frequent estimation and exaggeration of the secondary recovery factor—the percentage of oil that can be forced from a deposit by steam soaking, water and gas injection, and other methods—without completing careful engineering studies of the reservoir, designing the appropriate recovery technique, and rigorously determining the secondary recovery coefficient.

Key PEMEX engineers, now retired, have confirmed to the author that the monopoly violates internationally accepted standards both by estimating the depth of a deposit when the bottom of the reservoir has not been located, and by mixing proven and probable reserves by assuming that a geologically similar formation would yield as much oil and gas as an adjacent one already under production.

These questionable practices may explain PEMEX's reluctance to invite outside consultants to assess its holdings independently. The last time it did was in 1977 when DeGolyer & MacNaughton, a prestigious Dallas company, certified 14.7 billion barrels of proven deposits. Soon thereafter, PEMEX boosted the figure to 40 billion barrels—a quantity that James W. Watson, senior vice-president of DeGolyer & MacNaughton, insisted that his firm had "never substantiated." When asked if Mexico's proven holdings might be as high as 28 billion, Watson exclaimed, "Oh, no. Oh, no." He also said, "We've reminded [the Mexicans] over and over about the danger of losing credibility. We've been trying to hold them back."[8]

If not an unbiased source, then who has been validating PEMEX's figures? As it turns out, the monopoly has relied upon another state agency: the Mexican Petroleum Institute (IMP), a highly regarded Mexico City training center, think tank, and research and development facility, with scores of patents to its credit.

Yet, the IMP's head of production during the López Portillo administration refused to verify PEMEX's figures because of inadequate data. Thus, his boss, Agustín Straffon Arteaga, then-director of the institute, finally confirmed PEMEX's holdings in a personal act based on political expediency, not scientific considerations. In an unreleased internal study completed in late 1982, the IMP estimated Mexico's reserves, including natural gas but excluding the Chicontepec field, at approximately 48 billion barrels.

A confluence of reasons may have inspired Díaz Serrano to advance the highest amounts possible. Domestically, the prospect of massive deposits strengthens the monopoly's position with respect to bureaucratic competitors, bolsters the pride of a highly nationalistic people who for four decades have viewed the oil industry as a sacred symbol of national dignity, and enhances public confidence in an economy beset by surging inflation and ubiquitous unemployment. Upon taking control of PEMEX Díaz Serrano said that Mexico stood at the threshold of wealth not seen since the glory of Tenochtitlán, the Aztec capital. He later told his nation's chamber of deputies: "For the first time in its history, Mexico enjoys sufficient wealth to make possible not only the resolution of economic problems facing the country, but also the creation of a new, permanently prosperous country, a rich country where the right to work will be a reality."[9]

During the Napoleonic wars, ambitious soldiers reportedly carried a marshal's baton in their knapsacks. Similar stories abound about presidential sashes resting in the briefcases of Mexican cabinet members and heads of state firms, and the director-general's political fortunes appeared linked to the growth and performance of his agency.

Large reserves also justify the rapid exploitation of deposits—a tendency that alarms petroleum engineers conversant with the excesses of earlier periods in the nation's history because of the damage done to wells in Bermúdez, Cactus, and other fields in Chiapas and Tabasco. An accelerated flow of oil gives rise to more contracts, which provide opportunities for sub rosa "commissions" in an industry where graft and corruption flourish. Even corporations founded by Díaz Serrano landed lucrative contracts. One such firm, Perforaciones Marinas del Golfo, drilled the well that suffered the "blowout" and fire in June 1979, pouring 3.1 million barrels of oil and 3 billion cubic feet of gas into the seafood-rich Bay of Campeche. Detractors doubt the PEMEX chief's claim to have severed all financial ties with these companies. Similarly, the extraordinarily corrupt Oil Workers Union, which under a 1977 law enjoys 40 percent of all onshore well-drilling contracts, profited from the boom atmosphere to enrich its self-serving leaders who enjoyed direct access to López Portillo.

The possession of major reserves lofts a country's standing within the community of nations, improves its position with the World Bank, the Inter-American Development Bank, and other international financial agencies, and increases its attractiveness to private foreign lenders. Despite overtures from Venezuela, Algeria, and other members, Mexico declined to join OPEC. It perceived its sophisticated oil industry as quite different from that of cartel nations; insisted on preserving freedom of action in designing its domestic and foreign hydrocarbon policies; and preferred to enjoy the best of both worlds: the ability, thanks to lower shipping costs to the U.S. market, to charge more than many OPEC states for its oil, while avoiding the negative consequences of affiliation. Mexican officials no doubt anticipated that the inflated figures would bolster their leverage in negotiations with the United States on issues such as trade, illegal immigration, and the price of natural gas.

Key members of the generation of '38 had retired, and with them went any reticence about publicizing Mexico's reserves. Indeed, revelations of new holdings were made with a view toward gaining maximum attention in the United States. In mid-1978 Mexico's major newspapers mounted a campaign aimed in part at convincing the U.S. government and public of the importance of their country's oil riches.[10] Additionally, Díaz Serrano reported the Chicontepec discovery at a November 1978 meeting of the American Petroleum Institute in Chicago. Mexico was acutely aware of its neighbor's widespread interest in finding new sources of imports as reliance on OPEC supplies shot up from 17.3 percent (1973) to 30.5 percent (1978) of total consumption, while purchases from non-OPEC sources decreased from 18.9 to 13.9 percent during the same period.

OIL AND MEXICO'S STATUS

Mexico's oil wealth proved a magnet for presidents, prime ministers, and princes. High-level visitors from scores of nations streamed to this cornucopia-shaped nation to seek access to its petroleum. Heretofore, foreign policy for Mexico had meant ties to the United States and, to a lesser extent, other Latin American states. Echeverría's move to change that relationship aborted as economic difficulties intensified his country's need for financial assistance from the International Monetary Fund and North American banking sources. Hydrocarbon riches enabled López Portillo's Mexico to pick and choose from among dozens of offers to forge bonds with other industrialized countries, as well as those of the third world. At one time Mexico " 'had to go searching for money to borrow in New York, London, and Zurich,' said treasury under-secretary, Jesús Silva Herzog, 'now it's coming to us and we sometimes have had a hard time trying to select the best offer.' "[11] The president entered into especially attractive package deals with Japan, France, Sweden, and Canada that brought not simply dollars for crude, but guarantees of investment capital, loans, and technology transfers from these industrialized countries

For example, during a late 1978 visit to Tokyo, Japanese bankers were practically throwing money at López Portillo, who concluded two loan accords totaling $1.1 billion. These were the largest credits without strings ever arranged by Japanese banks for a foreign borrower. The money was later complemented by technical assistance for petroleum-related projects in which both countries displayed an interest; specifically, building a petrochemical plant, constructing port facilities on the Gulf (Tampico and Coatzacoalcos) and Pacific (Salina Cruz and Lázaro Cárdenas) coasts, and completing the Alpha Omega road-rail-pipeline link across the Isthmus of Tehuantepec. These agreements coincided with the arrival of the first shipment of Mexican crude in Japan. Revolutionary upheaval in Iran, formerly a major supplier of oil to Japan, whetted Japanese interest in exchanging dollars and know-how for PEMEX petroleum. In 1979 Mexico received $516 million in Japanese investment, compared to $694 million during the previous nine years. The figure for 1979 represented 42 percent of Japan's total investment in Latin America, whereas Mexico's proportion had traditionally been 4 to 5 percent.[12]

A 1980 trip by President Valéry Giscard d'Estaing to Mexico led to an offer by the French government to lend $227 million for 20 years at 3.5 percent interest for the purchase of French industrial equipment. Also promised were loans from French banks at attractive rates.

Government officials were not Mexico's only suitors. Representatives of international banks also competed fiercely to finance Mexico's oil-powered industrial development. A measure of Mexico's growing influence appeared in its ability to attract ever larger loans on increasingly favorable terms—that is, lower interest rates, longer repayment requirements, and generous grace periods. For instance, in 1976 Mexico had to pay 1.75 points over the London Inter-Bank Offering Rate (LIBOR), the benchmark figure that international banks charge one another. Three years later, Mexico could obtain 10-year loans for .625 of a point above LIBOR. The ease in obtaining credits, the lion's share of which come from U.S. financial institutions, helped to balloon the external debt of the public sector from $22.9 billion in 1977 to $85 billion by 1984.

Mexico's new status found López Portillo showered with invitations to visit foreign lands. All told, he made trips to 16 countries, meeting with such prominent statesmen as President Giscard d'Estaing, Premier Pierre Trudeau, Premier Masayoshi Ohira, and Chancellor Helmut Schmidt. Echeverría had excited Mexican aspirations for a new, more assertive position on the world stage. But the role that he could not secure with breathless globetrotting and flamboyant speeches was assured to López Portillo, *grâce à la* oil bonanza.

The International Monetary Fund also recognized Mexico's status as an emerging oil power. The organization had imposed a $3 billion limit on new foreign borrowing by the Mexican government in 1977—a figure that was to decline to $2 billion in 1978. The IMF's willingness to extend the $3 billion cap to 1978 permitted the country access to another $1 billion in credits, monies used largely by PEMEX to purchase oilfield equipment. Impressive earnings from hydrocarbon sales, success in meeting IMF targets, and the timely repayment of loans assured the removal of all restrictions on external indebtedness.[13]

On January 7, 1980, Mexico's prominence as an oil producer helped it win a nonpermanent seat on the U.N. Security Council as a compromise candidate after neither Cuba nor Colombia could muster the required two-thirds majority in the General Assembly. This was a major change in policy. Mexico, though an enthusiastic supporter of the United Nations, for which it recruited other Latin American members, had refused either to serve on the Security Council since 1946 or to participate actively in debates on controversial issues after cold war politics began to dominate the organization's agenda. Mexico preferred to steer clear of international disputes that might alienate the United States or cast it in a subservient role to its northern neighbor.[14] The oil-inspired confidence encouraged Mexico to promote multilateral policy initiatives in the U.N., especially with respect to energy, migration, transnational corporations, and global development issues.

Mexico's status as a regional leader was acknowledged when Foreign Minister Castañeda was asked to address the Nonaligned Movement's conference held in Havana in September 1979. Further recognition occurred when López Portillo assumed the chairmanship, with Austria's Chancellor Bruno Kreisky, of the International Meeting on Cooperation and Development.[15] This so-called North-South summit convened in the Mexican resort of Cancún on October 22, 1981. Its purpose (to be further discussed in Chapter 5) was to promote a large-scale transfer of resources and technology from the affluent North to the impecunious South. When asked if its new activism would affect relations with Washington, López Portillo said: "Mexico has its own foreign policy. It takes its decisions independently and it expresses them in a world in which, fortunately, Mexico's voice is being heard and will be heard more and more." That the group of 77 selected Porfirio Muñoz Ledo, Mexico's U.N. ambassador, as its president in 1983 provides additional evidence of Mexico's enhanced standing in international affairs.[16]

Mexico's becoming a significant aid donor also testifies to its elevation within the community of nations. During the first few years of its new oil boom, Mexico resisted pleas from Costa Rica and other less developed nations to supply crude on preferential terms. "Although they are needy," sympathized Patrimony Minister José Andrés Oteyza, "priority in selling them our oil will be determined by the terms of international trade rather than by any other consideration."[17] After all, Mexico was itself a developing country. Shipments of petroleum gratis to Nicaragua and an oil-for-bauxite swap with Jamaica proved harbingers of a changing attitude that was clearly revealed on August 3, 1980, when López Portillo met with Venezuelan President Luis Herrera Campíns in San José, Costa Rica, to announce an "Energy Cooperation Program for Central American and Caribbean Countries" designed to assist these nations with their energy needs. Under the plan, the first collaborative aid effort between an OPEC and a non-OPEC country, Mexico and Venezuela each pledged to dispatch up to 80,000 bpd of oil on favorable terms to nine nations of the area (the Central American republics, Panama, Barbados, the Dominican Republic, and Jamaica; Haiti was added in 1980, Belize in 1982). The exporters promised to grant the importers credits amounting to 30 percent of the commercial price of their purchases for a period of five years at an annual rate of 4 percent. Should the resources derived from these credits flow to "economic development projects of priority interest," notably those spurring domestic energy production, the loans could be extended to 20 years at a 2 percent interest, with a five-year grace period. These credits were offered at a fraction of the commercial rate; for instance, the Eurodollar interest rate at that time was 10.625 to 10.5 percent.

In theory, Mexico and Venezuela would equally supply the needs of recipients through petroleum shipments made in accordance with commercial contracts entered into bilaterally by Mexico and Venezuela, on the one hand, and the individual purchasing nation, on the other. During the first year of the facility, Venezuela furnished 84,030 bpd and Mexico 37,925 barrels; in the second year, the volumes were 67,262 bpd and 54,150 bpd, respectively; by the third year, Mexico had become the chief supplier because of severe economic and political problems affecting Venezuela in 1983, a presidential election year. A deepening worldwide recession exacerbated the domestic economic difficulties of the debt-ridden donors, forcing them in August 1983 to increase interest rates to 8 percent on short-term credits and to 6 percent on long-term loans. Henceforth, the assistance would cover 20 percent of the commercial value of the sale.

Although conceived and promoted by Venezuela, the oil mechanism satisfied a number of Mexican foreign policy goals. It expanded the purchasing power of countries that run chronic trade deficits with Mexico; demonstrated that Latin Americans can help each other without Washington's involvement; enhanced the donors' international prestige; encouraged energy nationalism through government-to-government accords in the oil sector; and promoted economic stability—or, at least, militated against instability—in a region afflicted by civil strife. It also enabled López Portillo to manifest his genuine concern for the energy problems of poorer countries, which he had proposed to cure with a "global energy plan" unveiled in a September 1979 speech to the United Nations. Above all, it permitted Mexico to associate itself with revolutionists such as the Nicaraguan Sandinistas, while helping to improve economic conditions in a region where guerrillas intend to do to political systems what OPEC price increases have done to their economies. The price of admission to the program was relatively low—at most, only between 3 and 4 percent of production—in comparison with the prestige and benefits derived from promoting stability in a volatile area close to Mexico's major oil fields.

THE UNITED STATES TRIES A NEW APPROACH

Mexico's announcement of large oil holdings attracted the attention of the United States. Table 1 reveals the increased interest in Mexico by several leading U.S. newspapers. Both the *New York Times* and the *Wall Street Journal* gave the first year of López Portillo's administration twice the coverage bestowed upon Echeverría's first 12 months in office. In addition, ranking U.S. officials paid many more visits to Mexico during López Portillo's administration

TABLE 1: Number of Articles about Mexico in Six Major U.S. News Sources

Source	1970	1971	1972	1973	1974	1975	1976	1977	1978	1979	1980	1981	1982
New York Times	110	94	102	118	138	139	157	203	74	216	122	139	184
Washington Post	*	*	87	112	72	55	120	120	102	152	66	38	111
Wall Street Journal	19	43	40	46	70	72	105	99	79	125	121	107	221
U.S. News & World Report	1	0	5	1	3	0	6	3	4	11	2	6	11
Newsweek	1	0	0	2	1	0	3	3	2	10	2	3	10
Time	2	3	1	3	1	0	3	2	1	2	0	5	17

*No index published this year

Sources: *New York Times Index* (New York: New York Times Co., 1970–1982); Times Company; *Washington Post Index* (Wooster, Ohio: Bell & Howell, 1972–1982); *Wall Street Journal Index* (New York: Dow Jones, 1970–1982); *Public Affairs Information Bulletin* (New York, 1970–1982); *Readers' Guide to Periodicals* (Bronx: Wilson, 1970–1982).

than during that of Echeverría's—a fact most certainly related to the oil boom.

President Gerald Ford held two uneventful meetings with Echeverría that produced no major policy changes. In fact, at a session on October 21, 1974, Ford suggested the formation of a commission to study immigration and related topics, thus sidestepping Mexico's request to allow greater freedom for Mexican nationals to work in the United States. Three months before assuming office, López Portillo visited Washington, where Ford courteously received him. The Mexican leader skillfully presented the agenda of issues between the two countries. In reply, the U.S. leader made a pro forma suggestion that these matters be taken up with the appropriate cabinet members. After the president-elect and his party returned to Mexico, the Republican administration made no attempt to follow up on questions raised at the White House session.

Former Secretary of State Henry Kissinger's memoirs demonstrate the low priority assigned U.S.-Mexican relations in this period. His sole reference to Mexico comes in a description of the unobtrusive appointments scheduled to minimize suspicion before departing on his secret trip to Peking. Included on this "nonchalant" schedule was a meeting with Mexico's Foreign Minister Rabasa.[18]

There were indications that Carter might forge a close relationship with his Mexican counterpart because of superficial similarities between the two men. Both shared a penchant for administrative reform, exhibited a moderate political philosophy, saw themselves as restorers of public confidence, and were newcomers on the national political stage, having won election to the presidency with relatively few debts to traditional power brokers. As discussed above, López Portillo garnered his party's support thanks to Echeverría's endorsement; Carter captured his nomination by impressive showings in primaries and caucuses held throughout the country. As might be expected of a president with a provincial background who evinced, at best, a modest grounding in foreign affairs, Carter showed the greatest interest in those countries bordering the United States. Moreover, he had often traveled to Mexico and knew some Spanish. Also auguring well for improved ties with Mexico were Rosalyn Carter's highly publicized interest in Latin America and her assiduous attempts to learn Spanish. In addition to a 12-member official delegation headed by Secretary Kissinger, Mrs. Carter attended López Portillo's inauguration as a private guest of the new chief executive and his wife. She brought a message of "special friendship" for Mexico from her husband, who himself would take office on January 20, 1977. Once in the White House, President Carter invited López Portillo to become the first foreign head of state to visit Washington during his administration. Before leaving Mexico, he set the tone for his visit by offering 40,000 thousand cubic feet (Mcf) per day in emergency natural gas exports to the United States. These shipments, which continued for 60 days, were especially welcomed because gas-related shortages had triggered layoffs of more than 800,000 workers during the bitterest winter in recent memory. Upon greeting his generous guest on February 14, Carter pledged to work closely on a personal and official basis to bind the two countries in a "continual demonstration of common purpose, common hope, common confidence, and common friendship."[19]

The two leaders reportedly got along quite well. In a White House meeting with several staff and cabinet members, Carter assumed a more active role than had Ford. He presided over the session, voiced a keen interest in bilateral subjects, exhibited impressive knowledge of outstanding issues, and pledged to keep abreast of matters of mutual concern. The leaders identified energy, trade, immigration, narcotics, and tourism as questions of great importance to their countries. President Carter complemented symbolic gestures and effusive words with the proposal that a cabinet-level consultative mechanism be created to focus on major issues and pave the way for future discussions between senior representatives of the two nations. During a visit by ranking Mexican officials on May 26, 1977, Carter pleased his visitors by signing Protocol I of the Tlatelolco Treaty, which forbids the introduction of nuclear weapons into Latin America.

This session also spawned three working groups with responsibility for politics, social matters, and finance. Chaired by the U.S. secretary of state and the Mexican minister of foreign relations, the political group met every six months, with sessions held alternately in Washington and Mexico City. Its discussions ran the gamut of bilateral relations.

The economic group was originally headed by Richard Cooper, undersecretary of state for economic affairs, and Jorge de la Vega, López Portillo's first minister of commerce. The complexity of the issues confronting this entity led to the formation of four subgroups to concentrate on finance; tourism; trade; and energy, minerals, industry, and investment.

The working groups compiled a mixed record of achievement. With the exception of the political group, they were large, unwieldy ad hoc bodies with a changing cast of characters who, on each side, had competing interests and sometimes rather indefinite agendas. In the absence of a commitment by one or both nations to settle major disputes, the groups often busied themselves with peripheral matters. Generally speaking, the participants lacked authority to set policy, and the most important bilateral issue in 1977—the terms for a natural gas deal—was handled outside the consultative framework to involve only those individuals and agencies possessing a specific interest in the transaction.

The groups did enable bureaucrats from a number of agencies to make trips abroad to acquire firsthand knowledge of the problem under discussion and become acquainted with the Mexican perspective. Nevertheless, regularly assigned embassy personnel in continual communication with Washington might have handled such talks, at least in the preliminary stages, with appropriate civil servants of the host government. But many U.S. agencies, which in recent years have expanded their own international affairs capabilities, view the State Department as a rival that does not serve their interests and should not act as their representative. Detractors, who argue that the department can make but a limited contribution on energy, investment, and other matters discussed with Mexican counterparts, claim that Foggy Bottom is riven by competing stands on key issues. After all, over a dozen offices and more than fifty foreign-service officers, many in responsible positions, help fashion the department's position on questions relating to Mexico. Wary of the State Department's pivotal role, but mindful of the strong interest in Mexico that Carter had conveyed to his cabinet, other agencies sought to take up important measures outside the consultative mechanism. For its part the State Department, anxious to guard its bureaucratic turf, often appeared reluctant to turn matters over to the working groups where competing agencies had representatives. For example, the department's Bureau of Economic and Business Affairs tried to minimize the role of the Department of Energy in oil and gas issues affecting the two countries. Still, the mechanism provided an interagency forum for representatives of both nations to discuss selected issues and gain familiarity with each other and the difficult nature of the questions involved. It fostered the exchange of information and research and actually helped resolve several problems.

Even as the working groups labored with their assignments, bilateral relations deteriorated. Three actions hastened this process: a sweeping proposal by the Carter administration, presented in August 1977 (to be analyzed in Chapter 7), to deal with illegal immigration; the United States' refusal in May 1978 to return uranium that had been enriched under contract with Mexico, unless it jointly supervised the storage of the radioactive element; and the collapse of negotiations for a natural gas deal.

THE NATURAL GAS CONTROVERSY

The natural gas controversy proved the sharpest thorn pricking the two countries.[20] The Reforma wells contained prodigious quantities of associated natural gas. Most wells in Mexico registered a gas-to-oil ratio of 1,000-to-one; that is, 1,000 cubic feet of gas mingled with each barrel of oil. At first, the central Reforma fields (Sitio Grande, Cactus, Samaria, Río Nuevo, Iride, Cunduacán, and Níspero) maintained this ratio. Later, 6,000 to 7,000 feet of associated gas per barrel issued from some wells, although the average for the area approaches 2,500. As a result, proven natural holdings jumped from 9.1 trillion cubic feet in 1973 to 26.7 trillion cubic feet in 1977.

These impressive ratios, added to the development of the offshore Campeche oil province and the apparent presence of abundant gas in the northern fields of the Sabinas Basin and Monclova in Coahuila state, led PEMEX to estimate that gas production, 2.1 billion cubic feet per day (cfd) in 1976, would climb to 5.4 billion cfd by 1982. Disappointing yields from Sabinas meant that output averaged only 4.3 billion cfd in 1982. In light of the domestic market's inability to absorb production—consumption in 1977 was 684 million cfd—what possibilities existed for handling the surplus?

PEMEX had six possible ways of disposing of its surplus gas: boosting domestic consumption; expanding petrochemical production; conserving the fuel by reinjecting it in the ground or shutting in wells with high gas-to-oil ratios; liquefying the gas and shipping it to

Europe and Japan; burning it off; or exporting it overland to the United States.

Díaz Serrano agreed with the IMP, which endorsed the export alternative because significantly higher domestic use meant modifying and enlarging the entire infrastructure necessary for transforming and delivering gas. Thus, PEMEX began negotiating the sale of gas with U.S. transmission companies in early 1977, and those discussions crystallized into a "Memorandum of Intent" signed between Petróleos Mexicanos and six firms on August 3, 1977.

The memorandum contemplated the largest importation of natural gas in U.S. history. It provided for the initial delivery of approximately 50 million cfd from the fields of northeastern Mexico, possibly as early as the 1977–78 heating season, and for deliveries of 2 billion cfd by 1979 when Reforma gas could be shipped. This amounted to 3 percent of the United States' annual consumption of 20 trillion cubic feet—60 percent of which is used by industry and utilities, 40 percent in commercial and residential heating. The parties contemplated a six-year accord, renewable for a similar term, with Mexico exercising the option to lower or halt exports as required by domestic exigencies. The companies agreed to a Mexican request to peg the initial price and subsequent quarterly increases to the heat equivalent of No. 2 distillate fuel oil, a roughly comparable energy source, delivered in New York Harbor. The accord fixed the price of the first shipments at approximately $2.60 per Mcf, or eight times the Mexican domestic price, and permitted adjustments on a quarterly basis. Should the price of No. 2 fuel decline, another yardstick would be chosen. A "take-or-pay" provision meant that the transmission companies would have to buy the gas regardless of market conditions prevailing in the United States.

The transmission companies purportedly acceded to the Mexican-initiated price. Two scholars have argued that the firms "did not want to be a party to a price hassle with the Mexican government. They had much to lose and nothing to gain by such a hassle."[21] Persuasive evidence contradicts this assertion and indicates that the Tennessee Gas Transmission Company, a Tenneco subsidiary and the leading prospective purchaser of Mexican gas, completed a multivolume study for PEMEX in which it recommended the link to No. 2 fuel oil, even though the resulting price ran counter to Carter administration policy recommendations and the immediate pocketbook in-

terests of U.S. consumers.[22] A separate report, prepared by an economist associated with Tennessee Gas, justified the tie to No. 2 fuel oil,
the price for which was determined by OPEC, because it was economically feasible for Mexico to convert its own industrial sector to
gas and, thereby, obviate the need to flare this clean, desirable energy source. Hence, PEMEX could peg exports to cartel-priced crude
or, alternatively, if gas were sold abroad, it should be viewed as a
major competitor to fuel oil and priced accordingly.[23]

Confident of a deal with the U.S. firms, PEMEX decided on October 6, 1977, to construct a National Gas Trunkline System from the
Reforma fields to the Texas border. All told, the 48-inch-diameter
conduit would extend 685 miles along Mexico's alluvial plain, running from Cactus in Chiapas state to the northern industrial belt
around Monterrey. A special line would stretch 74 miles to Reynosa,
the sister city of McAllen, Texas. From the border terminus, the gas
would flow through existing lines to 26 states across the sunbelt and
southern states, reaching as far north as Chicago and New York City.
The *gasoducto*, compared favorably in Mexico to the trans-Alaska oil
pipeline, was scheduled to reach its full capacity of 2.7 billion cfd in
1981 when the last of 18 pumping stations would begin operations.

Díaz Serrano regaled his country's congress with descriptions of
the proposed facility's advantages. It would serve, he argued, as a
steel spinal column connecting the production system and 12,400-
mile gas distribution network of the Southeast, the Federal District,
and the Central Valley with the production-distribution network of
the North, converging on Monterrey. This linkage would provide vital flexibility and ensure supply of high quality associated gas to
scores of markets outside the production centers. Nonassociated gas,
whether from northern or southern fields, would be available to adjust the total natural gas production in order to satisfy the current
requirements of the same. The system would also create new poles of
industrial development along the Gulf coast, drawing people away
from—or, at least, restraining the flow into—Mexico City, Guadala-
jara, and Monterrey. Moreover, the *gasoducto* would allow exploitation of a series of gas deposits that had previously not been opened
because of their small size. In addition, 24,000 to 35,000 jobs would
be created during the construction phase.[24] Above all, its advocates
claimed that the new facility would permit gas exports worth $5 mil-
lion per day, enabling PEMEX to recoup in 200 days its construction
costs of $1 billion (later raised to $1.5 billion).[25] Neither figure, however, took into consideration the substantial investment required to

process the gas for shipment to market. Nor was it pointed out that modifying the existing gas pipeline system (adding a 30-inch line from Minatitlán to Mexico City; enlarging the 12-inch line between Querétaro and San Luis Potosí; and building a San Luis Potosí-Saltillo link) would have obviated the need for this incredibly expensive facility, whose construction generated enormous legal and illegal profits.

The many problems that plagued the gas deal between the six U.S. transmission firms and PEMEX have been discussed elsewhere and are beyond the scope of this book. Suffice it to say that the accord raised the hackles of the Mexican left. These outcries precipitated a rare debate over public policy in a country renowned for secretive, authoritarian decisionmaking. Díaz Serrano, who denied that Washington had applied pressure to obtain his country's gas, led the government's counterattack, focusing on the sensitive question of Mexico's relations with its neighbor to the north:

> Energy defends us, frees us from economic aggression and makes us increasingly less dependent. . . . The strongest and most powerful country on earth has made a veritable cult of human rights, and I believe it would be stupid to think of its engaging in territorial aggression in the latter part of the twentieth century.[26]

As Mexico attempted to devise its own strategy, the U.S. Congress wrestled with an energy plan submitted by President Carter and James R. Schlesinger, secretary of the recently created Department of Energy. A key provision called for an immediate jump in the wellhead price of newly discovered natural gas to $1.75 per Mcf, a figure loosely based on the price of the energy equivalent of domestic crude. Deregulation of newly discovered gas and of gas sold in interstate commerce would take place in stages, culminating with the removal of most government controls on December 31, 1984. To pay Mexicans $2.60 per Mcf seemed unfair and politically artless when domestic producers could look forward to just two-thirds of that amount. Moreover, the higher price to Mexico would strengthen the argument of those who wanted complete deregulation of domestic gas to take place immediately. "How can you justify holding our prices down when you are willing to let foreign gas enter at such high levels?" thundered industry representatives.

Senator Adlai E. Stevenson III attacked the proposal from a different perspective; namely, that approval of the Mexican price would encourage the Canadians, who supplied gas to the upper Midwest and Pacific Northwest at $2.16 per Mcf, to demand parity, thus driving up the cost to U.S. buyers. Stevenson insisted that at $1.75 per Mcf Mexico could recover the gas, operate the pipeline, finance its debt, and still enjoy an attractive profit. The additional 85¢ would represent a bonanza for PEMEX, adding $620 million annually to the United States' deficit in fuel imports. "Natural gas prices in excess of $1.75 produce no more natural gas. They do produce inflation, recession, political instability, and windfall profits," he insisted. By the time the Mexican gas was integrated into the pipeline grid and transported to New York, added Stevenson, it would cost about $3.60 per Mcf.[27]

Senator Lloyd M. Bentsen of Texas and other legislators from the gas-producing states took strong exception to Stevenson's arguments and supported an import arrangement with Mexico. Nonetheless, Stevenson used his position as chairman of the Banking Committee's Subcommittee on International Finance to persuade the U.S. Export-Import Bank to postpone action on $588.2 million in credits that would finance the acquisition of U.S. goods and services for the pipeline and other hydrocarbon ventures. In response to the bank's action, the Mexican government canceled a $33-million order with the U.S. Steel Corporation, which, along with Canadian, French, Italian, Japanese, West German, and Mexican firms, had been asked to supply 48-inch steel pipe for the *gasoducto*. Although the aura of an economic reprisal surrounded this action, a backlog of requests, limited capacity to manufacture the appropriate pipe, and a fire in U.S. Steel's Baytown, Texas, plant made it unlikely that the order could have been filled on schedule.

Secretary Schlesinger also opposed the tentative agreement with Mexico. His opposition was both to the price, which might interfere with passage of the pending gas deregulation bill, and the proposed link to the middle distillate No. 2. Not only is the price of No. 2 volatile and subject to manipulation by OPEC, it can be shipped to any market, thus producing a worldwide price. For natural gas, in contrast, there is no single market: before the shah's ouster, Iranians sold gas to the Soviets for less than 50¢ per Mcf; in 1977, Canadians were able to get $2.16 from the United States; Algeria had negotiated a sale to U.S. transmission companies at $3.37, although it failed to win government approval; and Indonesians have supplied gas to Japan for between $3.50 and $5.00. Thus, it seemed economically unsound to peg the price of this energy source to fuel oil, a move that

would only reinforce or legitimize OPEC's position and favor the establishment of an international gas price determined by the cartel. Finally, wary of the sharp changes that can attend the transfer of presidential power every six years in Mexico, Schlesinger believed that any accord should be for 20 years, a period often agreed to in natural gas sales contracts.

As early as April 1977, U.S. officials had advised their Mexican counterparts that federal regulatory agencies would have to approve any sales accord with U.S. firms and that the price would be a point of contention. Despite repeated warnings, the Mexicans—accustomed to the dominant role enjoyed by their chief executive and emboldened by Tennessee Gas's pricing recommendations—seemed baffled by the administrative process. "They thought that Carter could wave a magic wand and the deal would go through," confided Robert A. Pastor, a member of the staff of the National Security Council with responsibility for Latin America. Yet, it was politically impossible for Carter to back the accord when, during the fall of 1977, he was strenuously lobbying Congress on the natural gas bill. In view of Mexico's revolutionary tradition, including the 1938 expropriation of the oil industry, it was ironic that Mexican policymakers should choose to believe the capitalists in the transmission firms rather than government representatives concerning the prospects for the deal.

In a pre-Christmas meeting, Díaz Serrano and Foreign Minister Santiago Roel García again pressed Schlesinger to tie the gas price to that for No. 2 fuel oil, then equivalent to $2.76 per Mcf. The U.S. secretary of energy, known to treat subordinates with all the delicacy of Cromwell ruling Ireland, adamantly refused to agree to more than $2.16, lest Canadian suppliers insist on raising their export price to obtain any higher amount received by Mexico. The ensuing impasse prompted PEMEX to announce on December 22 that it would not renew the Memorandum of Intent, due to expire at the end of 1977. The Mexicans justified this action on the grounds that their country, a champion of nonintervention, did not wish to meddle in the energy debate taking place in the United States.[28] Privately, they railed against Schlesinger's abruptness and arrogance. The gas companies, they felt, were using the pending deal as a lever to push up the fuel's price on the U.S. market. The Mexican government also expressed its intention to lay the gas pipeline as far as San Fernando, 75 miles south of the Texas border, but without the 18 compressors, thereby halving the construction cost.[29] After the memorandum had expired, Schlesinger told the transmission firms that "sooner or later" Mexico, which, except for the small amount during the winter of 1977, had not shipped gas to the United States since 1964, would have to sell in the U.S. market for lack of any other choice.[30] In response, Díaz Serrano expressed his nation's willingness to wait two or three more years rather than lower its price.[31]

VIRULENT REACTION

Mexico reacted swiftly and shrilly to the collapsed discussions. The president averred that he had been left "hanging by his paintbrush" when Schlesinger knocked over the ladder—a phrase more clever than accurate in light of the repeated warnings of potential pricing problems. Nonetheless, Mexican journalists, intellectuals, and officials vented their nation's collective anger at the U.S. energy secretary. One of the most undiplomatic statements came from the country's chief diplomat: "Schlesinger is a liar," said Roel García, "and you can quote me on that."[32] In January 1978 Díaz Serrano reported that Mexico would substitute the gas previously earmarked for the United States for oil in generating electricity at home and making petrochemicals. It would be able to export the 147,000 barrels of oil made available, thereby generating $700 million annually.[33]

In January 1978 Vice-president Walter F. Mondale received a polite reception during a three-day visit to Mexico for general talks. He was prepared to discuss a multilateral development project aimed at uplifting poor areas from which millions of Mexicans unlawfully migrate to the United States.[34] The vice-president was even ready to explore a possible package deal that might have included guaranteed financing and short-term bridging loans for the Mexicans, but the subject—which was first raised by a high-level Mexican official—never surfaced. The desultory recriminations following the cancellation of the natural gas deal spurred the drafting of a Presidential Review Memorandum (PRM-41) to crystallize administration thinking on U.S.-Mexican relations and to provide President Carter with options to consider before his meeting with López Portillo, scheduled for early 1979. The National Security Council, which supervised the writing of the document, never released it to

the public. Yet, according to the *Washington Post*, the PRM described Mexico as "the most promising new source" of oil in the 1980s and proposed inter alia that to overcome suspicions and misgivings below the Rio Grande, Washington should view Mexico as a world-scale partner, accord it significant concessions on vegetable and textile exports, approve quotas for the legal immigration of workers, and conclude a gas agreement. The last step would spur oil production in and shipments from a country that "could fill 30 percent of U.S. import needs by the mid-1980s, thus enhancing security of supply, and more than compensating for the decline of Venezuelan and Canadian supplies." Carter, who took a keen personal interest in the memorandum, said in early December 1978: "I consider our relationship with Mexico to be as important as any other that we have, and my personal relationship with President López Portillo has been very good."[35]

Anxious to strengthen these ties, raise bilateral relations to a higher plane, and unsnarl the embarrassing loose ends from a natural gas sale, Carter planned to fly to Mexico on February 14, 1979. His departure coincided with crises in two other countries. Terrorists kidnapped and killed Adolph Dubs, U.S. ambassador to Afghanistan, and left-wing gunmen attacked the U.S. embassy in Teheran. As a result, the president, who suffered from a bad cold, stayed up the entire night of the thirteenth as did Secretary of State Cyrus B. Vance and National Security Advisor Zbigniew Brzezinski. "We would probably have postponed a trip to any other country and indeed, under less urgent circumstances, the president put off a trip to Canada in the fall," stated Pastor. "We were all aware of how sensitive the Mexicans were to any perceived slight, and thought that postponing the trip might have so offended them that our relations might never have recovered. So we went ahead," he added.[36]

Carter reached Mexico City in mid-morning only to be drawn into a whirlwind of activities. These included a long private conversation with López Portillo, who expounded at length on international economic and political problems. He employed Delphic statements to blame the United States for the sorry state of world conditions, accuse Carter of not playing the role of the free world's leader, and assert that the Soviets had placed the West on the defensive. López Portillo used "stiff, harsh language, blaming the United States for everything that had gone wrong since the beginning of man," observed a member of the Carter entourage who asked not to be identified. His guest, an engineer eager to find practical solutions to bilateral problems, found the Mexican's accusatory monologues unwarranted and irritating.

President Carter was taken aback by the strident language heaped on him during the tête-à-tête. Still, he tried to break the ice in an afternoon luncheon toast. So fatigued and preoccupied that he appeared as "a man with a terminal illness" to one diplomat, the U.S. chief executive launched into a rambling discourse that praised López Portillo for his efforts to promote peace, alluded to the interest that he and his host shared in jogging, and, reflecting upon an earlier visit to Mexico, tastelessly referred to a bout of "Montezuma's Revenge" that he had suffered. This comment was extemporaneous and ignored by the Mexicans. The White House press corps, who were relatively uninformed about Mexico and were looking for a prism through which to view a complicated trip, found it in the anecdote.

The Mexican chief executive made no effort to relieve the tension that suffused the ceremony. Anxious both to strike back at the man he presumed had torpedoed the natural gas deal and to posture for his own audience, he chided his guest with a reference to the gas fiasco in his toast: "Among permanent, not casual neighbors," he said, "surprise moves and sudden deceit or abuse are poisonous fruits that sooner or later have a reverse effect." With respect to his nation's oil wealth, the Mexican president noted that: "Mexico has . . . suddenly found itself the center of American attention—attention that is a surprising mixture of interest, disdain and fear, much like the recurring vague fears you yourself [the United States] inspire in certain areas of our national subconscious."[37]

The remainder of the three-day trip proceeded without public acrimony. Apparently, López Portillo realized he had deeply offended the haggard U.S. leader, who made no effort to disguise his annoyance in subsequent private sessions. Carter diplomatically told the Mexican Congress that "Mexico will produce oil at a rate suited to your developmental objective" and added that "we are prepared to pay a fair and just price for the gas and oil you wish to sell."[38] The presidents signed agreements on housing, the development of arid and semi-arid lands, and scientific and technical cooperation. More important, Carter extracted from his host a pledge—incorporated in the joint communiqué after difficult negotiations—to begin government-to-government negotiations on gas. Furthermore, López Portillo softened his language toward the United States in a lengthy air-

port press conference following Carter's departure. But the Mexican chief executive had forcefully communicated the message that interdependence and mutual respect should replace paternalistic and patronizing attitudes in binational affairs.

Press stories, many of which were written by White House reporters, focused on the initial luncheon and portrayed the meeting as a disaster. Hugo B. Margaín, Mexico's ambassador to the United States, later asserted that the unfavorable image projected by North American newspapers was "totally false" and that relations between the two countries were "excellent, better than in a long time."[39]

The whole episode convinced U.S. diplomats that major policy announcements or the unveiling of programs should be done early in a visit to set the tone of media coverage. Moreover, written toasts should be exchanged by the two governments in advance of presidential meetings, a policy now followed.

In any case, the Carter-López Portillo meeting did lead to the resumption of talks on the natural gas issue, called the "Mexican Albatross" within the State Department. Prolonged negotiations, at times occurring in a "bazaar atmosphere," produced an eventual accord quite favorable to Mexico. The United States agreed on the purchase of 300,000 Mcf of gas at an initial price of $3.625 per Mcf. With an election year on the horizon, the Carter administration was anxious for improved U.S.-Mexican relations, which, in turn, might enhance the vote-getting appeal of Democrats among Mexican-Americans. Ironically, good relations with the country on the other side of the Rio Grande help a U.S. president politically but tend to harm his Mexican counterpart.

As often occurs when limited achievements take place in substantive matters, bureaucratic changes were made. The consultative mechanism was revamped to infuse the device with "more dynamism, cohesion and flexibility for its more effective operation."[40] In this instance, according to a plan developed by the State Department's Office of Mexican Affairs, the three original working groups gave way to nine, each cochaired—on the U.S. side—by one State Department official and an appropriate representative of another agency. A new "Multilateral Working Group," consisting of the secretary of state and his Mexican counterpart, replaced the political group. An official at the assistant-secretary level headed each of the other eight. These, including the agency working in tandem with the State Department, were: trade (Office of the Special Trade Representative), energy (Department of Energy), industry (Commerce), finance (Treasury), migration (Justice), border (Commerce), law enforcement (Justice), and tourism (Commerce). Representatives of U.S. and Mexican agencies that had an interest in the subject matter constituted the full membership of the nine bodies.

United States Ambassador Patrick J. Lucey entered a Washington meeting of U.S. government entities concerned about Mexico only to find some 70 agencies represented. Thus, he urged Carter to appoint a high-level official to coordinate Mexican affairs and, as it turned out, serve as the executive secretary for the U.S. side of the consultative mechanism. The president named as ambassador-at-large and Coordinator of Mexican Affairs Robert C. Krueger, a 43-year-old Texas politician who had excellent contacts on Capitol Hill and with the executive branch.

A former Rhodes scholar and Shakespeare specialist at Duke University, Krueger served two terms in Congress before narrowly losing a bid to unseat Senator John G. Tower in 1978. Supposedly responsible for the day-to-day conduct of affairs with Mexico, the special coordinator had difficulty carving out a role for himself. The anomalous character of his position and the absence of a clear mandate sparked tension between his staff and both the Bureau of Inter-American Affairs, in which the Office of Mexican Affairs is located, and the Bureau of Economic and Business Affairs. In addition, he remained at the margin of bilateral energy policy as high officials in the Department of Energy increasingly cultivated personal contacts and pursued policy alternatives with their Mexican counterparts. Krueger's continuing interest in politics led him to travel frequently, often to Texas. Absences from Washington made it difficult for him to keep on top of policymaking, which he sometimes complicated with off-the-cuff statements that appeared designed to win support in Texas rather than advance overall U.S.-Mexican interests. Krueger's proper relationship with the U.S. ambassador in Mexico City remained a source of confusion because of his ambassador-at-large title. Mexican foreign policy elites criticized the ambiguous situation, stating: "Two ambassadors are less than one."[41] In retrospect, any Coordinator of Mexican Affairs, a post abolished by President Reagan, could have functioned more effectively in the White House than in the State Department, where bureaucratic detractors readily impeded his work.

Purchasing natural gas, reorganizing the consultative mechanism, and naming a special coordinator could not stem the erosion in U.S.-Mexican relations that followed Mexico's refusal to allow the shah to return to his rented home in Cuernavaca, where he stayed from June 10 to October 22, 1979, before receiving medical treatment in New York. Washington's decision to admit the shah to the United States sprang partly from the Mexican president's personal assurance, which he later denied, that the deposed monarch could count on "security and asylum" in Mexico. Carter was livid upon learning of the Mexican volte-face. "López Portillo is a liar!" the chief executive exclaimed. "They just double-crossed us, and I doubt there's any other reason than just wanting to cause problems, unless they think they are currying favor with the Third World by mistreating the shah."[42] One Carter official expressed contempt for the Mexican leader: "We understand that on several occasions López Portillo visited the shah when he was in Cuernavaca and recommended several private entrepreneurs to him," he said. "López Portillo attempted to get the shah to invest some money in the enterprises."[43]

To add insult to injury, the Mexican president excoriated the United States' freezing of Iranian funds as an "aggressive decision." Such treatment of assets would make oil-producing countries "think twice before they exchange a real source in the ground for a currency which devaluates and besides is frozen."[44] Reportedly, Carter's anger at López Portillo's words and actions led him to request an option paper on how to retaliate against Mexico. Cooler heads within the White House prevailed and no such document was prepared. Yet, after leaving the White House, Carter confided to scholars visiting him in Georgia that López Portillo was one of the most intractable heads of state with whom he had to deal.

NATIONAL ENERGY PROGRAM

Bristling toasts and inhospitable treatment of the shah enabled Mexico's president to demonstrate his nation's sovereignty and independence vis-à-vis the United States. The fourfold increase in oil prices registered in 1979 sharpened Mexico's assertiveness toward its neighbor. This same assertiveness appeared in a National Energy Program (NEP) that Oteyza announced in November 1980.

López Portillo's term might have been called the *sexenio de planes*, for the government unveiled plans for employment, urban development, industrial development, tourism, food production, and other economic activities. Although not the first published—a Global Development Plan embraced a blueprint for the various sectors of the economy—The National Energy Program was designed to fit within the framework of this comprehensive document.

Oteyza hailed the NEP as the first attempt to set priorities, encourage rational development, and evaluate the use of the nation's energy resources. He stressed two specific objectives of the program: to guarantee an adequate and timely supply of energy to fuel Mexico's "independent and integral economic development," thereby achieving a broad-based industrial capability that will endure after oil supplies have been exhausted and to use energy sources more rationally while diversifying primary sources, particularly renewable ones. The production of energy "would depend upon the country's development needs and not on reserve volumes *per se*, nor on the requirements of other economies or interests foreign to ours."[45] The second objective reflected the patrimony minister's disenchantment with Díaz Serrano's ambitious development efforts, which Oteyza believed would make their nation too dependent on both a single export and the U.S. market.

The plan recommended price increases and technological improvements to stimulate efficiency, with a view to reducing the ratio of energy consumption growth to GNP growth from its high level of 1.7-to-one to one-to-one by 1990. It also emphasized the need to focus on nonoil fuels: annual coal consumption would grow from the current 8.5 million tons to 23 million tons by 1990; electricity generation would expand at an average yearly rate of 12 to 13 percent over the decade; and greater attention would be directed toward solar and geothermal opportunities. Finally, the program identified atomic power as the bridge to "the new energy era" of the twenty-first century and called for the building of 20 nuclear plants in as many years.

As mentioned above, the NEP emphasized that oil and gas output should be keyed entirely to national needs. Petroleum production, which surpassed 1.9 million bpd in 1980, was to reach 3.5 million bpd in 1985 and 4.1 million bpd in 1990, based on the assumption that the economy would register an 8 percent annual growth. During the same period, daily natural gas output would climb from 1,300 million cubic feet to 4,300 million cubic feet to 6,900 million cubic feet. Confident that hydrocarbon prices would continue to soar, the architects of the plan fixed a ceiling on exports at 1.5 million bpd of oil and 300,000 Mcf of natural gas. For security reasons, Mexico would sell no more than 50 percent of its exports to a single country. This provision was unmistakably aimed at the United States, which then imported 77 percent of the crude that PEMEX shipped abroad and was perceived by radical nationalists as being prepared to dispatch troops south of the Rio Grande to keep the supply lines open. In a further precautionary step, it was stipulated that no country should depend upon Mexico for more than one-fifth of its total oil imports. Excepted from this restriction were Caribbean and Central American countries that benefited from the joint oil facility (Israel also imported more than 20 percent of its petroleum from Mexico).

In early 1981 the Mexican government gave credence to its market diversification goal by publishing a list of countries with which sales contracts had been signed. The United States remained the largest customer, even though its portion of exports had declined to 49.8 percent. As seen in Table 2, Canada, Japan, France, Spain, Brazil, and nations aided under the San José agreement recorded impressive gains, while Sweden and India became new purchasers.

Several assumptions underlay the NEP: a continued, robust international demand for oil; ever higher revenues from energy exports; and the use of these monies to attain both self-sustained growth and economic and political freedom of action from Washington.

CONCLUSIONS

Mexico hoped to use oil and gas as levers to increase its influence over the United States in such nonpetroleum areas as trade, immigration, and investment. Its prospects were enhanced by its becoming an exporter in a seller's market dominated by OPEC, from whose grip Washington longed to escape. Rather than employ the "big stick," President Carter showed sensitivity and restraint in dealing with a country whose stability was more important to U.S. vital interests than sharply higher oil output.

Lack of knowledge of U.S. decisionmaking, reliance on the advice of private firms, and refusal to heed U.S. government warnings led Mexico to demand a politically unrealistic price for its natural gas. The collapse of negotiations in 1977 infuriated López Portillo and other leaders whose decision to construct a Chiapas to Texas *gasoducto* divided public opinion at home.

TABLE 2: Mexico's Exports of Crude by Country of Destination, 1977 to 1981 (thousand barrels per day)

Country	1977 Volume	1977 Percent	1978 Volume	1978 Percent	1979 Volume	1979 Percent	1980 Volume	1980 Percent	1981* Volume	1981* Percent
United States	178.5	88.4	325.0	89.0	448.7	84.2	564.8	68.1	733.0	49.8
Canada	0.9	0.4	2.4	0.7	—	—	4.2	0.5	50.0	3.4
Spain	2.4	1.2	13.6	3.7	42.9	8.0	92.7	11.2	220.0	15.0
Israel	20.2	10.0	22.0	6.0	40.9	7.7	56.7	6.8	45.0	3.1
Netherlands	—	—	1.2	0.3	—	—	—	—	—	—
Japan	—	—	0.9	0.3	—	—	35.3	4.3	100.0	6.8
Costa Rica	—	—	—	—	0.3	0.1	4.9	0.6	7.5	0.5
France	—	—	—	—	—	—	42.2	5.1	100.0	6.8
Brazil	—	—	—	—	—	—	16.9	2.0	50.0	3.4
Nicaragua	—	—	—	—	—	—	2.3	0.3	7.5	0.5
Yugoslavia	—	—	—	—	—	—	3.1	0.3	3.0	0.2
Sweden	—	—	—	—	—	—	—	—	70.0	4.8
India	—	—	—	—	—	—	—	—	20.0	1.4
Jamaica	—	—	—	—	—	—	—	—	10.0	0.7
Others	—	—	—	—	—	—	6.8	0.8	55.0	3.7
Total exports	202.0	100.0	365.1	100.0	532.8	100.0	829.9	100.0	1,471.0	100.0

*Contractual obligations as of August 1980.

Sources: Secretaría de Programación y Presupuesto and Petróleos Mexicanos, *La Industria Petrolera en México* (México, D.F.: S.P.P., 1980), pp. 284, 286, 288; Jaime Corredor, "Oil in Mexico," Mexico City, 1980 mimeo).

The chief executive reacted angrily to perceived U.S. efforts to project its influence by frustrating Mexico's obtaining a fair price for its hydrocarbons. To consolidate his support, vindicate his personal honor, and uphold national sovereignty, he announced that the country's natural gas would be consumed at home. This action, which won widespread approval in his country, was complemented by efforts to persuade U.S. public opinion of the vastness of Mexico's hydrocarbon riches and by a publicly administered tongue-lashing of President Carter. Concern grew in Washington that the cumulative impact of unmanaged tension could chill relations between the United States and Mexico. Hence, interest in building institutions to structure bilateral affairs resulted in the consultative mechanism and the appointment of Robert Krueger as a special coordinator. Still, little progress occurred on substantive issues and none on fashioning the kind of package arrangement that Mexico entered into with other industrial nations. Three factors explained this failure: the decentralization of U.S. policymaking coupled with a preference for handling issues separately; Mexico's similar disinterest in linking issues, though Washington was disposed to consider such an approach; and President Carter's annoyance, evolving into hostility over the incident with the shah, toward López Portillo.

Strained political ties and Mexico's commitment to diversifying export markets aside, market forces assured that the United States would remain the largest importer of PEMEX crude, with purchases rising from 178,500 bpd in 1977 to 733,000 bpd in 1981. Meanwhile, U.S. loan and equity capital poured into Mexico, whose oil-fueled growth depended on the influx of dollars and whose oil sector purchased about 60 percent of its equipment from U.S. suppliers. The incremental growth in output envisaged in the NEP coupled with the constraints on sales to the United States made clear that Washington should not expect Mexico to replace the Mideast as its principal source of imported oil.

On balance, expanded PEMEX shipments to the U.S. market sprang less from astute maneuvering by the Carter administration than from the imperative for Mexico to earn hard currency to finance an expensive and expansive development program. Even as it acted more assertively with respect to its northern neighbor, the groundwork for greater Mexican dependence on the U.S. was laid. As will be seen in Chapter 8, rising PEMEX crude exports put pressure on OPEC-fixed prices that began to fall in the early 1980s, thereby reducing the earnings of cartel and noncartel producers. The decision to divert gas to the domestic market carried opportunity costs in the form of reduced dollar revenues that were important to financing Mexico's development. Also harmful to Mexico was the tendency to react to a perceived U.S. threat rather than set its own goals and pragmatically pursue them. Such hypernationalism manifested itself in the take-it-or-leave-it posture assumed on natural gas prices. This same intractable style, exacerbated by Mexico's inexperience in bargaining with the United States on crucial matters, carried over to oil prices and proved disastrous when a worldwide glut appeared in 1981, another subject embraced in Chapter 8.

NOTES

1. An excellent biographical sketch of López Portillo appears in *Current Biography Yearbook 1977* (New York: Wilson, 1977), pp. 271–74.
2. David Gordon, "Mexico: Survey," *Economist*, April 22, 1978, p. 19.
3. October 12, 1974, pp. A-1, A-4.
4. *New York Times*, September 18, 1980, p. D-11.
5. *Offshore* 38 (January 1978): 44.
6. "Mexico: Crisis of Poverty/Crisis of Wealth," *Los Angeles Times* supp., July 15, 1979. As reported in the *Washington Post* (October 16, 1974, p. A-18), Cuba was the first country to which Mexico offered to sell its "new oil." Castro refused the proposal, preferring—instead—to continue receiving oil on concessionary terms from the Soviet Union.
7. The following material draws heavily on George W. Grayson, "Does Mexico Have as Much Oil as It Says," *Los Angeles Times*, December 2, 1982, Part II.
8. *Los Angeles Times*, May 18, 1979, p. 1.
9. *Christian Science Monitor*, August 8, 1979, p. 22.
10. Olga Pellicer de Brody, "Oil and U.S. Policy toward Mexico," in Jerry R. Ladman et al., *U.S.-Mexican Energy Relationships* (Lexington, Mass.: Lexington Books, 1981), p. 190.
11. *Fortune*, July 16, 1979, p. 138.
12. *Latin America Weekly Report*, January 9, 1981, p. 4.
13. *Latin America Economic Report*, November 4, 1977, p. 197.
14. Edith B. Couturier, "Mexico," pp. 132–33.
15. Illness prevented Kreisky's actually cochairing the meeting. Canada's Prime Minister Trudeau took his place.
16. *New York Times*, April 24, 1980, p. 2.
17. *Daily Report (Latin America)*, April 5, 1979, p. M-1.
18. Cited in Arturo Gándara, "An Assessment of Carter Administration Relations with Mexico," a study published by the Rand Corporation, Santa Monica, Calif., May 1980, P-6490, p. 1; see also, Henry Kissinger, *White House Years* (Boston: Little, Brown, 1979), p. 731.
19. *Facts on File*, February 26, 1977, p. 136.
20. For an analysis of this controversy, see George W. Grayson, "The U.S.-Mexican Natural Gas Deal and What We Can Learn from It," *Orbis* 24, No. 3 (Fall 1980): 573–607.
21. Richard R. Fagen and Henry Nau, "Mexican Gas: The Northern Connection," in Richard R. Fagen (ed.), *Capitalism and the State in U.S.-Latin American Relations* (Stanford: Stanford University Press, 1979), pp. 403–4, footnote 43.

22. David Rulison Palmer, "American Politics and Policies in the Regulation of Mexican Natural Gas Imports" (Ph.D. diss., Business Administration, University of California, Berkeley, 1982), pp. 301ff.

23. *Ibid.* Palmer, "American Politics and Policies."

24. Jorge Díaz Serrano, *Linea troncal nacional de distribución de gas natural: el director general de petróleos mexicanos ante la h. cámara de diputados* (Mexico City: Petróleos Mexicanos, 1977), p. 19.

25. *Daily Report (Latin America)*, October 12, 1977, p. V-5.

26. *Excelsior*, October 26, 1977.

27. U.S. Congress, *Congressional Record (Senate), October 19, 1977*, p. A19937.

28. *Excelsior*, January 6, 1978, pp. 1-A, 14-A.

29. *Excelsior*, December 23, 1977, p. 5-A; *Latin American Economic Report*, January 6, 1978, p. 1.

30. *Excelsior*, January 7, 1978, pp. 1-A, 10-A.

31. *Keesing's Contemporary Archives*, April 13, 1979, p. 29549.

32. *Washington Post*, February 4, 1979, p. A-17.

33. *Excelsior*, January 13, 1978, p. 10-A.

34. *Washington Post*, January 21, 1978, p. A-13; and January 22, 1978, p. A-18.

35. *Washington Post*, December 15, 1978, p. 26.

36. Interview with Dr. Pastor, College Park, Maryland, February 1, 1983.

37. *Keesing's Contemporary Archives*, April 13, 1979, p. 29549.

38. *Keesing's Contemporary Archives*, April 13, 1979, p. 29549.

39. *Excelsior*, March 15, 1979, p. 1-A.

40. Excerpts from the presidents' joint communiqué appeared in the *New York Times*, February 17, 1979, p. A-5.

41. Arturo Gándara and César Sereseres, "U.S.-Mexican Relations: Too Important to be Left to Presidents?" (Santa Monica: Rand Corporation, October 1979), p. 5.

42. *Washington Post*, December 21, 1979, p. A-13.

43. Hamilton Jordan, *Crisis: The Last Year of the Carter Presidency* (New York: Putnam's, 1982), p. 72.

44. *Washington Post*, December 4, 1979, p. A-16.

45. Secretaria de Patrimonio y Fomento Industrial, *Programa de Energía: Metas a 1990 y Proyecciones al año 2000 (Resumen y Conclusiones)* (Mexico City: Secretaria de Patrimonio y Fomento Industrial, 1980), p. 8.

5
THE CARIBBEAN BASIN
AND CUBA

INTRODUCTION

The United States and Mexico have an overriding interest in promoting economic growth, effective governments, the containment of conflict, and regional cooperation within the Caribbean basin.[1] Both nations also desire stability; however, while Mexico accepts ideological pluralism and recognizes the legitimacy of regimes led by leftist revolutionaries, the Reagan administration bristles at the presence of Marxist states in the region, especially those enjoying military support from Moscow or Havana. President Reagan views the area as constituting "a vital strategic and commercial artery" essential to U.S. security. Approximately half of U.S. trade, two-thirds of imported oil, and over 50 percent of strategic minerals purchased abroad pass through the Panama Canal or the Gulf of Mexico, he told the OAS on February 24, 1982. The region, referred to as the "third border" of the United States, is second only to Mexico as a source of illegal immigration. The "economic disaster" besetting the area has provided "a fresh opening to the enemies of freedom, national independence and peaceful development." Specifically, Reagan warned against Cuban and Soviet moves to exploit the situation by training, arming, and directing extremists in guerrilla warfare and economic sabotage, leading toward the creation of totalitarian regimes.[2] The emergence of Marxist-Leninist governments could force a diversion of U.S. defensive strength from Europe and Asia to erect an expensive military shield where none had previously existed.[3]

After seeking rapprochement during much of the Carter administration, Washington has attempted to advance its interests in the region by threatening Nicaragua militarily, intervening in Grenada, and attempting to isolate Cuba. The United States has also given strong diplomatic—and, in some instances, military—support to individual countries that are democratic, potentially democratic, or viewed as a barrier to leftist expansionism. Washington has also lavished support on groupings of democratically oriented countries that might contribute to a containment effort. Above all, the Reagan administration has launched a Caribbean Basin Initiative (CBI) to provide aid, investment, and export opportunities to some two dozen nations in a region marked by linguistic, cultural, economic, and political diversity.

Mexican leaders have been equally explicit concerning their interests in the region. In his sixth report to the nation, López Portillo reiterated his country's insistence on self-determination, the peaceful solution of disputes, nonintervention in the affairs of other states, and a prohibition on the use of force.[4] A combination of factors—Mideast-sized oil holdings near the country's southern border, severe domestic economic problems, and a rising tide of refugees from a convulsed Central America—has heightened Mexican concern about instability. López Portillo peppered his last major speech with allusions to a "regional conflagration," "catastrophe," and "cataclysm"—prospects for which he clearly believed were heightened by U.S. intervention in Central America. Yet, Mexico has fashioned policies that are quite different from those of the United States even though generally pursuing similar goals. For instance, rather than trying to isolate Cuba, Nicaragua, and Grenada, Mexico has emphasized close relations with these nations. At the same time, it has projected its political influence in the region by providing economic assistance, organizing through the PRI a Permanent Conference of Latin American Political Parties (COPPPAL), and undertaking joint activities with France and Venezuela. The latter include the San José Accords discussed in Chapter 3. Not only does it want to have a hand in shaping policies followed by individual countries, but Mexico has attempted to position itself so, if called upon, it can act as a mediator between the United States and leftist nations of the area.

RELATIONS WITH COUNTRIES OF THE CARIBBEAN BASIN

United States economic, political, and military penetration of the Caribbean basin has given rise to scores of books and articles and need not be discussed here.[5] Scholars have devoted considerably less attention to Mexico's involvement in the region.

In terms of population, wealth, industrial capability, culture, and institutions, Mexico is as imposing to other countries of the area as the United States is to Mexico. During the viceroyalty and for a brief period in the last century, Central America formed part of Mexico; and even now when Guatemalans or Hondurans speak of the "colossus of the North," they are probably referring to Mexico, not the United States. Many residents of the region, and Central America in particular, have studied at Mexican universities, read books distributed by Mexican publishers, attended motion pictures made in Mexico, watched Mexican-produced television programs, and taken part in cultural exchanges with their northern neighbor. Even as its own citizens illegally flock to the United States, Mexico has suffered an influx of as many as 450,000 refugees from Guatemala and, more significantly, El Salvador.[6]

A giant among pygmies, Mexico's GNP is larger than that of the other nations of the region combined, even when Colombia and Venezuela are included. Yet, until recent years, it played a modest role in an area deemed a "natural" sphere of influence by many Mexicans.[7] It was absorbed by the political and economic problems associated with nation-building in the nineteenth century, the protracted social revolution early in the twentieth century, and the "economic miracle" of the post-World War II years. Moreover, "democratic" Mexico looked askance at the military dictatorships that flourished in Central America and the island nations. Even if it had desired to play a visible role in the area, such activism would have been preempted by the United States, which regarded the region as the center of its sphere of influence and, as recently as the 1930s, relied on dollar diplomacy and the big stick to keep the countries in line.

President López Mateos asserted his country's independence by maintaining diplomatic and economic ties with Castro's government, which other OAS members treated as a pariah after 1962. Despite both his pronounced anticommunism and efforts to strengthen bilateral relations with Washington, Díaz Ordaz decried U.S. military intervention in the Dominican Republic and sought to cultivate Central American leaders. The convergence of two factors produced this initiative: Mexico's new attempts at market diversification and the country's concern about being left out of a regional plan of economic integration manifest in the formation of a Central American Common Market (CACM).[8] In early 1966 Díaz Ordaz made official visits to Central American countries and Panama in what was the first official trip of a Mexican president to the region. He took this opportunity to inaugurate a program of economic and technical cooperation, which embraced an offer to open Mexico's market to Central American exports. The chief executives of Honduras (1966), Guatemala (1967), Costa Rica (1967), and El Salvador (1968) reciprocated the Mexican leader's visit. The meetings involved economic or commercial diplomacy and evinced the Central American preoccupation with strengthening the CACM and reducing their trade deficits with Mexico.[9] Mexico bought $2 million in bonds of the Central American Bank for Economic Integration, made available credits totaling $5 million to that same institution for the purchase of Mexican goods, and proposed preferential treatment of CACM and Panamanian exports (an initiative vetoed by the other members of the Latin American Free Trade Association). During this same period, Mexican entrepreneurs, often in joint ventures with local counterparts, expanded their investments in Central America to avoid tariff barriers against third parties erected by the new integration treaty. "Contact with Central American rulers grew rapidly enough to engender suspicion on the part of some political elements in the region that Mexico was becoming a sub-imperial power."[10] The Guatemalans were especially wary of Mexico when Díaz Ordaz used the occasion of his 1966 visit to affirm the right of British Honduras, now Belize, to self-determination.[11]

Mexico's involvement in Central America declined apace with the crisis and deterioration of the CACM caused largely by the 1969 Salvadoran-Honduran "soccer war." In the final analysis, the Mexican and Central American economies proved more competitive than complementary. Although trade expanded greatly in the 1960s, by the end of the decade Central America accounted for only a modest share of Mexico's total exports (1.8 percent) and imports (0.11 percent). Similarly, Central American exports (0.15 percent) to and imports (1.8 percent) from Mexico were negligible.[12]

After taking office, Echeverría welcomed to Mexico several Central American and Caribbean heads of state, and in 1972 he visited Venezuela, Colombia, Costa Rica, Guatemala, Honduras, and Panama to expand his nation's modest commercial relations with the area. During 1973 and 1974 he exchanged ambassadors with Barbados, Guyana, and the Bahamas in Mexico's first attempt to establish a dialogue with the English-speaking Caribbean. In 1974 he traveled to Jamaica and initiated warm relations with Prime Minister Manley.[13] Frustrations at the lack of success of reforms in Mexico itself found Echeverría increasingly turning to foreign affairs to generate support at home and legitimize domestic political objectives. Echeverría encouraged the participation of all Caribbean area nations in the Latin American Economic System. Yet, as discussed in Chapter 2, he enjoyed little credibility as a regional or third world leader because of his mercurial behavior, unpredictable actions, identification with the 1968 massacre, and sagging popularity within Mexico. He left office without having crafted a coherent, well-defined, and comprehensive policy toward the Caribbean basin as a whole or toward individual neighboring states.[14]

López Portillo's reputation as a serious, responsible technocrat combined with his country's highly publicized oil wealth to enhance Mexico's political and economic influence in the region. To a large extent, Mexico's initiatives occurred in reaction to U.S. policies. Internal economic problems dominated Mexico's agenda during the first half of his administration; still, by 1979 López Portillo had fashioned a strategy that brought his country into diplomatic conflict with Washington. Even so, the country's economic and technical dependence on its neighbor meant that Mexican authorities "could not afford to allow foreign policy disputes . . . to spill over into, or damage, Mexico's economic relationship with the United States."[15]

CUBA

López Portillo moved Mexico closer to Cuba than ever before in the history of the two nations. Visits, accolades, and bilateral protocols nourished this relationship. In May 1979 Castro returned to Mexico for the first time since setting sail from Veracruz 23 years before to spark a revolution in Cuba. López Portillo invited the leaders of four leftist opposition parties, including the *Partido Comunista Mexicano*, to join him in welcoming "one of the personalities of this century" to the resort island of Cozumel. In sharp contrast to the reception received by Carter three months before, the Mexican president lauded the "fraternal and indestructible" friendship between Mexico and Cuba; deplored Washington's economic embargo of the Pearl of the Antilles; decried the continued existence of the Guantanamo Bay naval facility; and scorned the U.S. suggestion that Cuba played a key role in the success of Nicaragua's Sandinistas.

For his part, Castro praised Mexico for defining its energy policy "not in terms of the oil needs of the United States but as an instrument for the development of your own country," noting that he had not "come to seek Mexican oil or gas which seems to be fashionable these days." He also urged "just, civilized, and humane treatment" for Mexico's undocumented workers in the United States. Such migration, he insisted, was "the bitter and inevitable fruit of the mutilation of Mexican territory and the underdevelopment imposed by the force, arrogance, and domination of the United States in the past."[16]

The two countries established a Joint General Intergovernmental Commission to foster collaboration in trade, science, health, education, and cultural affairs. Some 250 Cuban technicians flew to Mexico to assist in sugar cultivation and livestock raising; a like number of PEMEX oil experts have advised Cuba's state oil company.

Early in López Portillo's administration, rumors suffused Mexico City that, under a Soviet-Mexican agreement, PEMEX would ship crude to Cuba in return for Soviet exports to Spain, Mexico's principal European market. The arrangement would have yielded substantial savings on transportation costs. A U.S. weekly magazine reported in mid-1978 that the flow would eventually reach 70,000 bpd, almost one-third of Mexico's crude exports, with the Soviet Union supplying Greece, Turkey, and Mexico's Eastern European customers in return for PEMEX shipments to Havana.[17]

Despite the effusive welcome accorded Castro in Mexico, the quadrilateral deal has yet to materialize. This was in part because Venezuela, before withdrawing its ambassador from Cuba in 1980, entered into such a four-party arrangement and in part because of the difficulty Mexico experienced in working out a satisfactory compensation formula with the Soviets, who stood to benefit most from freight savings. Furthermore, the Soviet Union may have preferred the nuisance of dispatching tankers from the Black Sea to Havana rather than relinquishing the political leverage that comes from controlling their satellite's energy lifeline. In 1981 Moscow provided Cuba, which then produced only 5,000 bpd from its own wells, 95 to 98 percent of its petroleum under a swap arrangement for sugar that is renegotiated every five years.[18] Moreover, the Soviet bloc supplies virtually all of the island's oil technology.

López Portillo's July 31-August 2, 1980, visit to Cuba demonstrated solidarity with Castro's regime at a time of deepening economic problems illuminated by an exodus of refugees to the United States. An estimated crowd of one million turned out to hear Castro praise the steadfastness of Mexico as an ally. In one of his speeches during the visit, López Portillo insisted: "We will allow nothing to be done against Cuba." To him, acts against Cuba were tantamount to acts "against ourselves."[19] The meeting paved the way for a far-reaching accord on energy entered into the following January. This agreement, considered the most comprehensive energy deal between Cuba and any noncommunist nation, called for collaborative oil and gas exploration onshore and on the undersea shelf off the country's western coast where Soviet and Rumanian engineers reportedly found traces of hydrocarbons. It was also agreed that PEMEX would help renovate the Nico López refinery in Havana and assist in the construction of a new propane gas plant to overcome the severe shortage of bottled domestic gas besetting Cuba. Mexico pledged to supply equipment and materials on a cost-plus-expenses basis and aid the country in gaining access to Western technology. While no provisions were made for the shipment of PEMEX crude, Mexico promised to sell its "dearest friend" 10,000 tons of propane. Cuba's Vice-president Carlos Rafael Rodríguez extolled Mexico's generosity as setting the stage for his country's "second independence."[20]

The provisions of the understanding dealing with offshore seismic work precipitated a controversy between Washington and Mexico City. The United States attempted to spike the contract because it could not allow U.S.-manufactured equipment purchased by Mexico to be resold to the Castro government. In a display of intransigence, Mexico publicly declined to honor the U.S. protest.[21] Privately, however, high-level Mexican officials assured Washington that their country would not violate the U.S. embargo by transferring prohibited oil technology to Cuba.

While Mexico might speak defiantly on a matter of marginal concern to the United States, it proved less bold when faced with an issue deemed nonnegotiable to a U.S. president. Reagan made clear he would not participate in the October 1981 summit of 22 indus-trialized and developing nations unless Castro were excluded from the guest list. Despite his vaunted friendship for the Cuban presi-dent, López Portillo acquiesced in this demand to assure the presence at Cancún of the country best able to make resources available to the third world. As chairman of the so-called Nonaligned Movement, Castro was eager to attend the conference. To salve the Cuban's wounded pride, López Portillo invited him back to Cozumel in early August 1981. He received his visitor with a 21-gun salute and offered a toast that the talks would "strenghten and solidify the links be-tween Mexico and our beloved Cuba."[22]

Severe domestic economic problems and the new chief execu-tive's muted enthusiasm for the Sandinistas suggested that Miguel de la Madrid's administration, which took office on December 1, 1982, would forego diplomatic activism to concentrate on the troubles at home. Foreign Minister Bernardo Sepúlveda Amor, whose last post had been ambassador to the United States, did pursue his country's goals with a less abrasive style than that of his predecessor; yet, Mex-ico did not waiver in its belief that the struggle of rebels in Central America should be extricated from the East-West conflict, even as President Reagan in an April 27, 1983, address to a joint session of Congress stressed the Cuban-Soviet threat to the area. Indeed, Mex-ico found support for its position from the Contadora Group (named for the Panamanian island where it first met in January 1983), which advocated an immediate halt to fighting and arms shipments, the withdrawal of all foreign military advisers, adoption of mutual non-aggression pacts by the states in the region, and recognition of the sovereignty and right to self-determination of each of those nations. Membership in this ad hoc body, which also included Colombia, Venezuela, and Panama, blended Mexico's voice into a chorus of crit-icism of U.S. involvement in the region in contrast to the solo cri-tiques of the past. Nevertheless, Sepúlveda lashed out at the Grenada intervention—an indication not only of Mexican sentiment but that his country had not knuckled under to the Reagan administration.

MEXICO AND NICARAGUA

López Portillo continued and deepened a policy with Cuba in-herited from his predecessors. Oil wealth encouraged him to pursue a new line with respect to Nicaragua that also brought Mexico into diplomatic conflict with the United States. Following the abortive popular uprising against General Anastasio Somoza Debayle in September 1978, Mexico's embassy in Managua opened its doors to hundreds of political dissidents, including several who later gained key government posts. At the same time, Mexican diplomats maintained close contacts with a pro-Sandinista amalgam of well-regarded professors, priests, and businessmen known as the "Twelve."[23] Moreover, Gustavo Iruegas, who was then in charge of Mexico's embassy in Managua, unobtrusively aided the rebels by setting up "safehouses." Shortly after his May 1979 meeting with Castro, the Mexican chief executive welcomed Costa Rica's president Rodrigo Carazo Odio, whose government had suspended relations with Nicaragua in November 1978 after a series of border incidents. At a luncheon for the visiting dignitary, López Portillo denounced the "horrendous genocide" in Nicaragua and publicly severed diplomatic ties with the Somoza dictatorship, urging its replacement by the Sandinista-led "government-in-exile," then residing in San José.[24] The rupture signalled to other military regimes in the region that Mexico intended to play a more activist role.

López Portillo doubted the possibility of centrist democratic forces emerging triumphant from the authoritarian, oligarchic, and militaristic tradition of the area. Thus, he felt it imperative to foster ties with leftist movements that were destined to topple conservative regimes in hopes of moderating their policies and obtaining their friendship for his country. After all, a pluralistic, single-party-dominant government chosen through elections had emerged from Mexico's revolutionary tradition. Further, good relations with Castro had kept the Cuban leader from fomenting guerrilla activities in Mexico. Such "surfing on the wave of the future," as one Reagan adviser later characterized López Portillo's approach toward insurgencies, became apparent when Mexico sent two high-ranking missions to five countries—Venezuela, Colombia, Panama, Jamaica, and the Dominican Republic—to urge them to withdraw their ambassadors from Managua. Costa Rican representatives accompanied the Mexican envoys. PEMEX also terminated the sale of all petroleum products to Nicaragua.

Mexico spearheaded the fight against a U.S.-sponsored plan to dispatch an inter-American peace force to Nicaragua to restore order and pave the way for free elections after Somoza left the scene. This issue symbolized both Washington's diminished influence in the region and the strong opposition of Latin American governments to the concept of a peacekeeping detachment. Fourteen years earlier, the OAS had pliantly endorsed the occupation of the Dominican Republic by U.S. forces. In 1979 it turned thumbs down on similar involvement in Central America, even after Washington cited alleged Cuban involvement with the Sandinista guerrillas. Cuba was no longer the outcast it had once been, inasmuch as 14 Latin American countries had diplomatic ties with the Castro regime.

López Portillo moved swiftly to fill the influence vacuum in the region left in recent years both by the United States' preoccupation with Europe, the Soviet Union, and Asia, and by Cuban adventurism in Africa. For example, after Somoza's downfall in July 1979, the Mexican president showered praise and aid on the Nicaraguan revolutionaries, but Washington provided more aid than any other nation during the new regime's first year and a half in power.

In October 1979 Mexico—through the PRI—hosted 22 "nationalistic, democratic, and anti-imperialist" parties from 14 nations in Oaxaca where they endorsed "Revolutionary Nationalism" as the guiding philosophy of a Permanent Conference of Latin American Political Parties.[25] The new grouping included parties of different ideological orientations; namely, socialists such as Costa Rica's National Liberation Party; populists such as the Brazilian Workers' Party; Eurocommunist-oriented parties such as Venezuela's Movement toward Socialism; and the Sandinistas, who refer to themselves as a people's politicomilitary front. While welcoming Social Democratic groups, the organization rejected Communists and Christian Democrats on the grounds that they were "under foreign influence"—a specious conclusion in the case of the latter. The result was to divide Christian Democrats and Social Democrats, thereby weakening two of the most important democratic groupings in the hemisphere.

> Furthermore, combining the Social Democratic leadership in the Caribbean area with the extremist and anti-democratic leftists such as [Tomás] Borge of Nicaragua under Mexican sponsorship, blurs the fundamental distinction between democratic and dictatorial political goals. Indeed, the actions of López Portillo will substitute "revolutionary nationalist" rhetoric for solid commitments to pluralist democracy as the test of legitimacy and support from Mexico.[26]

COPPPAL committed itself to the vague and noncontroversial goals of joint action, mutual support, open communications, and a formalization of relations. In fact, at its founding session and subsequent gatherings, the organization has furnished a forum for members to denounce multinational corporations, the IMF, and the United States and other developed countries. Communiqués issued at the conclusion of COPPPAL meetings often appear as disjointed compilations of grievances focusing on external forces deemed manipulative and imperialistic.

At first blush, COPPPAL seems to have advanced Mexican goals by enhancing the country's stature, giving a rhetorical fillip to López Portillo's World Energy Plan, and bringing its ruling party into contact with a number of small, left-wing movements that someday might prove to be as significant to their countries as the Sandinistas have been to Nicaragua. Above all, Mexico sought through the newly formed body to domesticate the Sandinistas by surrounding them with moderate parties that might temper their revolutionary zeal. "We want the Nicaraguans to feel they can look to us if they need anything," explained one Mexican diplomat. "They don't have to think the Cubans are their only friends."[27] Although designed to further Mexican interests and invariably headed by the president of PRI, the organization at times seemed to be the proverbial tail that wags the dog. Specifically, the ease of including items in COPPPAL's declarations has found Mexico identified with radical positions that are in tension with its own national interests.

On January 24, 1980, López Portillo flew to Managua for a nine-hour visit with the country's new leaders. He called their revolution a path that other countries could follow to escape Latin America's "pitiful labyrinth"—just as the Mexican and Cuban revolutions had served as models in earlier decades. In a demagogic reference to the Somozas and the United States, he urged nations of the hemisphere to fight "against internal demons and the satanic ambition of imperial interests."[28]

López Portillo promised to send technical aid to modernize the Nicaraguan fishing fleet, dispatch two teams to drill geothermal wells, and provide 315 tons of material and equipment to rehabilitate the country's telephone and telegraph system. He also turned over a Mexican-owned fertilizer plant, offered credits to finance the purchase of 150 Mexican buses, excused repayment of a $17 million loan contracted by the Somozas, and supplied technical assistance for schools and health services. However, as in the case of Cuba, the most valuable aid took the form of oil and related technology. In April 1980 Mexico began supplying 7,500 bpd to Nicaragua. This

volume, termed "indispensable for [the country's] survival," constituted approximately half of the nation's consumption. The "concessionary price" at which it was sold may have been a euphemism for a
gift inasmuch as Nicaragua has never paid for these early shipments
nor for oil furnished under the San José Accords. A pact between PE-
MEX and the Nicaraguan, Conde Minas, assured Mexican assistance
in "all aspects" of the hydrocarbon industry, especially in exploration
and drilling. In return for this help, the Nicaraguans pledged to sell
Mexico hides, meat, sugar, oil seeds, gold, and precious stones.[29]

Mexico's relations with the government of National Reconstruction grew even warmer as a chill developed between Washington and
Managua. In the spring of 1981 the United States suspended most of
the $75 million in aid for Nicaragua because of that country's alleged
support for the Salvadoran insurgents. Mexican officials jumped into
the breach, signing an agreement that would raise their assistance by
approximately $200 million within two years. Other aid came from
Libya and the Soviet Union: the former provided a $100 million
loan; the latter furnished $4 million in wheat shipments.

The U.S. reprisal against Nicaragua stimulated even greater
Mexican-Venezuelan cooperation on regional matters. At the conclusion of a three-day visit to Mexico City in early April 1981, President
Herrera Campíns joined with López Portillo in reiterating a commitment to continued aid for Nicaragua and offered the combined effort
of the two countries to help find a political solution to the Salvadoran
conflict. On March 23, 1982, the Venezuelan chief executive excoriated recent NATO naval exercises in the Caribbean about which his
country had not been notified in advance, as well as reported plans
for U.S.-backed paramilitary operations against Nicaragua. The
Reagan administration should "make an effort to comprehend"
Latin American problems "in order to act in a realistic way," he
said.[30]

Clearly, López Portillo viewed joint action as a means to enhance the influence of the two countries in the area where the intervention of both the United States and the Soviet bloc was growing.
"Collaboration between Venezuela and Mexico is vital to achieve the
stability of the 27 nations in the Caribbean basin," he stated. "I am
sure that we will find the necessary points of coincidence to create a
framework of negotiations to resolve the region's problems."[31] By
discouraging U.S. military involvement in the area, the Mexican
leader hoped to avert an East-West conflict whose escalation might
force Mexico to choose sides. This would be an extremely costly deci-

sion for any Mexican president because—rhetoric aside—his country's national interests would dictate aligning with Washington.

Nicaragua's failure to pay its bill provoked the financially burdened Venezuelans to cease oil exports, made under the aegis of the San José Accords, in mid 1982. Despite their own economic woes, the Mexicans agreed to meet all of this Central American nation's crude oil needs. Threatened attacks on tankers by *contras*, armed opponents of the Sandinistas led EXXON to refuse to transport oil into Nicaraguan ports—a move that complicated PEMEX deliveries. By July 1983 the de la Madrid administration was pressing Nicaragua both to pay for its oil purchases and renegotiate its $300 million debt with Mexico.

Mexico's support has had a significant impact. To begin with, it assures the Sandinistas oil and other badly needed resources at little or no cost. It also increases their legitimacy in the eyes of West European governments that are often skeptical about U.S. warnings of Cuban or Soviet influence within Nicaragua's ruling elite. That the PRI belongs to the Socialist International affects the perceptions that Europe's Social Democratic parties have of the area. If the Mexicans who live cheek by jowl with Central America and stand to lose most from an upheaval cast their lot with the revolutionary junta, they reason, can the danger be as great as U.S. officials have warned? "Many of the European Social Democrats think of this as similar to their shift toward the Palestinian Liberation Organization as a means of moderating its terrorism and ultimate objectives."[32]

Mexico's stance could hearten extremists who scorn elections in Nicaragua and elsewhere in the Caribbean basin. As critical as the Mexicans were of Somoza's repressive practices, they remained silent as Nicaragua's revolutionaries postponed elections "for about four years," curtailed civil liberties, and applied pressure to the Church, the business community, opposition political parties, *La Prensa*, and the noncommunist labor union. Meanwhile, the Sandinistas have developed one of the region's most formidable militaries, with a 40,000-strong army supplemented by a militia of 200,000 men and women. As one scholar observed of the post-Somoza period: "Cuba sent more than 2,000 people within a few months, but Mexico and other Latin American nations essentially became spectators hoping for the best while witnessing the pattern of subtle but obvious expansion of communist power through the Directorate."[33]

López Portillo's visit to Managua betokened a shift from spectator to generous uncle. In its avuncular generosity, Mexico emphasized that, based on the principle of "nonintervention," its aid would be "unconditioned." As a consequence, Mexico refrained from publicly admonishing the Sandinistas to respect civilian primacy over the armed forces, pluralism, and democratic principles.

During a November 1981 meeting, López Portillo reportedly told then-U.S. Secretary of State Alexander Haig that he shared the United States' concern over the "increasing extremism" of the Nicaraguan junta, and that he would intercede with the Sandinistas on Washington's behalf. The Mexicans have never denied this report. Yet, one Mexican official was quoted in a British newsletter as saying: "The *gringos* are the only ones who are putting the pressure on. We don't use pressure against anyone, and we don't accept its use against ourselves."[34]

While in Managua on February 21, 1982, López Portillo proposed a three-pronged peace plan whereby: Washington would end "threats" of intervening militarily in Nicaragua and cease the clandestine military training of anti-Sandinista exiles; Nicaragua would reduce the size of its armed forces; and the Managua regime would sign a nonaggression pact with its neighbors and the United States. Five weeks later Foreign Minister Castañeda helped secure a promise from the United States and Nicaragua that the two countries would resume direct negotiations. If any talks resulted from this pledge, they had not borne fruit by early 1984. Meanwhile the Reagan administration gave lip service to the goals of the Contadora Group, while financing a not-so-thinly-veiled war by the *contras*. In September 1983 Washington launched large-scale military-naval exercises with Honduras, seen as a bulwark against Sandinista expansion and from whose territory the best equipped segment of *contras* operated. This containment policy found increased economic and military assistance flowing to Honduras, El Salvador, Costa Rica, and Guatemala. The perceived success of the Grenada affair led some right-wing U.S. policymakers to urge abandoning containment for intervention in Nicaragua.

EL SALVADOR

As guerrillas increased their efforts to seize power in El Salvador, Mexico again associated itself with the insurgents, while decrying U.S. support for the Christian Democratic-military junta and publicly advocating "self-determination and non-intervention." Despite reforms in landholding, banking, and foreign commerce advanced in 1980 by the center-right coalition headed by Christian Democrat José Napoleon Duarte, Mexico treated it as if it were indistinguishable from Guatemala's venal dictatorship. While continuing to extend diplomatic recognition to the San Salvador regime, the PRI showed itself anything but neutral as it used COPPPAL to nurture ties with the opposition Democratic Revolutionary Front (FDR), recruiting it into COPPPAL. In theory, the government of Mexico conducted business with its counterpart in El Salvador. In practice, the stronger bilateral relationship involved the PRI and the Salvadoran Social Democrats, the most important component of the FDR, which in turn became the civilian arm of a guerrilla coalition known as the Faribundo Martí National Liberation Front (FMLN).

Mexico also showed its contempt for El Salvador's legal government by changing ambassadors to San Salvador in mid-1980 and announcing, through Foreign Minister Castañeda—a vociferous advocate of the rebel cause—the possibility that it would recognize both a state of belligerency and the FDR as the rightful government. The Frente would have to have demonstrated "certain control over territory and . . . [be] habitually obeyed by a substantial part of the population," he said.[35] As it turned out, Mexico's new envoy to El Salvador was Iruegas, who was chargé d'affaires in Managua when Mexico City broke relations and yanked the diplomatic rug from under Somoza's booted feet.[36]

El Salvador's insurgents launched a major offensive in late 1980 in hopes of seizing power before the Reagan administration could establish itself in office. Events in Mexico seemed to harmonize with rebel operations. In late November the Confederation of Mexican Workers (CTM), a federation of the nation's most powerful unions, issued a demand that the government halt oil shipments to El Salvador and sever diplomatic ties with the Duarte regime. Later, a conference on world solidarity with El Salvador took place in Mexico. It has even been argued that the Mexican armed forces commenced maneuvers on the country's southern border on December 5, 1980, to distract Guatemala's army and prevent its aiding the Salvadoran regime.[37] While possible, this interpretation seems unlikely because major actions of the so-called final offense of the Salvadoran insurgents did not begin until January. Moreover, other reasons— "showing the flag" to Guatemala, eliminating any Guatemalan guerrilla camps on Mexican soil, and above all enhancing the familiarity of Mexican forces with the frontier area—explain the military operations. In any case, the training exercise coincided with "an enormous increase in Mexican government and media support for the Salvadoran guerrillas, along with additional funds for propaganda and permission for a 'government in exile' to be based in Mexico."[38]

Mexico's animus toward the Salvadoran junta also appeared in the FDR's use of Mexico City as a propaganda base, which could only have occurred with López Portillo's blessing. A case in point was the January 14, 1981, news conference at which Guillermo Manuel Ungo, head of the Social Democratic Party, announced formation of a seven-member "political-diplomatic" commission that had "plenipotentiary power" over the various insurgent groups fighting in El Salvador. Ungo took advantage of his forum to advocate negotiations for a cease-fire and a political solution arranged directly between the left and the United States, since the latter "had been demonstrated to be the power behind the Salvadoran throne. It has contributed to the radicalization and the polarization of the process. It therefore has a quota of responsibility."[39]

The following month, López Portillo reiterated this demand for a political solution, while warning Washington against military intervention. He lamented that El Salvador had become "a zone of hegemonic confrontation," having been "elevated to the undesirable rank of a strategic frontier"—an obvious reference to the State Department's insistence that the Salvadoran civil war could affect U.S. national security. "We are certain," the Mexican leader said, "that a military solution is not viable and that only a political solution will allow a resumption of peace." Meanwhile, the president refused to meet with a visiting U.S. delegation, led by General Vernon Walters, former deputy director of the CIA, that offered documentation of Soviet, Vietnamese, and Cuban participation in the conflict.[40]

In September 1981 Mexico abandoned its Janus-like approach and unmistakably sided with the insurgents. In a communiqué to the U.N. Security Council, Mexico joined with France in recognizing the FDR and the FMLN as a "representative political force." The proposal for the collaborative statement apparently came from Castañeda, who met with Foreign Minister Claude Cheysson during his late July stopover in Mexico City. The French diplomat, fresh from a trip to Nicaragua, Honduras, and Costa Rica, proved receptive to impelling a negotiated settlement lest the explosive situation in El Salvador attract superpower intervention—a euphemistic reference to U.S. involvement. Thus, the two nations laid aside differences over oil pricing that had embittered bilateral relations a few weeks earlier to place their imprimatur on the foes of the Christian Democrat-military regime in hopes of enhancing the rebels' legitimacy and promoting peace talks between the warring parties.

Nine Latin American countries, headed by Venezuela's Christian Democratic government, condemned the declaration as interference in El Salvador's domestic affairs by supporting "one of the subversive extremes" that sought the armed overthrow of the Salvadoran government. The critics also took issue with that portion of the Franco-Mexican statement that demanded a restructuring of the Salvadoran armed forces before elections had been held. While Argentina, Bolivia, Colombia, Chile, Guatemala, Honduras, the Dominican Republic, Paraguay, and Venezuela signed the condemnation, it also is believed to have enjoyed the support of Brazil, Costa Rica, Ecuador, and Peru.[41] State Department officials insist that the outcry revealed a spontaneous expression of its sponsors' sentiments and not an instance of the United States' acting through surrogates.

The rebuke to Salvadoran policy in no way softened Mexico's support for the Sandinista regime. At the time of Secretary Haig's visit to Mexico City in late November 1981, Mexican leaders warned that any U.S. military action against Nicaragua or Cuba would be a "gigantic historical error" and suggested that Washington temper its rhetoric to defuse a dangerous political situation in the Caribbean basin.[42] López Portillo told his guest of Mexico's insistence "on the need to reduce the volume" of "discordant declarations" and to "create a sort of truce of silence to improve the atmosphere." Haig reportedly assured the president "openly, categorically and unconditionally that for the moment the United States would not intervene militarily in Nicaragua or Cuba."[43]

Unimpressed by the victory achieved by moderates and conservatives in the March 1982 constituent assembly elections, López Portillo six months later argued that the Franco-Mexican proposal for a dialogue between the government and the rebels demonstrated more "realism," for "no other solution had proved viable."[44] The Contadora Group echoed this call for a negotiated settlement in El Salvador.

GUATEMALA

Events in Nicaragua and El Salvador have spurred insurgents to renew their drive to capsize Guatemala's military rulers. To avoid capture, Guatemalan rebel bands sometimes flee into the Mexican border state of Chiapas. The Guatemalan government is reasonably strong and the economy, aided by recent oil discoveries, balanced. Still, the murder of moderates and Indians has become a contagion—with mounting bloodshed, human-rights violations, and the polarization of forces. A victory by guerrillas in El Salvador would put even more pressure on Guatemala's generals, for whom the Mexicans have no love lost.

López Portillo's minister of defense, General Félix Galván López, had become friends with his Guatemalan counterpart, General Oscar Mejía Victores, when the latter attended Mexico's military academy as a young man. Border disputes, antithetical forms of government, and Mexico's determination to preserve Belize's sovereignty in the face of territorial claims by Guatemala have chilled relations between the neighboring countries. Despite this official coolness, the two regimes reached a modus vivendi during the López Portillo *sexenio*, thanks to the friendship of the top generals and a political decision taken in Mexico City to minimize confrontations. To avoid clashes in Chiapas between their respective forces, the Mexican army agreed to remain approximately two miles from the frontier. Such positioning not only created a buffer, but made it easier for Guatemalan troops to track down guerrillas who cross into Mexico, often attempting to hide among the 100,000 or more refugees who had streamed across the sievelike border of mountains, jungle, and forests by early 1984 and over 30,000 of whom were crammed into 27 camps. Mexican troops are also under orders to "apprehend, subdue, and deliver" to the proper authorities any rebel infiltrators with whom they come into contact.[45] Reported raids by the Guatemalan army against refugee camps in January have further strained ties between the neighboring states. These attacks, verified by eye-witnesses, raise the chilling possibility of a Guatemalan-initiated massacre in Chiapas similar to that which produced hundreds of deaths in the Palestinian camps of Sabra and Shatila located in West Beirut. Such a bloodbath could propel Mexico and Guatemala into war.

Mexico also regards with trepidation Guatemala's enthusiasm for the renewal of the Central American Defense Council generally referred to as CONDECA. Created in 1965 with U.S. blessings, CONDECA originally included the five Central American republics plus Panama. The old organization, employed chiefly as a clearinghouse for information on guerrillas and as a framework for occasional joint maneuvers, became defunct after the 1969 war between

El Salvador and Honduras. The newborn CONDECA is intended to present a credible "deterrent" against former member Nicaragua and, as such, enjoys the fulsome backing of Washington which boasts a staunch ally in General Mejía, who took over his country following an August 1983 coup.[46]

In case diplomacy, oil shipments, and a tenuous understanding with Guatemala don't immunize their nation from the turmoil afflicting Central America, Mexican authorities have attempted to win the allegiance of the Chiapan peasantry, ethnically akin to their Guatemalan counterparts, by providing roads, health clinics, government stores, potable water, farm equipment, and agricultural extension services. That General Absalon Castellanos Domínguez, elected governor of the state in 1982, supervises these activities epitomizes the civil-military cooperation in the area.[47]

The delicacy of the border situation combined with concern over the growth of military establishments in Guatemala, Nicaragua, El Salvador, Honduras and other nations of the Caribbean basin figured in the decision by Galván López to enlarge garrisons in Chiapas and to revitalize the 99,000-man army, which embraces the 6,000-man air force. These include such measures as improving training and replacing World War II vintage museum pieces with some of the most up-to-date equipment in the Caribbean basin. The navy (27,000 men), which bears responsibility for protecting a 200-mile "economic security zone," has also undergone modernization. Among the developments are the following:

- Mass-producing the German-patented G-3 automatic rifle for eventual distribution to all 71 infantry batallions;
- Obtaining from the United States an LST and two Gearing-class destroyers;
- Replacing horses with motorized vehicles in at least 18 (perhaps 23) of the 24 cavalry regiments;
- Purchasing from France 40 Penard light tanks;
- Buying from Switzerland 50 PC-7 turboprop trainers, each adorned with two machine gun pods;
- Acquiring from Spain training vessels and six extremely fast patrol boats; and
- Manufacturing at home several types of rocket launchers and a dozen DN-III armored vehicles.[48]

A flyover by seven newly secured F-5 jet fighters proved the main attraction at the September 16, 1982, Independence Day parade. By late October the Northrop Corporation had delivered a dozen of these supersonic aircraft. The F-5s form the core of an air defense system that may eventually be fleshed out with a radar network, air-to-air missiles, "hard" bombs, and improved communications.

Sophisticated matériel requires sophisticated officers and men. Courses—from those taught at the ultramodern Heroico Colegio Militar, Mexico's West Point, to those at the National Defense College attended by specially selected colonels and brigadier generals—have been more rigorous.

Still, the Mexican military is hardly a Prussian force. Its weaknesses include a crazy patchwork of weapons and vehicles even within the same unit, faulty command and control within units, a personnel system rife with cliques and favoritism, a poor intelligence capability, primitive coordination between the army (and air force) and the navy, and inadequate support and logistics functions. The air force has yet to acquire the missiles, bombs, and radar to complement the F-5s; thus, it would have to depend on visual sighting should foreign aircraft attack the Southeast oil fields or other PEMEX installations. Nevertheless, the acquisition of new equipment and improved training have boosted morale, while the presence of petroleum deposits and the establishment of the economic security zone have given the armed forces a mission that transcends civic action, peasant pacification, and antismuggling campaigns. Of concern to Mexican politicians is the likelihood that protracted strife in Central America will lead to a greater role in decisionmaking by the ever more professional officer corps.

CARIBBEAN BASIN INITIATIVE

Escalating petroleum charges, falling prices of coffee, sugar, bauxite, and other primary products, and flights of capital provoked by political uncertainties have ravaged the economies of the Caribbean basin. Even though the joint oil facility has mitigated conditions, countries of the area still suffer from declining gross domestic products, rising prices, chronic and dangerously high unemployment, low productivity, and a pressing liquidity crisis. Whether civilian or military, the governments of the region face enormous balance-of-payments deficits that require cutbacks in public spending and feed social discontent. For example, Panama and the five countries of

Central America required $1 billion in 1981 just to import necessary goods and service an $8.5 billion external debt. Even Guatemala, which boasts one of the area's strongest economies, saw its foreign reserves evaporate in 1981 and 1982. Panama was the only nation of the Central American region to register even a slight growth in per capita income in 1981.[49] In 1980 Edward Seaga and Tom Adams, the ministers of Jamaica and Barbados respectively, began promoting the concept of a "mini-Marshall plan" for the Caribbean. Seaga, the first state visitor to Washington after Reagan's inauguration, found the U.S. chief executive sympathetic to a bold new scheme that would spur economic development and promote social and political stability.

Thomas O. Enders, assistant secretary of state for inter-American affairs, took the lead in shaping what became known as the Caribbean Basin Initiative (CBI). The Carter administration had taken steps that set the stage for this program. It nearly doubled U.S. assistance to the area from $96 million in 1977 to $184 million in 1981; established in 1977 the Caribbean Group for Economic Cooperation and Development, which is comprised of 31 donor and recipient governments and 16 financial institutions such as the IMF (the group has funneled more than $300 million to the Caribbean since 1978); and helped to launch a "private sector entity" Caribbean/Central American Action—backed by 51 U.S. corporations and staffed in part by Foreign Service officers on leave—to improve U.S. relations with the area.[50]

While anxious to uplift the states of the region, Enders rejected comparisons between the new venture and the post-World War II Marshall Plan or President John Kennedy's Alliance for Progress. These efforts evoked images of huge U.S. development grants and concessionary loans extended to thwart the spread of communism. Both a conservative president and a Republican Senate were eager to cut, not expand, foreign aid. The White House asked for $350 million more than the $474.6 million already earmarked for the area in fiscal year 1981. To enhance the security of the region, administration officials requested $60 million in military aid to supplement the $50 million already sought for fiscal year 1982. Nonetheless, they emphasized that the "centerpiece" of the U.S. program was one-way free trade; namely, Congress would be requested to eliminate duties on all imports from the basin for 12 years, except those on textiles, wearing apparel, and shoes. Duty-free treatment would be accorded sugar imports, but only up to a certain limit to protect the price of domestically produced supplies. Finally, the initiative contemplated five-year domestic tax credits of up to 10 percent of the amount of new equity investment made by U.S. entrepreneurs in the countries of the region. By permitting firms to reduce their domestic tax liability, it was hoped that U.S. investors would take risks that heretofore seemed forbidding because of high start-up costs in developing new markets, training new local employees and managers, and overcoming transportation bottlenecks to insure a steady flow of raw materials and export items.

Rather than "going-it-alone," Washington persuaded Mexico, Canada, Venezuela, and (later) Colombia to take part in this joint effort to funnel aid, trade incentives, and investments to the region—a decision reached at a July 1981 foreign ministers meeting in the Bahamas. However, Mexico insisted that the program should not involve military aid; be directed against the Soviet bloc; or exclude any nation in the region—an unmistakable allusion to leftist regimes in Cuba, Grenada, and Nicaragua. At a meeting in New York in March 1982, Colombia joined the core donor group. The State Department reported that the commission of the European Community expressed interest in cooperating with the initiative.

Various dilemmas seemed to imperil the initiative before it was even established, such as how could donors with conflicting foreign policy interests and different sets of friends and foes among potential benefactors pull in harness. Only Canada, a relative newcomer to Caribbean involvement that recently had tripled its development assistance to Central America, seemed prepared to get along with everyone. While friendly to El Salvador and Guatemala, the United States was overtly contemptuous of Cuba and Grenada and increasingly estranged from Nicaragua. Mexico's relations were just the opposite, while Venezuela—congenial to El Salvador and Nicaragua—was tepid toward Guatemala and hostile toward Cuba and Grenada.

The solution lay in fashioning the CBI as a broad umbrella, under which bilateral transactions could occur according to the mutual interests of the parties involved. Each nation would develop its own program, with coordination occurring among the sponsors to avoid duplication and to eliminate gaps. Mexico's commitment to aid Cuba would not obligate Washington to help the Castro regime, and the United States could assist El Salvador without requiring the Mexicans to follow suit. Indeed, the lip service paid to the CBI by Herrera Campíns and López Portillo aside, their countries' major contribution entails folding the San José Accords into the program. Such a move enables participation in a much-heralded plan without excessive identification with the political and military strategy of the Reagan administration.

Even if multilateralism and bilateralism blend into an innovative framework, other dilemmas also cloud the initiative's future. First, uneasiness characterizes cooperation among the donors because of a fundamental disagreement over the causes of the unrest afflicting the region. While noting the importance of indigenous factors, the United States has assigned primary blame to Marxist-Leninist forces, such as the Cubans. In contrast, the Mexicans insist that the unrest is essentially an internal response to problems that have domestic roots. "In our continent, social injustice is the true womb of unrest and revolutionary violence," López Portillo declared. "The theory that foreign subversion is the origin of our ills is unacceptable to the democratic nations of the area."[51]

Second, funds pose more of a problem than format. Conceived as a long-term social and economic development program, the Caribbean nations see it instead as a possible source of new credits with which to overcome an immediate crisis. For example, the Central American countries have called for $20 billion in loans throughout the remainder of the 1980s, with three-fourths of the monies earmarked for energy development and the promotion of regional cooperation and integration. The remainder would be for balance-of-payments assistance and other pressing needs.[52] Such a resource transfer runs counter to the Reagan administration's emphasis on trade and investment and is beyond the reach of other sponsors.

Third, it is difficult, perhaps naive, to attempt to design a single program for an entire region. Generalizations are dangerous; still, the needs of the island nations are basically economic, and attracting even two or three medium-sized firms could have a significant impact on the postage stamp-sized countries of the eastern Caribbean. However, attention to the economic problems of—and drawing private capital to—Guatemala, Nicaragua, and El Salvador must await the resolution of political and military conflicts. St. Lucia's ambassador to the OAS expressed the fear that the development needs of the Caribbean may be "lost or reduced" when considered in the context of the "larger Basin perspective."[53] Needless to say, leftist leaders throughout the region, concerned about dependence on the industrial world, remain wary of U.S.-championed capitalism and President Reagan's "magic of the marketplace" philosophy as appropriate means to improve the lot of their populations.

Fourth, some observers doubt that unexplored opportunities remain for private firms, which, after all, are not strangers to the region. Are there undiscovered oil reservoirs? Have money-making ventures been ignored? The *Wall Street Journal* reports that Jamaica's conservative prime minister has had difficulty interesting businesses in purchasing hotels that the government has been operating. Perhaps the main obstacle to private investment lies not in ignorance of what is possible, but in the lack of adequate roads, electric power, or water supplies combined with the fear of political upheaval and nationalizations. Only government or institutional aid will finance infrastructure projects. Yet, the danger of nationalization can be alleviated if local governments sign pledges to protect property rights or if U.S. taxpayers are willing to subsidize risk insurance coverage through the Overseas Private Investment Corporation, which is expanding its activities in the region. Bilateral investment treaties, contemplated between the United States and each CBI participant, would also help to immunize investors against expropriation, war, and other unsettling events.

Finally, Secretary Enders stressed favorable access to the U.S. market as a means to stimulate trade between countries of the region and the United States. But this is not as easy as it seems. About 87 percent of exports from the Caribbean basin already enter the U.S. market duty-free. Proposed concessions on the remaining 13 percent, which include leather and rubber goods, automobile parts, tuna, fruit, farm products, and other politically sensitive items, provoked strong opposition from unions, agricultural groups, and their representatives in Congress and the Department of Commerce.[54] Moreover, despite safeguards included in the legislation, Puerto Rican government officials and business leaders feared that relaxation of import rules for other countries would deprive the Commonwealth of its current privileged status, especially with respect to rum exports that earned more than $200 million for the island in 1980.[55] In fact, Puerto Rican leaders worried lest the Commonwealth find itself at a competitive disadvantage by having to adhere to occupational safety, environmental, and minimum wage laws that did not apply to independent nations of the basin.

Congress approved the $355 million aid component of the CBI in late 1982. Yet, it waited another eight months before passing the emasculated trade and investment provisions. Although retaining the 12-year, duty-free treatment of imports from the Caribbean basin, the legislators excluded from coverage textiles and clothing, petroleum products, luggage, flat goods, handbags, footwear, work gloves, leather apparel, and tuna. Quotas may be imposed on perishable agricultural products, including citrus fruit concentrate, should such items injure U.S. industry. The final bill eliminated tariffs from all Caribbean rum imports, a benefit that only Puerto Rico and the U.S. Virgin Islands previously enjoyed. Eligibility for the CBI preference requires at least 35 percent local content, including up to 15 percent U.S. content.

The Reagan administration failed to win approval of the 10 percent across-the-board tax break on new investment that formed part of the original bill. Instead, businessmen attending conferences in beneficiary states may deduct their expenses from U.S. federal income taxes. Cuba is specifically barred from the initiative as is any other country considered communist.[56]

CONCLUSIONS

Mexico reacted strongly to U.S. maneuvering in Nicaragua as guerrillas challenged the Somoza regime. Emboldened by increased oil earnings and his country's enhanced stature, López Portillo jettisoned any pretense of adhering to his nation's much-acclaimed nonintervention policy. Specifically, he responded to Washington's efforts to promote a transition from *somocismo* to a centrist government by backing the Sandinistas who seized power following the dictatorship's mid-1979 collapse.

Mexico relied upon a number of tools in projecting its influence in Central America in particular and the Caribbean basin in general. It increased its economic assistance, deployed the PRI to mold an organization of leftist and populist political parties, and embarked upon joint activities, including the formation of an oil facility with Venezuela, the issuance of a communiqué on El Salvador with France, and participation in the Contadora Group. It also began modernizing its military as the Guatemalan insurgency spilled across its southern border into Chiapas and armies of the area expanded.

These actions attracted support from across Mexico's political spectrum, thereby strengthening the hand of the country's chief executive in advancing national interests.

Preventing the internationalization of the conflict in the region emerged as a keystone of Mexican policy. López Portillo's strident opposition to superpower involvement may have helped delay Washington's use of military means to destabilize the Sandinista government, but it failed to deter the dispatch of troops to Grenada. In contrast to the consensus among Mexican elites on their country's policies and goals in the region, adverse public opinion in the United States, the skepticism of career military officers, and the hostility of key members of Congress who were attentive to Mexico's views served as a more potent restraint on the Reagan administration's use of the CIA and the Pentagon in Central America. Additionally, a lack of cohesion among interest groups meant that only the foreign assistance and trade components of the Caribbean Basin Initiative became law. Left unaddressed was the investment element in the proposal conceived to promote stability and economic development in the convulsed region. Mexico's participation in the CBI appeared more symbolic than substantive. Yet, by incorporating the joint oil facility into the program, López Portillo could resist Washington's turning the initiative into a blatantly anticommunist instrument.

The United States prevailed over Mexico on the relatively inconsequential issue of Castro's exclusion from the Cancún summit. Reagan placed his personal reputation on the line by emphasizing that he would not attend a North-South conference to which the Cuban leader was invited. López Portillo knew that his own reputation would have suffered had the vaunted meeting taken place without the participation of the U.S. chief executive. Nonetheless, Mexico's oil-motivated activism, which gained support from key nations of the region, troubled the efforts of the Reagan administration to muster support for its policy at home, among European allies, or within the Caribbean basin. Increasingly, Mexico acted as a middle-level power, inviting comparisons with Brazil, India, Sweden, and Yugoslavia. Yet, it avoided a confrontation with the superpower on which it was so dependent and which, in the final analysis, would ignore advice to the contrary and employ military means to achieve foreign policy goals.

NOTES

1. Ambassador Thomas O. Enders, assistant secretary of state for inter-American affairs, cites five vital U.S. interests advanced by the Basin's development: alleviating the poverty that has stimulated migration to the United States; reducing the need for future U.S. aid and expanding markets for U.S. goods; strengthening regional cooperation and burden-sharing; enhancing the security of and prospects for "democratic political evolution" in the area, thereby offering an alternative development strategy to that proposed by Marxist-Leninists; and protecting strategic and economic interests by promoting stable neighbors friendly to the United States. See, "A Comprehensive Strategy for the Caribbean Basin," *Caribbean Review* 11, No. 2 (Spring 1982): 13. For an excellent analysis of the Caribbean Basin Initiative, see David Scott Palmer's "The Caribbean Basin Initiative: Economic, Social, and Political Aspects of U.S. Policy Issues in the Region in the 1980s." A draft paper delivered at the 1983 Conference of the Mid-Atlantic Council of Latin American Studies, Williamsburg, Virginia, April 8, 1983 (mimeo.).

2. The text of President Reagan's speech to the OAS appears in U.S. Department of State, Bureau of Public Affairs, *Caribbean Basin Initiative*, Current Policy No. 370, Washington, D.C., 1982; see also, U.S. Department of State, Bureau of Public Affairs, *Background on the Caribbean Basin Initiative*, Special Report No. 97, Washington, D.C., 1982. Robert A. Pastor presents a lucid and comprehensive analysis of the Caribbean Basin Initiative in "Sinking in the Caribbean Basin," *Foreign Affairs* 60, No. 4 (Summer 1982): 1038–58.

3. Enders, "A Comprehensive Strategy for the Caribbean Basin," p. 11.

4. *Excelsior*, September 2, 1982, p. 16-A.

5. See, for example, Whitney T. Perkins, *Constraint of Empire: The United States and Caribbean Interventions* (Westport, Conn.: Greenwood, 1981).

6. Bruce Michael Bagley, "Mexican Foreign Policy: The Decline of a Regional Power?" *Current History* 82, No. 488 (November 1983): 409.

7. Susan Kaufman Purcell, "Mexico-U.S. Relations: Big Initiatives Can Cause Big Problems," *Foreign Affairs* 60, No. 2 (Winter 1981/1982): 388.

8. Rene Herrera and Mario Ojeda, "The Policy of Mexico in the Caribbean Basin," unpublished paper, 1982, p. 4.

9. John F. McShane, "Emerging Regional Power: Mexico's Role in the Caribbean Basin," in Elizabeth G. Ferris and Jennie K. Lincoln (eds.), *Latin American Foreign Policies: Global and Regional Dimensions* (Boulder, Colo.: Westview, 1981), p. 195.

10. Anthony T. Bryan, "Mexico and the Caribbean: New Ventures into the Region," *Caribbean Review* 10, No. 3 (Summer 1981): 5.

11. Bryan, "Mexico and the Caribbean," p. 5.

12. Herrera and Ojeda, "The Policy of Mexico in the Caribbean Basin," p. 6.

13. McShane, "Emerging Regional Power," p. 196.

14. McShane, "Emerging Regional Power," p. 196.

15. Bagley, "Mexican Foreign Policy," p. 406.

16. *New York Times*, May 18, 1979, p. A-3.

17. *Business Week*, July 3, 1978, p. 44.

18. *World Oil*, August 15, 1981, p. 198; *Facts on File*, February 20, 1981, p. 111.

19. *Regional Reports: Mexico & Central America*, August 15, 1980, p. 4.

20. *Facts on File*, February 20, 1981, p. 111.

21. *World Oil*, August 15, 1981, p. 114.

22. *New York Times*, August 8, 1981, p. 5.

23. *New York Times*, August 20, 1980, p. A-8.

24. *Latin America Political Report*, May 25, 1979, p. 154.

25. The organization is discussed in "COPPPAL: An Appreciation of the Regional Political Situation," *Comercio exterior* 28, No. 5 (May 1982): 173–79.

26. Constantine Christopher Menges, "Concurrent Mexican Foreign Policy, Revolution in Central America and the United States," paper prepared for the Hudson Institute, Washington, D.C., June 1980 (mimeo.), p. 43.

27. *New York Times*, August 20, 1980, p. 8-A.

28. *Excelsior*, January 25, 1980, pp. 1-A, 10-A.

29. *Excelsior*, January 25, 1980, pp. 1-A; 10-A; *Latin America Regional Report: Mexico & Central America*, February 15, 1980, p. 4.

30. *Facts on File*, March 26, 1982, p. 198; and *Washington Post*, March 24, 1982, p. 1.

31. *New York Times*, April 9, 1981, p. A-14.

32. Menges, "Current Mexican Foreign Policy," pp. 47–48.

33. Menges, "Current Mexican Foreign Policy," p. 40.

34. *Latin America Weekly Report*, December 4, 1981, p. 4.

35. *Washington Post*, August 18, 1980, p. A-21.

36. *Regional Report: Mexico and Central America*, August 15, 1980, p. 4.

37. Constantine C. Menges, "Mexico's Central America Strategy," *Christian Science Monitor*, July 13, 1981.

38. Menges, "Mexico's Central America Strategy."

39. *Facts on File*, January 23, 1981, p. 39.

40. *Facts on File*, March 6, 1981, p. 135.

41. *Facts on File*, September 11, 1981, p. 655.

42. *Washington Post*, November 25, 1981, p. A-16.

43. *Washington Post*, November 25, 1981, p. A-16.

44. *Excelsior*, September 2, 1982, p. 16-A.

45. General Galván López, quoted in *Proceso*, March 29, 1982, p. 6.

46. *Latin American Weekly Report*, October 14, 1983, p. 3.

47. Edward J. Williams, "Mexico's Central American Policy: National Security Considerations," unpublished paper (mimeo.), p. 32.

48. *Baltimore Sun*, October 31, 1982, p. K-1.

49. *New York Times*, September 2, 1981, p. 5.

50. Abraham F. Lowenthal, "The Caribbean," *Wilson Quarterly* 6, No. 2 (Spring 1982): 115.

51. *New York Times*, April 9, 1981, p. A-14.

52. *New York Times*, September 9, 1981, p. 5.

53. *Latin America Weekly Report*, December 18, 1981, p. 7.

54. *Wall Street Journal*, July 13, 1981; also, see, Pastor, "Sinking in the Caribbean Basin," pp. 1045–46.

55. *Latin America Weekly Report*, December 18, 1981, p. 7.

56. *Latin America Weekly Report*, August 15, 1983, p. 11.

6

MEXICAN MEMBERSHIP
IN THE GATT

INTRODUCTION

In the aftermath of World War II, the United States was frustrated in efforts to create an international trade organization that would enforce a far-reaching code, legally binding on member nations, to abolish nontariff barriers to commerce, promote the reduction of all tariffs through multilateral negotiations, and thereby achieve the goals of free, nondiscriminatory trade.[1]

In the absence of a comprehensive system, 23 nations signed a General Agreement on Tariffs and Trade (GATT) that took effect in 1948. The compact has established the framework for seven major tariff conferences, the most recent of which, referred to as the Tokyo Round for the city in which it took place, occurred between 1973 and 1979. Before this series of negotiations, attention had been directed to tariffs, although some concern had been focused on eliminating or liberalizing such nontariff barriers as licensing, quotas, and quality standards.

These conferences provided an opportunity for agreements on trade concessions that are normally made, according to the concept of reciprocity, only in return for reciprocal concessions from other GATT members. No contracting party is required to reduce any tariff or refrain from raising an existing one; however, once a concession is made on a given item, that good is deemed "bound" against increases above the stipulated level. The most-favored-nation (MFN) principle means that a tariff reduction or any other commercial benefit conferred upon one member by another is automatically extended to all contracting parties, thus multiplying the impact of reciprocal benefits. An escape clause does permit the withdrawal of a concession if that concession unexpectedly injures a domestic industry. Such withdrawals or even violations of the General Agreement do not trigger the imposition of penalties. Rather, they allow the contracting parties that were hurt by the action either to be compensated by receiving alternative concessions or to retaliate by withdrawing equivalent concessions.[2]

Only three developing countries (Brazil, Chile, and Cuba) numbered among the original signatories of the treaty constituting the General Agreement. The organization became more attractive to less developed countries (LDCs) in the 1960s as a Part IV was added to the three elements of the original accord. This section, entitled "Trade and Development," authorized nonreciprocity by LDCs toward other members and exhorted developed states to diminish trade barriers affecting exports from the third world.[3] This action enhanced GATT's appeal to developing nations, 52 of which had joined the organization by 1981.

United States trade policy in the 1970s focused on encouraging Mexico's entry into the General Agreement. After all, by the latter part of the decade, it had become the United States' third largest trading partner (after Japan and Canada), and Washington wanted greater access to one of the most protected markets in the world at a time when substantial trade deficits were anticipated as a result of rising petroleum imports. United States trade experts advanced arguments, many of which are cited below, stressing the advantages that GATT affiliation would hold for Mexico. Of the several issues treated in this book, none better illustrates that the perceived effort by the United States to influence Mexico's adopting a given position believed by many United States authorities to be in Mexico's own best interests often provides powerful ammunition to the opponents of that policy and greatly imperils its adoption.

BACKGROUND

López Portillo, then finance minister, attended the September 1973 ministerial meeting that launched the Tokyo Round of negotiations. These talks, which lasted six years and coincided with the vertiginous increase in international oil prices, gave rise to several provisions tailored to assist developing countries. For example, the industrial nations strengthened the legal status of the nonreciprocity component of Part IV of the GATT by pledging to provide "special and differential" treatment to the developing countries with respect to various nontariff codes and by agreeing to a package of GATT reforms. Despite these concessions, an overwhelming majority of third world delegates boycotted the signing of the documents drawn up at the conclusion of the round. They criticized the failure to devise a new "safeguards" code enabling a country to immunize its industries from a flood of imports. They also insisted that tariff reductions agreed to in the negotiations favored "have" over "have-not" countries. Finally, some nations resented the United States' having won approval of "graduation"—a procedure for attenuating the preferential treatment accorded products of such "advanced developing countries" as Brazil, India, Hong Kong, Taiwan, South Korea, and Mexico.

While not signing the final document, Mexico participated actively in the Tokyo round, notably in helping to draw up the nontariff measures negotiated in the Multilateral Trade Negotiations (MTN). Mexican influence was particularly evident in the developing country provisions of the subsidy, licensing, and customs valuation codes. Mexico also played a conspicuous role in talks related to tariff reductions and, within the context of these negotiations, reached trade agreements with the United States, Japan, and the European Community. A student of these negotiations has called the accords, in which Mexico offered concessions on 328 products valued at $503 million in 1976, "quite favorable" to the Mexicans. Yet, these concessions posed little danger to domestic industries, for they involved lowering tariffs on only 21 items and removing import licenses on but 34 products during a lengthy transition period. In contrast, the industrial nations, accepting the obligation to provide better treatment to less-developed states and anxious to coax Mexico into the GATT, offered substantial concessions on 248 products worth $612 million.[4]

By the conclusion of the Tokyo Round, López Portillo had won the presidency on a platform that, among other things, called for spurring the efficiency of Mexican firms and encouraging higher industrial output by diminishing protectionism. By mid-1980 Mexico had abolished import permits on over two-thirds of the goods that it purchased abroad. The year before, it had replaced a subjective system of "official prices" used for customs purposes with a more rational means of employing "normal value" to evaluate imports. These actions were "wholly congruent" with GATT principles.[5]

The emphasis on liberalization and rationalization also found expression in Mexico's willingness, announced by Commerce Minister Jorge de la Vega Domínguez on January 16, 1979, to explore accession to the General Agreement. This move probably sprang both from an attempt to be responsive to López Portillo's apparent predilection to join the GATT and from urging by officials in Mexico's Ministry of Commerce who believed that they had done well for their country in the Tokyo Round. Despite efforts by the U.S. government to leave the question of membership entirely up to Mexico, the overenthusiasm of certain U.S. officials, coupled with pro-affiliation articles in leading U.S. newspapers, made it appear that the decision was taken, at least in part, at the behest of Washington, which had long sought its neighbor's abandonment of isolationist trade policies.[6]

A working group formed within the GATT met five times in 1979 to discuss Mexican membership. At these sessions, Mexico was represented by Hector Hernández Cervantes, undersecretary of commerce, and Abel Garrido, the ministry's director of international negotiations. In October the group published a Protocol of Accession whose principal provisions were as follows:

- Establishing a 12-year transition period in which to abolish remaining import permits;
- Including the bilateral tariff agreements negotiated during the Tokyo Round;
- Accepting the new Mexican tariff valuation scheme;
- Permitting Mexico to continue to use export subsidies and import controls;
- Approving the implementation of the National Industrial Development Plan of March 1979 and authorizing certain tax incentives to be granted to industry, provided no harm is done to other GATT members;
- Giving full rights to manage domestic development policies, including the protection of industry and agriculture;
- Recognizing the Mexican protectionist policy with respect to the agricultural sector, particularly basic foodstuffs; and
- Allowing Mexico to ignore any elements of Part II of GATT (nontariff commercial barriers) that conflict with current Mexican laws.[7]

The U.S.-Mexican MTN accord negotiated during the Tokyo round embraced staged U.S. concessions to Mexico totaling $536 million, $304 million in industrial products and $232 million in agricultural items, $100 million of which represented tariff ceilings on winter vegetables. Mexico agreed to $312 million in concessions, of which $159 million were in agricultural products and $153 million in manufactured goods. The MTN package included most of the concessions contained in the Tropical Products Agreement, a bilateral treaty negotiated between the United States and Mexico in 1978, but never ratified by the Mexican Senate.[8]

PROPONENTS AND THEIR ARGUMENTS

López Portillo's experience during the Tokyo Round, his advocacy of freer trade, his courting of large industrialists alienated by Echeverría, the protracted discussions over an extremely generous protocol, and his attempts to expand Mexico's trading horizons beyond the Rio Grande through meetings with European and Japanese leaders convinced U.S. experts that his country would join the GATT. The force of presidential power in Mexico's authoritarian political system further enhanced the likelihood of membership. Amid such speculation, the president took an unprecedented step. In early November 1979 he announced that a "national consultation" would precede any decision on affiliation.

In view of López Portillo's obvious sympathy for the GATT, why did he invite the kind of freewheeling discussion that seldom occurs in Mexico? Several theories have been offered to explain his action. The most sympathetic suggests that he wanted to deepen the political reform of 1977 by encouraging greater "government in the sunshine," to use a North American cliché, or that he was "stalling for time" in order to mobilize public support in behalf of the treaty.[9] The most cynical explanation supposes that he perceived that the political liabilities of membership outweighed the political advantages, at least during the remainder of his term; he knew that opponents of affiliation would be more vocal than proponents and planned to use their anticipated dissent to justify a graceful retreat. Finally, new unforeseen questions may have arisen in his mind during the negotiations and he simply wanted more time to gather information and have them answered before leading Mexico into the international organization. Cabinet members hostile to the GATT are believed to have cautioned him that the Ministry of Commerce had not disclosed the full consequences to the country of membership.

Spokesmen for trade groups that principally represented large firms and multinational corporations gave speeches and participated in forums in an effort to promote entry. The most important of these were the Conference of Industrial Chambers (CONCAMIN), the Mexican Employers Federation (COPARMEX), the Confederation of National Chambers of Commerce (CONCANACO), the National Association of Importers and Exporters of the Mexican Republic (ANIERM), and the Chamber of Transformation Industries of Nuevo Leon (CAINTRA). CAINTRA assumed more importance than a mere regional trade association because its membership roster includes huge corporations dominated by the Garza Sada family, whose interlocking boards compose the Monterrey Group. The group itself kept a low profile during the public debate either because its leaders had more important items on their agenda of national issues or because they feared that active lobbying by the Monterrey industrialists, who are viewed as pariahs by leftist parties, unions, and intellectuals, would prove counterproductive. Even though more outspoken than the Monterrey Group, the American Chamber of Commerce of Mexico, a staunch advocate of membership, showed marked discretion in expressing its views.

Less discreet were several foreign diplomats. Even before the public dialogue began, Dr. Hector Gross Espies, Uruguay's ambassador to Mexico, insisted that his hosts had nothing to fear from affiliating with the GATT,[10] while Michael Delafosse, France's commercial attaché, argued that entry was in Mexico's best interests.[11] United States ambassador Patrick J. Lucey was even more persistent. He wasted no opportunity to voice his country's belief in the wisdom of membership, behavior that was out of step with the generally circumspect posture of his government. Moreover, in a letter made public in early 1980, Special Trade Representative Reubin Askew wrote President Carter that "Mexico has a growing importance in the world trading system, and I agree that it should be encouraged to join the GATT."[12]

Rolando Vega, president of the Association of Bankers of Mexico, strongly endorsed entry, insisting that the question of membership must transcend ideologies.[13] The Ministry of Commerce, the lead agency with respect to negotiations, received little or no direction from the presidency and got involved conspicuously only near the end of the consultation. The ministry's lack of coordination and efficiency may help explain this tardiness. More important was the belief by de la Vega, Hernández, Garrido, and others that López Portillo was firmly committed to joining the GATT, thereby obviating the need to drum up support. Belatedly, they perceived his misgivings and jumped into the fray, but not until opponents had shaped and dominated the discussion.

The ministry's advocacy sometimes seemed more scholarly and technical than compelling. For instance, on February 16, 1980, it purchased two pages in *Excelsior* to convey "Information to the People of Mexico [about] GATT."[14] Instead of extolling clearly the advantages of membership, the advertisement bombarded readers' eyes with column after column of numbers, designed to show concessions received from and granted to Australia, Canada, the European Community, the United States, Finland, Japan, Norway, New Zealand, Sweden, and Switzerland. The presentation may have convinced an international trade specialist, but it seemed like a treatise in obfuscation to anyone else.

Within the public sector, representatives of the Bank of Mexico, especially the director-general of the Fund of Exports of Manufactured Products (FOMEX), were more visible in recommending entry than their colleagues in the Ministry of Commerce. Proponents of accession stressed the gradual assumption of obligations, the explicit recognition of the role of its National Industrial Development Plan, and the other liberal elements contained in the protocol negotiated between Mexico and the GATT. For instance, FOMEX's Luis Malpica de la Madrid termed the negotiations "magnificent" because they called for concessions on just 8.4 percent of the country's total imports.[15] He turned the table on nationalists by pointing out that the GATT would permit Mexico, then highly dependent on trade with the United States, to diversify its markets. Furthermore, he observed that it made good sense to accept the rules adhered to by countries with which Mexico conducted 80 percent of its trade.[16] Other advocates joined him in noting that the GATT would offer Mexico, which frequently alleged discrimination and arbitrary treatment at the hands of the United States, the opportunity to participate in an international body where disputes could be resolved objectively. "There's more protection inside than out of the organization," they said.[17] Even more specific was Manuel Clouhtier, president of COMPARMEX, who claimed that affiliation would "benefit and increase agricultural, forestry, and fishing production." Moreover, it would "counteract the harmful effects of the United States' anti-dumping law which affects Mexican vegetables," he said.[18]

A leading U.S. official observed that Mexico could look forward to more concessions as a signatory of the General Agreement than if it remained outside. Additionally, the country's size and economic strength meant that it would not only safeguard its own interests within the organization but that it could become a spokesman for LDCs in general. Put briefly: Mexico would help shape international commercial relations during the next decade.[19]

Hernández and the trade association underlined the GATT's importance in diversifying exports, attracting private investment, and even redistributing income. They also emphasized that affiliating with the organization would give the country's pampered manufacturers a cold shower. Membership, they insisted, would bring competition, militating against the high prices and uneven quality of many goods produced domestically under monopolistic conditions. Planning and Budget Minister de la Madrid averred that the "protection of inefficiency cannot be tolerated."[20] A bit of doggerel published in *Excelsior* gave humorous expression to this view:

Ojalá que el GATT suspenda el tradicional descaro . . . de que en México se venda lo mal hecho a precio caro . . .[21]	Oh that the GATT would stop the imprudent tradition . . . by which Mexico sells the poorly made at a high price

OPPONENTS AND THEIR ARGUMENTS

Critics of membership pressed their case months before the negotiations had concluded. The National College of Economists (CNE), an organization composed largely of academic and government economists, many of whom had gained a Marxist perspective on society as students at UNAM, spearheaded the opposition. The association lambasted Mexico's proposed entry through speeches by its successive presidents; carried its message to opinion leaders through press interviews and newspaper advertisements; held discussions with government officials; and convened highly publicized forums, "Mexico Before the GATT," in which foes of affiliation generally outnumbered advocates. Economists at the Centro de Investigaciones y Docencia Económicas, the members of the small League of Revolutionary Economists, and professors throughout the country fleshed out what might be termed the academic component of opposition.

Important publications not only printed—and sometimes embellished—the views of critics, but joined in the dissent. For example, editorials in *El Día, Unomásuno*, and *Proceso* warned against the dangers of membership. While *Excelsior*, the country's most respected newspaper, failed to take a clear position, its columnists observed no such neutrality. Of the 19 columns devoted to the GATT question between January 1 and March 18, 1980, opponents to joining outnumbered proponents by a two-to-one margin, while one writer failed to take sides. Most strident in his criticism was Manuel Buendía, a militant leftist whose "Private Network" column appears on *Excelsior's* front page and is syndicated across the nation. He often used his rapier-like wit in articulating many of the arguments listed below. In a particularly acerbic essay, he compared chief negotiator Hernández's attempt to sell GATT to the huckstering of a cemetery lot salesman. "I don't want you to die," Buendía mockingly reported the official as saying, "but that is inevitable. Permit me to show you a good place from where to await the resurrection."[22]

Various trade associations contended that Mexico's joining the GATT would produce hardships and even bankruptcies among their affiliates. The largest of these was the National Chamber of Transforming Industries (CANACINTRA), which claims to represent 75,000 member-firms concentrated in the automobile, chemical, food-processing, and metallurgical industries. An inveterate champion of protectionism, CANACINTRA was instrumental in securing Mexican opposition to the postwar International Trade Organization. It also lobbied successfully for its country's abrogation in 1950 of the 1942 Trade Agreement with the United States.

Neither the PRI nor its labor sector, the CTM, took an official stance on the GATT question. The leader of the House of Deputies noted the lack of consensus within that body. As a result, more attention flowed to the small political parties and trade unions that opposed membership. In the former category were the Mexican Communist Party, the Popular Socialist Party, the Coalition of the Left, the Movement of Socialist Action and Unity, and the Mexican Democratic Party; the latter included the General Union of Workers and Peasants of Mexico. By early February 1980 the Confederation of Labor, an umbrella group that includes the CTM and other labor federations, receded from its initial anti-GATT position to one of neutrality.

Within government circles, the Ministries of Finance, Patrimony, and Foreign Relations raised the most searing objections to membership. Finance Minister David Ibarra Muñoz described the putative restriction of GATT's benefits to industrialized countries, which were impeding imports from poor nations and failing to implement the original Tokyo Round principles that favored LDCs.[23] Oteyza focused on the alleged conflict between the General Agreement and the country's National Industrial Development Plan, unveiled in March 1979. Foreign Minister Castañeda and his subordinates concentrated on the danger that the GATT posed to their country's sovereignty.[24]

Critics unleashed a fusillade of arguments against membership. They claimed that the GATT favored large, capital-intensive multinational corporations at the expense of artisans and small- and medium-sized companies. Many such firms, which generate 90 percent of the nation's jobs, could not compete successfully against foreign goods, according to Heberto Castillo, an influential columnist for *Proceso* and president of the nationalistic, non-Marxist Mexican Workers Party.[25]

León García Soler, an *Excelsior* columnist, insisted that wiping out the small- and medium-sized industries would concentrate even more economic and political resources in the hands of giant industries. In 1970, he noted, less than 1 percent of corporations in Mexico held 67 percent of fixed industrial assets, boasted 63 percent of invested capital, and generated 63 percent of the value of production. In contrast, 92 percent of the firms accounted for only 5.2 percent of fixed industrial assets, 5 percent of invested capital, and 6 percent of production.[26]

Some opponents frankly recognized the Mexican dilemma of producing only a few products in which the country enjoyed a comparative advantage; that is, an ability to produce and sell goods with relative efficiency vis-à-vis its trading partners. David Márquez Ayala, an economist and UNAM professor, argued that membership would obligate greater production for export when the country should be channeling its resources to internal goals. Joining the

GATT would be imprudent, he stated, for Mexico "has little or almost nothing to sell abroad."[27] The increasing overvaluation of the peso before the February 1982 devaluation lent credence to this conclusion.

Bureaucratic detractors of membership may have been less candid in describing their objection. The administration of Mexico's elaborate system of import permits, quotas, and tariffs provided jobs for thousands of government workers. For instance, it's not unusual to hear businessmen complain of having to obtain 15 or 20 signatures from bureaucrats just to get an export permit. Affected civil servants, particularly in the Ministry of Commerce, may have resisted entering an international organization devoted to the goal of reducing and eliminating the very commercial barriers that justified their employment. Gustavo Vega, one of Mexico's most promising young scholars and a faculty member at the Colegio de México, will test this hypothesis of bureaucratic self-interest in a book that he is currently writing on his country's relationship to the GATT.

Almost every adversary emphasized the theme that, on the one hand, entry would enhance the influence over Mexico of the United States, multinational corporations, and international financial agencies and, on the other hand, curtail Mexico's freedom of action. García Soler reminded his readers that the GATT emerged from the same post-World War II structure embracing the IMF and the World Bank. The powerful nations that control these organizations and the international economic order "never respect the rules of the game."[28]

Similarly, Javier A. Matus Pacheco, the foreign ministry's director-general of multilateral economic relations, claimed that the GATT used a smokescreen of multilateralism to disguise bilateral economic arrangements dictated by wealthy countries. He insisted that inside the GATT, Mexico's position would be "weak because [like other LDCs] it lacks political and economic power." Yet, outside the organization, it could promote its interests by working collectively with other third world nations, possibly to establish a New International Economic Order. Matus also minimized the attractiveness of the Protocol of Accession, arguing that concessions for Mexico only affected 10 percent of the 1976 value of the country's total exports.[29]

It was further maintained, though not proven, that the GATT did not give sufficient consideration to the problems of developing countries and was inconsistent with the National Industrial Development Plan. Above all, the General Agreement was depicted as a Trojan Horse that would enable the avaricious, energy-short *gringos* to gain control of Mexico's oil. As the National College of Economists expressed it:

> Mexico must not accept pressures applied by superpowers like the United States and international financial organizations like the World Bank and the International Monetary Fund in order to enter the General Agreement on Tariffs because it could sacrifice its petroleum industry and never cease being dependent.[30]

Deputy Jesús Puente Leyva, a former president of the CNE and then chairman of the Energy Committee of his nation's congress, warned that membership posed a "sophisticated provocation"; specifically, it threatened not just the oil sector but the flooding of the Mexican economy with U.S. goods. In his words:

> This must be interpreted as the predictable strategy of the neighboring country to the North to liberalize Mexico's commercial frontiers so that . . . foreign exchange generated by Mexican oil can be spent easily and without obstacles on massive imports from the United States.[31]

Among others, Minister Oteyza championed a policy of bargaining with Mexico's oil wealth to extract commercial concessions, investment packages, and technological transfers from developed countries such as had been done with France and Japan. Membership in the GATT, he argued, would militate against such bilateral arrangements. Moreover, it might prevent PEMEX's reducing exports unless internal consumption were also curtailed.

THE DECISION

On March 18, 1980, López Portillo announced that: "After receiving various contradictory opinions I have resolved that it is not the opportune moment" for Mexico to accede as a contracting party of the GATT or to join any of the nontariff codes. He explained that the General Agreement did not offer the protection and flexibility necessary for Mexico's economic development,[32] an apparent expression of the concern that PEMEX would not be able to alter its level of oil exports deemed appropriate for the national interest. His statement, which recognized that Mexico had been offered the most favorable terms that it could expect to receive, followed a meeting with selected cabinet members in Los Pinos, the presidential residence. At this session, the ministers of finance, patrimony, foreign relations, and labor opposed affiliation, while the ministers of commerce, interior, and budget and planning recommended membership.[33] As is the custom in Mexico, advocates and adversaries closed ranks behind the chief executive, whose decision was greeted by virtually unanimous approval. Commerce Minister de la Vega, the strongest proponent of entry, observed that the presidential decision was based "not only in his full and vast knowledge of the subject, but in the exactness of the national consultation that had taken place." Oteyza, an inveterate opponent of affiliation, called the action a reinforcement of Mexico's independence and self-determination and "a rejection of the sirens' song and the use of its resources in a fashion that would not add to its strength."[34]

What accounted for López Portillo's veto of membership? Why did he reverse a position apparently taken when Mexico agreed to negotiate the terms of accession?

Only the former president and his confidants can answer these questions. Still, the timing of the announcement—March 18 was the forty-second anniversary of the expropriation of the oil industry and López Portillo's speech was made before an audience of petroleum workers—underlined the importance of safeguarding his nation's sovereignty. Neither big business nor the Ministry of Commerce made a convincing case for membership. In general, proponents were significantly less vocal and effective than opponents, who seized the initiative in the national consultation. Critics drew upon their nation's traditional reticence to join international organizations, especially those considered under the sway of the United States and other developed countries. Further strengthening their hand was the reaction against Washington's position. They warned against increasing their nation's dependence on its northern neighbor or, as they called it, "selling out to imperialism." Such dependence was especially feared because it might circumscribe PEMEX's ability to maximize benefits from its petroleum, a natural resource that has a special significance to Mexico and that was regarded as the key to sustained economic growth.

Mexico's wariness of any attempted assertion of foreign influence manifested itself in allegations of U.S. "retaliation," "threats," and "pressures" following the GATT pronouncement. Even though

U.S. representatives publicly recognized that the "decision was one for Mexico to make unilaterally,"[35] the active advocacy by the U.S. ambassador and unfortunate press reports nourished claims of U.S. intervention. President Carter, who was angered by López Portillo's caustic luncheon toast on February 14, 1979, and the refusal to readmit the shah to Mexico at year's end, took umbrage at Mexico's failure to affiliate with the General Agreement.

Mexico's failure to join the GATT nullified the bilateral trade concessions subscribed to during the Tokyo Round. Furthermore, Mexico and the United States have no agreement covering the treatment of imports from each other, although, in general, both countries provide MFN treatment to the other's goods. However, in the area of unfair trade practices this situation encouraged U.S. producers to bring countervailing duty suits with the Department of Commerce against Mexican products. A successful suit against a GATT subsidy code member requires not only proof of the subsidization of the item in question, but also a finding of an injury inflicted on a U.S. industry. (Even for a noncode signatory which is a GATT member, an injury test is provided for duty-free imports, which would be especially important to Mexico since a large number of its imports enter without tariffs under the GSP.) In the case of Mexico, only the presence of a subsidy had to be shown and that was relatively easy because the increasing overvaluation of the peso had led to the adoption of several export-promotion schemes, including tax credits known as CEDIs.

On April 10, 1981, the Department of Commerce determined that "the government of Mexico has given manufacturers, producers, and exporters of leather apparel benefits or grants within the meaning of the countervailing duty law." As a consequence, it applied a 5 percent ad valorem charge, to be paid by U.S. importers, to the roughly $20 million in Mexican leather clothing items sold annually to North American consumers.[36] Even after overvaluation of the peso ceased and CEDIs were eliminated, other practices such as subsidized export credits and regional assistance continued, thereby providing grounds for U.S. penalty duties. Steel, hydrous ammonia, asparagus, toy balloons, playballs, polypropylene, manhole covers, various lead products, and other items have become the targets of countervailing duty suits or are subject to agreements limiting Mexican government assistance.

According to Steve Lande, chief U.S. negotiator with Mexico between 1976 and 1982, U.S. laws to combat unfair trade practices are themselves unfair to developing countries. Whereas the GATT allows subsidies, these statutes provide that the offending nation must phase out all assistance to the product in question. Moreover, unlike the GATT, there is no appeals process. Remaining outside of the General Agreement deprives Mexico of both an injury test and the opportunity to appeal to GATT for relief (for example, India has used the pressure of a GATT complaint against U.S. policy to wring important trade concessions from the United States).[37] Lande, among others, contends that the United States should liberalize, not deliberalize, its trade policy since Mexico offers a dynamic market for U.S. exports, and insufficient export earnings constitute its main constraint on purchasing.

Further complicating relations was Mexico's deliberalization of its trade policies. At the beginning of 1981, prior import licensing affected only 1,668 tariff classifications, representing 58.5 percent of the previous year's imports. A deteriorating current account position with other countries, notably the United States, persuaded Mexican officials to reinstitute permits on industrial and, to a lesser extent, agricultural items, thereby raising to 2,053 (85 percent of 1980 imports) the number of tariff classifications subject to prior licensing. In mid-1981 Mexico raised the import duty on 409 items, with levies on capital goods increasing from 10 to 15 percent and those on luxuries up to 100 percent. Furthermore, the selective reinstitution of official import prices also served to curtail imports.[38] Oteyza warned that, if necessary, supplemental emergency trade barriers would be erected to slow the flood of foreign goods that "threatens the nation's economy."[39]

Another bone of contention was Mexico's seizure, in July 1980, of U.S. tuna clippers allegedly fishing in Mexican waters. In retaliation, Washington imposed an embargo on Mexican tuna products, whose value approached $20 million in 1980.

In mid-1981, Presidents Reagan and López Portillo expanded a previously constituted working group into a Joint Commission on Commerce and Trade in order to fashion a mechanism for managing bilateral trade, whose value reached $30 billion that year. Although forming working groups on automobiles, petrochemicals, and computers and electronic goods and discussing issues ranging from the

Generalized System of Preferences to border traffic, the commission failed in its first two-and-one-half years to construct a comprehensive framework for resolving trade problems. Mexico's worsening economic crisis found bilateral efforts riveted on both the plight of firms hard hit by currency restrictions in Mexico and on the need to improve the information flow between the two governments.

In an April 1983 meeting with high-level U.S. officials, Hernández Cervantes, whom de la Madrid had named minister of commerce, criticized U.S. protectionism and called for a bilateral trade accord enabling Mexican goods to enter the United States with reduced tariffs or none at all. This proposal fell on deaf ears even though a decline in buying power had seen Mexican purchases of U.S. goods plummet from $18 billion in 1981 to $12 billion in 1982, causing a loss of some 200,000 jobs north of the Rio Grande.[40] Nineteen-eighty-three witnessed another precipitous drop in U.S. exports to Mexico at a time when a reasonably valued peso and fewer resources because of an economic crisis militated against Mexico's subsidizing its own goods shipped abroad. Addressing commercial matters in a multinational forum such as the GATT would have diminished the inevitable political tensions that suffuse joint efforts to resolve trade matters.

CONCLUSIONS

United States' advocacy of Mexican entry into the GATT provided ammunition to opponents who claimed, among other things, that membership would limit opportunities to use their nation's oil wealth to advance its interests. They raised the spectre of Mexico's economic vassalage to the United States, an unlikely prospect in view of the exceedingly generous terms negotiated for the country's joining the 89-state organization. López Portillo's initial support of membership persuaded proponents, whose advocacy was generally late and ineffective, that the matter was settled. Yet, the president reversed himself in the aftermath of a spirited public dialogue that both revealed the divisions besetting the country over GATT and gave detractors of affiliation a splendid opportunity to voice the "gringos-are-out-to-get-us" refrain.

Ironically, Mexico would be in a stronger position vis-à-vis the United States had it entered the General Agreement. First, it would enjoy the injury test, a formidable weapon against countervailing duty suits. Second, its balance-of-payments and foreign exchange problems would have provided GATT-approved grounds for discontinuing trade liberalization, as well as assuring it full control over oil export levels. Third, even though President Reagan is well disposed toward Mexico, his administration has yet to fashion a bilateral trade mechanism. Affiliating with the GATT would have offered an opportunity for Mexico to advance its commercial interests in a multilateral, less politically charged environment. Finally, Mexico has attempted to exert leadership in economic matters through the United Nations Conference on Trade and Development, an international organization composed of poorer nations to which industrialized countries pay little heed. The GATT would have furnished Mexico a more respected and respectable forum in which to champion its own and third world interests.

NOTES

1. Kenneth W. Dam, *The GATT: Law and International Economic Organization* (Chicago: University of Chicago Press, 1970), pp. 10–16.

2. Dam, *The GATT*, pp. 17–19.

3. Dale Story, "Trade Politics in the Third World: A Case Study of the Mexican GATT Decision," *International Organization* 36, No. 4 (Fall 1982): 769.

4. Story, "Trade Politics in the Third World," pp. 769–70.

5. Story, "Trade Politics in the Third World," p. 770.

6. U.S. official quoted in the *New York Times*, February 2, 1979, p. D-1.

7. Story, "Trade Politics in the Third World," p. 773.

8. John Michael Garner, "Outlook for Mexican-U.S. Trade," in John H. Christman (ed.), *Business Mexico* (Mexico City: American Chamber of Commerce of Mexico, 1981), p. 172.

9. *Economist*, November 10, 1979.

10. *Excelsior*, April 1, 1979.

11. *Excelsior*, February 12, 1980.

12. *Times of the Americas*, March 1980.

13. *Visión*, April 7, 1980, p. 37.

14. *Excelsior*, February 16, 1980, pp. 16-A, 17-A.

15. *Excelsior*, February 8, 1980, p. 23.

16. *Excelsior*, February 8, 1980, p. 23.

17. *Excelsior*, February 8, 1980, p. 23.

18. *Visión*, April 7, 1980, p. 37.

19. C. Fred Bergsten, assistant secretary of treasury for international affairs, quoted in *Excelsior*, March 16, 1979.

20. *Latin America Economic Report*, June 15, 1979, p. 178.

21. Campos Díaz y Sánchez, "Epigrama," *Excelsior*, February 15, 1980.

22. *Excelsior*, February 12, 1980.

23. *Latin America Economic Report*, June 15, 1979, p. 178.

24. See, for example, Javier A. Matus Pacheco, "Elementos para evaluar la conveniencia del ingreso de México al GATT," *Comercio exterior* 30, No. 2 (February 1980): 118–22.

25. *Proceso*, November 19, 1979, p. 39.

26. *Excelsior*, January 12, 1980.

27. *Excelsior*, March 9, 1980.

28. *Excelsior*, January 12, 1980.

29. Matus Pacheco, "Elementos para evaluar," pp. 120–22.

30. *Excelsior*, March 5, 1979.

31. *Excelsior*, April 19, 1979, p. 4.

32. *Proceso*, March 24, 1980, p. 6.

33. *Novedades*, November 22, 1982, p. 11.

34. *Proceso*, March 24, 1980, p. 6.

35. Garner, "Outlook for Mexican-U.S. Trade," p. 172.

36. Garner, "Outlook for Mexican-U.S. Trade," pp. 174–75.

37. Telephone Interview, June 18, 1983.

38. Garner, "Outlook for Mexican-U.S. Trade," pp. 175–76.

39. *Journal of Commerce*, August 18, 1981.

40. *Facts on File*, April 29, 1983, p. 309.

7

IMMIGRATION AND INFLUENCE

INTRODUCTION

Immigration is the most sensitive and potentially explosive issue in U.S.-Mexican relations. It raises questions concerning the sanctity of borders, thereby reopening old wounds produced in past territorial conflicts. That citizens would wish to leave their country temporarily or permanently for another raises awkward, vexing questions about the home government's ability to provide employment and other opportunities for its own people. The prospect of absorbing millions of newcomers also forces a reexamination of the United States' vaunted reputation as a "melting pot," "island of freedom," and "beacon of hope" for the world's huddled masses. Moreover, immigration, unlike oil, investments, or agricultural products, directly affects human beings whose activities demand and command the attention of leaders on both sides of the Rio Grande.

When masses of people seek to migrate, neither politicians nor the press can remain indifferent to their efforts to enter a foreign nation, their hardships in earning a living there, and their struggle to decide whether to adopt a new homeland or return to their old one. Both dewy-eyed humanitarians and hard-hearted xenophobes are moved by roundups of sweat-drenched illegals in Arizona onion fields, the grisly starvation of migrants in the ballast tanks of ships, and the automobile deaths of unlawful aliens, attempting to flee the U.S. Border Patrol, along California's Highway 86, known as "blood alley" because of hundreds of collisions that occur there annually.

139

Above all, immigration touches a question that is central to a nation's independence, for controlling access to one's country is a universally recognized attribute of sovereignty in the international political system.

Despite opposition from segments of their constituencies, the Carter and Reagan administrations backed initiatives to reform immigration policy in general and to reduce illegal immigration in particular. While claiming that such legislation was strictly a U.S. concern, Mexican authorities unmistakably favored maintaining the status quo and preserving the border as an escape valve for their own people. This chapter focuses on U.S. attempts to revise immigration laws and the Mexican response to this effort. A brief history of Mexican immigration to the United States precedes this analysis.

HISTORY OF IMMIGRATION

Although the major surges of immigration to the United States have occurred in the twentieth century, employers began recruiting Mexican laborers to work on farms, in mines, and in laying and maintaining railroad lines as early as the mid 1880's. Wayne A. Cornelius reports that Mexicans constituted 17 percent of the maintenance crews for the nine most important western railroads in 1909. The significant Mexican communities in Chicago, Detroit, Gary, and Kansas City took root in this period, as migrants left railroad construction to seek stationary and better-paying jobs in factories and the stockyards.[1]

The protracted Mexican revolution and World War I gave impulse to migration. The former drove Mexicans north of the border in search of security and employment; the latter attracted field hands to replace U.S. farm workers mobilized to fight in Europe. The result was that the number of persons of Mexican birth residing in the United States expanded from 100,000 at the turn of the century to 650,000 by 1930. "Like Chinese coolies and the Japanese before them, Mexicans provided a steady supply of cheap labor. . . . Employers regarded them as dependable, submissive, hardworking."[2] Representatives for California fruit growers lauded the Mexicans for their indifference to politics, affinity for sunshine and adobe walls, and contentment with a modest tortilla diet. A member of the Los Angeles Chamber of Commerce explained that

> No labor that has ever come to the United States is more satisfactory under righteous treatment. The Mexican, as a result of years of servitude, has always looked upon his employer as his patron, and upon himself as part of the establishment.[3]

Pressures, harassment, threats, and bribes replaced any "righteous treatment" as approximately a half-million Mexicans and Mexican-Americans returned to Mexico during the 1930s. The Great Depression dried up employment opportunities and sharpened the antagonism toward foreigners who were scorned as competitors for scarce jobs and social welfare largesse. Prejudice, physical intimidation, and ethnic slurs abounded. Signs in restaurants and other public places revealed the ugly popular mood: "No Niggers, Dogs, or Mexicans Allowed."[4] Obviously impressed by the docility of the Spanish-speaking foreigners, a Kern County, California, deputy sheriff stated that "the Mexicans are trash. They have no standard of living. We herd them like pigs."[5]

Still, within a decade "Help Wanted" signs sprang up again. In 1942 the U.S. Congress enacted Public Law 45 that instituted the bracero program. This plan permitted Mexicans to enter legally southwestern states to fill agricultural jobs vacated by Americans conscripted into military service. The forced resettlement of Japanese-Americans further exacerbated the need for workers. Under the enabling legislation, the workers received free transportation to and from their homes; they were assigned to specific growers or growers' associations; they earned the minimum wage of 46¢ per hour (later increased to 57¢); failure to perform satisfactorily meant that the employee forfeited both his job and right to remain in the United States; and Mexican labor officials could conduct periodic inspections to certify that their people enjoyed fair treatment. Over the objections of organized labor, Congress expanded the program to embrace nonagricultural jobs in early 1943. For some two decades, the bracero experiment constituted the largest component of Mexican migration to the United States. As many as 400,000 Mexicans per year had worked in 25 states, including some as far north as Minnesota and Wisconsin. Numerous problems beset the program. Experts agree that the braceros earned higher wages than they would have obtained at home. Yet, they faced deep-seated prejudices and the lax enforcement of regulations concerning wages and working conditions.[6]

A coalition comprised of unions, Chicano groups, the Roman Catholic Church, and other religious organizations persuaded Congress and the Johnson administration to terminate the program on December 31, 1964. Unobtrusive allies of this move were manufacturers of cotton and tomato harvesting machinery, whose products substantially decreased the demand for stoop labor in the Southwest, and thus "dulled the growers' desire for braceros."[7]

While bread-and-butter considerations dominated the outlook of labor organizations, concern was also expressed that foreign workers suffered such exploitation and discrimination as to make them "second-class citizens" and victims of "legalized slavery" in a society that extolled the virtues of democracy, equality, and opportunity. Parallel to the flow of legal braceros was a rapidly expanding stream of illegal "wetbacks" who traded peonage in Mexico for only slightly better treatment north of the Rio Grande where, as renegades, they fell victim to unscrupulous manipulation and predatory employers.

The cessation of the bracero plan gave a fillip to the unionization of U.S. farm workers, culminating in the formation of the United Farm Workers' Union (UFW), an AFL-CIO affiliate headed by Caesar Chavez. After years of intense struggle that sometimes involved labor violence reminiscent of the brawling 1930s, Chavez— on January 31, 1978—called off boycotts, which had been launched to aid union organizing, against iceberg lettuce (begun in 1970), table grapes (1973), and Gallo wines (1973). Under a two-and-one-half-year-old California Agricultural Relations Act, the UFW, then 30,000 members strong, had signed contracts with more than 100 growers and was negotiating with 100 more. An additional 43 representational elections won by the UFW were awaiting certification by the state labor relations board. These gains benefited from a 1977 accord with the Teamsters, which had fiercely competed with Chavez to organize workers in California. The compromise gave the UFW jurisdiction over employees primarily engaged in farming, while the Teamsters had the right to sign up truck drivers, cannery workers, and others not directly working in the field.

Besides the stemming of the inflow of braceros and Chavez's charismatic leadership, the assistance tendered to the farm workers by the AFL-CIO, the Roman Catholic Church, the World Council of Churches, Gov. Edmund Brown, Jr., and other politicians, elements of the mass media, and liberal groups throughout the United States was a decisive factor contributing to the unionization of men and women deemed by many as "unorganizable." It must be remembered that earlier efforts to forge unions in California's Imperial Valley had often resulted in the organizers being pummeled, tarred, and feathered by growers and their allies.

The passage of time since the last bracero crossed legally into the United States has blurred memories of this initiative. It has also given rise to certain half-truths or erroneous assessments of what occurred during the 22-year duration of the program. Two flagrant misconceptions persist. The first is that the program abated the influx of illegal aliens. In the first decade of the bracero scheme, the number of wetbacks increased faster than the number of legal braceros. The unlawful flow subsided only after the Immigration and Naturalization Service (INS) launched what was inelegantly called "Operation Wetback." This paramilitary offensive involving draconian searches and massive deportations—methods unacceptable in today's human rights-conscious environment where Hispanics evince growing political influence and Mexico is treated with notable sensitivity. Second, some erroneously believe that the bracero program promoted closer ties with Mexico when just the opposite occurred. Zealous Mexican reporters filled their country's newspapers with "lurid tales" of mistreatment of Mexicans in the United States, particularly in California.[8] Hence, allegations of arbitrary or unjust treatment quickly transcended the domain of labor-management affairs to become perceived in Mexico City as insults to that proud country's national honor. A proposed treaty to address widely publicized abuses was loaded down with crippling amendments and thus progressed at a snail's pace through the U.S. Senate. Caustic comments about Mexicans often punctuated debate over this legislation, further embittering relations.

A combination of "push" factors (high population growth rates, inordinate unemployment and underemployment, inflation, maldistribution of income, and subsistence standards of living and wages) and "pull" factors (demand for and recruitment of such workers by U.S. employers, family ties, activities of a number of public and private organizations) led to the acceleration of unlawful immigration in the post-bracero period, as measured by the number of illegals apprehended by the INS. Table 3 embraces these figures.

TABLE 3: Illegal Aliens from Mexico Apprehended and Total Illegal Aliens Apprehended, 1960–1982

Fiscal Year	Total Apprehensions	Mexicans Apprehended	% Mexicans Apprehended
1960	70,684	29,651	41.9%
1961	88,823	29,817	33.6
1962	92,758	30,272	32.6
1963	88,712	39,124	44.1
1964	86,597	43,844	50.6
1965	110,371	55,340	50.1
1966	138,520	89,751	64.8
1967	161,608	108,327	67.0
1968	212,057	151,705	71.5
1969	283,557	201,636	71.1
1970	345,353	277,377	80.3
1971	420,126	348,178	82.9
1972	505,949	430,178	95.0
1973	655,968	576,823	87.9
1974	788,145	709,959	90.1
1975	766,600	680,392	88.8
1976	875,915	781,474	89.7
1977	1,042,215	954,778	91.6
1978	1,057,977	976,667	92.3
1979	1,076,418	988,830	91.9
1980	910,361	817,381	89.8
1981	975,780	874,161	89.6
1982	970,246	887,457	91.5

Source: Cornelius, *Mexican Migration to the United States: Causes, Consequences, and U.S. Responses* (Migration and Development Study Group, Center of International Studies; Cambridge, Mass.: M.I.T., 1978), p. 11; and *Annual Reports* of the U.S. Immigration and Naturalization Service.

LEGISLATION ON ILLEGAL IMMIGRATION

Throughout the late 1960s and early 1970s, Rep. Peter W. Rodino (D-N.J.) and others sponsored legislation to foreclose job opportunities for illegals by requiring employers to determine the eligibility for employment of persons hired, with escalating penalties for those knowingly hiring unlawful aliens. Such legislation died in the Senate, which became a burial ground for it and the similar measures subsequently offered by restrictionists. Keeper of the graveyard was the redoubtable James O. Eastland (D-Miss.). Born in 1905 and elected to the Senate in 1940, his extended service made him both the upper chamber's senior member and third in line of succession to the presidency. More important with respect to immigration policy, he chaired both the Subcommittee on Immigration and Naturalizaton and its powerful parent, the Senate Judiciary Committee. For a decade, Eastland apparently never called a subcommittee meeting, even when formally urged to do so by committee members. This inaction assured the interment of bills within its domain.

Respected observers attribute the senator's behavior to a desire to make "it easy for plantation owners to get cheap foreign labor."[9] Substantiating this theory is the action taken in 1972 by Eastland's office to halt raids by the U.S. Border Patrol against illegals working in Coahoma County, Mississippi, about 50 miles from Eastland's own cotton plantation. Before the forays were cancelled, agents had arrested 20 Mexicans, including 17 unlawfully working at a cotton gin.[10]

Preoccupied by Watergate, President Nixon devoted little attention to immigration reform. In contrast, President Ford agreed with his Mexican counterpart, Echeverría, "on the immediate necessity for each government to study the question with a view to finding a mutually satisfying solution."[11] Hence, he instructed his Domestic Council to prepare a report on the subject and to draft legislation. Even as this work proceeded, apprehensions of illegals rose from 345,353 in 1970 to over 1 million in 1977, with Mexicans accounting for most of the increase. General Leonard F. Chapman, Jr., commissioner of the Immigration and Naturalization Service, lacked the enforcement capability to police the Mexican border. Anxious to gain the attention of the executive and legislative branches, he decided to publicize the problem in the press. This may have motivated the INS news release of December 8, 1975, reporting that 8 million illegal aliens resided in the United States and that they saddled U.S. taxpayers with a burden of $13 billion or more. Although undocumented, the 8 million figure had its intended effect. Newspapers and magazines printed sensationalist articles about the "silent invasion." In turn, the INS annual budget boasted increases of 16.4 percent between fiscal year 1974, when Chapman began his "public education campaign," and 1977 when a new administration took office.[12]

Eight months after being sworn in, President Carter sent to Congress legislation built on the Ford administration's study and designed to help reduce markedly the increasing flow "and to regulate the presence of the millions of undocumented aliens already here." Among other things, the bill[13] provided a blanket amnesty for unlawful workers who entered the United States before 1970 and had resided here continuously since then. Those arriving between 1970 and January 1, 1977, would enjoy a "nondeportable" status as "temporary resident aliens"; that is, they could remain in the country, work, and even travel abroad. But they would not be eligible for welfare, food stamps, Medicaid, or other social benefits for five years. The government would reevaluate their position at the end of the period. Undocumented aliens who arrived in this country after January 1, 1977, would be ineligible for temporary resident alien status. Other provisions would have increased the size of the U.S. Border Patrol 40 percent by adding 2,000 agents. The centerpiece of the program was the imposition of civil penalties of up to $1,000 per illegal worker for employers who "knowingly" hired illegal aliens and criminal penalties on those who serve as brokers for such employers. The attorney-general could seek both a civil penalty and injunctive relief where "cause exists to believe that an employer has engaged in a pattern or practice of employing aliens" in violation of the law.

The Illegal Alien Control Bill failed because of opposition in the Senate Judiciary Committee and because of mounting apprehension on both ends of Pennsylvania Avenue that a resolute border program would offend Hispanic-Americans in a half-dozen populous states whose electoral votes are crucial to the outcome of presidential elections. Senator Edward M. Kennedy's 20-hour, highly publicized trip to Mexico, which included a meeting with López Portillo, came on the eve of the May 3, 1980, confrontation with President Carter in the Texas Democratic primary and epitomized the attempted use of contacts with Mexico for domestic political purposes. Mexico's emergence as a substantial oil-possessing nation further diminished enthusiasm—in the White House as well as in Congress—for action at the border.

This sentiment hardened into a negative reaction toward the repair of a security fence, twelve feet high and six-and-one-half miles long, between Juárez and El Paso, where the Border Patrol was arresting 11,000 illegal aliens each month. Authorities estimated that five times that number evaded detection. Critics viewed the "Tortilla

Curtain" as a powerfully offensive symbol of tension between the two countries. "I don't believe that we and Mexico should have any sort of Berlin [Wall] on our borders," said William P. Clements, who served as governor of Texas between 1978 and 1982.[14] Others decried the structure as useless because truly motivated migrants would surely walk around it. The Immigration and Naturalization Service, which had conceived the $2 million project, admitted that this would happen, but insisted that the wall would narrow the number of entry points and make patrols easier and more effective.

Because of the uproar in Texas and in California, where a similar fence was planned for San Ysidro, INS officials said in late 1978 that the undertaking had been "put on hold" and was being "reevaluated" by the Carter administration. The fence was later built after the design was changed to remove cutting edges that gave the structure the appearance of a military fortification.

Meanwhile, the president named former governor Reubin Askew, who was later succeeded by Father Theodore M. Hesburgh, president of the University of Notre Dame, to head the Select Commission on Immigration and Refugee Policy, which would recommend a new, comprehensive policy to Congress. The appointment of the commission effectively shelved the issue, and the subsequent postponement of its report removed the subject from the 1980 presidential campaign.

The Hesburgh panel released its findings on February 26, 1981.[15] This document emphasized the value of immigration to the nation's economic and cultural enrichment and identified three goals of immigration policy: family reunification, economic growth consistent with protecting the U.S. labor market, and cultural diversity compatible with national unity. A Census Bureau study accompanying the report estimated that between 3.5 and 6 million illegals resided in the United States. In their introduction, the commissioners "recommended closing the back door to undocumented/illegal migration," while "opening the front door a little to accommodate legal migration."

Means to close the back door included reinforcing the U.S. Border Patrol; devising a "more secure" form of worker identification to enable employers to determine whether job applicants were legally entitled to work in the United States; and recommending civil and criminal penalties for employers who hire illegal aliens. The report also recommended deporting "those persons who come to U.S. shores—even though they come in large numbers—who do not meet established criteria" as refugees.

The commissioners seemed to agree that the real problem springing from illegal immigration was not economics, bilingualism, ethnic tensions, or national security.

> Most serious is the fact that illegality breeds illegality. The presence of a substantial number of undocumented illegal aliens in the United States has resulted not only in a disregard for immigration law but in the breaking of minimum wage and occupational safety laws, and statutes against smuggling as well.[16]

More notable were means to open the front door. These included a one-time amnesty for most of the unlawful workers already in the United States and an increase in the ceiling on legal immigration from the 270,000 annual level to 450,000 for five years to clear up a backlog of applications. The commission rejected a proposal by environmental groups to impose a "cap or ceiling" on total immigration on the grounds that such a limit would diminish flexibility in the admission of refugees and relatives.

The Reagan administration reviewed the Commission's proposals and then advanced its own plan. But Sen. Alan K. Simpson (R-Wyo.) and Rep. Romano L. Mazzoli (D-Ky.) ignored Reagan's proposals and introduced the Immigration Reform and Control Act, which was closer to the Commission's recommendations. This measure, endorsed by the White House, advocated a ceiling on legal immigration at 425,000, a figure that would include 325,000 visas for "family reunification immigrants"; namely, the immigrant's spouse and children, the spouses of the immigrant's children, and the immigrant's own brothers and sisters. The sole "exceptions" to this cap were guest workers and "refugees." An amnesty section granted permanent resident status to aliens who had unlawfully entered the country before 1977 and remained continuously in the United States; those arriving between January 1, 1977, and January 1, 1980, would enjoy temporary resident status, with a three year waiting period required before they could be elevated to permanent status. Permanent residents had to wait five years before applying for citizenship, and all aliens accepting amnesty were barred for at least three years from receiving Medicaid, food stamps, or other federal social benefits. Persons unlawfully entering the United States since January 1, 1980, faced deportation.

Just as in the Carter bill, civil fines would be levied against employers who knowingly hired illegal aliens and, if the attorney-general ascertained a "pattern or practice" of violation, a criminal fine of up to $1,000 and a prison sentence of as much as one year could be imposed. It required the president to develop and implement within three years of the bill's passage a "secure system to determine employment eligibility"—possibly involving a national work card. The legislation increased criminal penalties for persons using fraudulent documents to evade the immigration law. Additionally, it streamlined the processing of employers' applications for temporary foreign workers under the so-called H-2 program, which had permitted 36,000 men and women to labor in the United States in 1981. Meanwhile, all workers hired after the bill became law would have to show their potential employers, as a condition of legal employment, documents prescribed by the attorney-general. Both employer and employee would be obligated to sign an affidavit that the required documentation had been provided.

Chairman Rodino stalled consideration of the measure in the House Judiciary Committee until the Simpson-Mazzoli bill passed the Senate by an 80 to 19 vote in September, 1982. The House Committee stripped it of an essential element—the comprehensive ceiling on legal immigration—which shattered a fragile compromise and opened the door to intensive lobbying by interest groups. That the bill reached the floor during the lame duck session increased its vulnerability to an onslaught of 300 amendments, the House version of a filibuster, to delay a floor vote. Neither Speaker Thomas P. O'Neill, Jr. (D-Mass.) nor Majority Leader James C. Wright, Jr. (D-Texas) was willing to steer it through the procedural obstacle course. Consequently, the legislation died on December 19, 1982.

The measure again died in the House in 1983. In May Senator Simpson masterfully used nonpolitical, bipartisan appeals to assure favorable Senate action, 78 to 18. However, Representative Mazzoli, who seemed to have lost interest in the issue, showed none of his Senate colleague's skill in the lower chamber. Opponents succeeded in emasculating the legislation in the House Judiciary Committee before Speaker O'Neill announced on October 4, 1983, that he would not allow the bill to be voted on in the current session.

O'Neill ignored public opinion polls, the report of a blue-ribbon federal commission, the Senate votes, and the growing number of newspapers endorsements of the Simpson-Mazzoli plan in claiming that "I don't think there's a constituency out there" to support its passage. In a burst of candor, the Massachusetts Democrat, himself a product of ethnic politics, disclosed another reason for scuttling this bill. Leaders of the 11-member Congressional Hispanic Caucus, O'Neill loyalists over years, sought his help. They told him that the reform would force Spanish-speaking residents to wear dogtags under conditions reminiscent of Nazi Germany, and O'Neill didn't want to jeopardize the Hispanics' traditional support of the Democratic Party. Moreover, he might push the measure through the House only to face a veto inspired by the desire of another clever Irish politician, the president, to appeal to Spanish-speaking voters. This theory seems implausible in light of the backing that both Reagan and Attorney General William French Smith expressed for the bill.

Representative Robert Garcia (D-N.Y.) hailed O'Neill's move as a "major victory for the Hispanic Caucus." Representative Edward R. Roybal (D-Calif.) praised O'Neill as "a profile in courage." On the other hand, Representative Henry J. Hyde (R-Ill.) said "the notion that majority rule has anything to do with the legislative process is absolutely wrong" because "if the Speaker doesn't want the bill to be debated or voted on, it's dead." Representative Daniel E. Lungren (R-Calif.) asked O'Neill: "How great does the problem have to get before you are going to allow us to act?"[17]

Following an October 25, 1983, meeting with Senator Simpson, O'Neill reportedly promised to allow the bill to go to the floor the following year.[18] Even though it could eventually pass in an attenuated version, the legislation may have little immediate impact on illegal entries. The Border Patrol, INS, and the Department of Labor lack the manpower with which to monitor the frontier and workplaces, and neither a Republican nor Democratic administration is likely to emphasize enforcement for reasons cited below. Furthermore, a recent report by the General Accounting Office, based on information supplied by officials in 20 nations, concluded that employer sanctions were "not an effective deterrent." It seems that employers either evaded the law or, once apprehended, suffered penalties too mild to deter such acts. Often the laws were not effectively enforced because of "strict legal constraints on investigations, noncommunication between government agencies, lack of enforcement resolve and lack of personnel."[19] For example, Canadian employers face fines of $4,000 and/or two years' imprisonment if convicted of "knowingly" hiring illegal workers. Still, officials of the Royal Canadian Mounted Police estimate that between 500,000 and 1 million aliens are in Canada unlawfully and that most of them are employed.[20] Hong Kong appears to be one nation which has used employer sanctions successfully to impede unlawful entries.

DOMESTIC INTEREST GROUPS AND OPPOSITION TO REFORM

It is not surprising that executive and legislative initiatives have focused on illegal crossing at the U.S.-Mexican frontier, which was compared by one congressman to a pre-World War II fortification: "We really have a Maginot Line. It is outflanked, overflown, and infiltrated. And you know what happened to the French."[21] What is amazing is the lack of forceful, determined action to regain control over the border, especially since an overwhelming percentage of U.S. residents voice support for such a policy. For example, an October 1983 Gallup Poll found that 79 percent of those interviewed believed it should be illegal to employ anyone who has entered the United States without the proper papers. This figure marked a slight but continuing increase over Gallup surveys in 1980 (76%) and 1977 (72%) when the same question was asked.[22] Ninety-one percent of respondents to a mid-1980 survey wanted "an all-out effort to stop" illegal entries.[23] Few subjects command such widespread support among U.S. citizens.

Survey figures notwithstanding, key groups in both parties have opposed—or evinced principally rhetorical interest in—concerted action to halt the inpouring of illegal workers. Despite the vigorous efforts of Senator Simpson and Attorney General William French Smith, many Republicans are cool toward tampering with the border safety valve. Their party enjoys strong support from large growers and factory owners in the sunbelt and South who pay low wages to migrants and face increasing difficulty recruiting legal residents to perform the work. These farmers and manufacturers flinch at stiff penalties on employers of illegal workers. Conservative senators such as Jesse Helms (R-N.C.) and John Tower (R-Texas) joined the U.S. Chamber of Commerce in condemning such sanctions as an unfair burden on farmers and small businesses. The GOP is also anxious to deepen inroads made in 1980 among Hispanics, who once voted Democratic en masse and are viewed by party strategists as the "Awakening Giant" in U.S. politics. While Ford captured only 24 percent of this vote in 1976, Reagan obtained 36 percent four years later, and in 1983 undertook a vigorous effort to woo the nation's 14.6 million Hispanic Americans, 56 percent of whom are old enough to vote.[24]

In addition, the belief of some party theorists in laissez-faire economics and a single labor market leads to a disdain for impediments to either Mexican workers seeking jobs in this country or to U.S. employers anxious to hire them, especially when an influx of aliens could weaken organized labor. Annelise G. Anderson, associate director of the Office of Management and Budget under Reagan, reflected this view in labeling the Simpson-Mazzoli bill's worker identification system as "typical of totalitarian societies." "One of the things that a totalitarian society can't abide is not being able to control the movement of people," she said. These remarks, termed "guerrilla warfare in Washington" by the New York Times, badly contradicted the administration's position.[25] Some conservatives endorse a stronger policy because they fear that the U.S. is losing control of its borders and its Anglo culture is being diluted.

Within Democratic circles, many liberals wish to redress the imperialistic abuses suffered by Mexico at the hands of the Marines, General Pershing, and predatory oil companies. They tend to equate limitations on migrants with xenophobia, racism, or selfishness in a country prized as a land of opportunity. Senator Kennedy represents this position. He voted against the Simpson-Mazzoli bill on the grounds that discrimination would result from an initiative that "started out to be immigration reform and has become, in too many provisions, immigration restriction." "That is a fine how-do-you-do for this nation," he said during the debate.[26] The American Civil Liberties Union, which emerged as a forceful critic of the legislation, reiterated Kennedy's misgivings and warned against Big Brotherism. "A secure verification system could very likely be built on a national data bank which would centralize personal data about all persons authorized to work in the United States," an organization spokesman told a congressional committee in 1982.[27]

Catholic spokesmen have advocated a generous amnesty provision in any immigration reform. In 1982 Monsignor Daniel Hoye, general secretary of the United States Catholic Conference, reluctantly supported the Simpson-Mazzoli legislation on the basis that, even if it were not perfect, it would legalize a large number of undocumented aliens who had arrived by the end of 1981 (a House amendment extended the cut-off date for amnesty to January 1, 1982). Typical of the pressure from Hispanics, which prompted the conference to oppose the bill in 1983, were the comments of Mario J. Paredes, executive director of the Northeast Catholic Center for Hispanics, a conference affiliate. He expressed concern over the tighter amnesty provisions in the Senate version of the bill. "Now over a million people who arrived in 1980 and 1981 are lost to the flotsam of underground society, fearful of exercising rights we deem the cornerstone of society." Moreover, he characterized the no-welfare provision as "meanspiritedness," and labeled the exclusion of unmarried sons and daughters of legal immigrants among admittable aliens as "nativist."[28] The *National Catholic Reporter* has also lamented nativist tendencies within the immigration reform movement. It referred to a *GEO* magazine interview with former ambassador Clare Booth Luce, who expressed "fear" that soon there will be "as many Mexicans in Texas, New Mexico, California and Arizona as there are natives. . . ." Jesuits at Loyola University's Institute of Human Relations attribute, in part, the growing concern about immigration to "*bigotry* begotten of a provincial nationalism" in the tradition of the American or "Know Nothing" party, which in 1854 castigated immigrants as "foreign conspirators . . . ignorant and priest-ridden slaves of Ireland and Germany or outcasts of Europe's poorhouses and prisons."[29]

Jewish leaders, including those influential in Democratic circles, decry any cap on immigration. This position springs from a sympathy nourished both by the migration of Jews throughout history and by the plight of Jews in the Soviet Union today. It is difficult for the United Hebrew Immigrant Aid Society and other Jewish organizations to oppose the exodus of Mexicans at the same time they are championing the resettlement of Soviet Jews in the United States in preference to Israel. Furthermore, now that the tourist boycott is past history, Jews seek good relations with Mexico in order to reduce U.S. dependence on Arab oil. They are also aware that PEMEX is Israel's principal supplier of crude, with shipments averaging 45,000 bpd.

Even though illegals compete with their constituents for jobs and other opportunities, most black leaders have not pushed for immigration reform. The National Association for the Advancement of Colored

People (NAACP) has passed annual resolutions and testified before the Select Commission on the need to strengthen "our defenses against illegal immigration."[30] Yet, neither the NAACP nor other black organizations have assigned a high priority to this goal, and a majority of the Black Caucus was reportedly prepared to vote against the Simpson-Mazzoli bill in 1983.[31] The Reverend Jesse Jackson and other black politicians harbor the dream of fashioning a "rainbow coalition" that embraces Hispanics, who, after Asians, are the United States' fastest growing minority and destined to become its largest. Both blacks and Hispanics "feel a bit like wallflowers in the Democratic party. Both face high unemployment, housing problems, and some ethnic discrimination. Both count heavily on public education to improve the lives of their children."[32] But columnist Carl Rowan, who holds no illusion of a happy alliance, has written about the "immigration nightmare," while William Raspberry has warned that foreign workers "constitute an additional barrier to the employment of low-skilled black Americans whose joblessness already is a national disgrace."[33]

Despite inaction by most of their national leaders, blacks at the local level have vented their anger over illegal entries. Resentment at the arrival of "Mariel refugees" from Cuba contributed to rioting that left 18 dead in Miami's predominantly black Liberty City section in May 1980.[34] Observers have also noted tensions between Hispanics and blacks in New Orleans, Los Angeles, and New York City.[35]

Chicano leaders treat immigration reform as the political version of fingernails scratching a blackboard. Many of their organizations fear that instituting a worker verification system, imposing stiff sanctions on employers hiring illegals, and upgrading the Border Patrol would result in abuses of the civil liberties of Spanish-speaking individuals legally residing in the United States. As Representative Edward Roybal (D-Calif.), a prime mover in the Hispanic Caucus, said during the 1982 House debate on the Simpson-Mazzoli legislation, "this bill is discriminatory and violates the civil rights of millions of individuals who will be affected the moment that [it] is signed."[36] Tommy Espinoza, president of Chicanos for La Causa, Inc., scorned the bill for turning employers into enforcement agents and for requiring Hispanic-Americans to endure the "humiliating and unfair" experience of proving their citizenship in their own country. He excoriated the prohibition on federal benefits for three years after obtaining permanent residence and six years for the newest aliens granted amnesty as consigning immigrants to "second class citizenship status" and representing "taxation without representation."[37] Some Chicano groups even welcome the newcomers as a means to enhance their own political influence. The leaders' opinions run counter to those of a cross-section of U.S. residents of Hispanic descent, 75 percent of whom endorse both restrictions on hiring illegal aliens and requiring worker identification cards.[38]

Labor unions might be expected to place the greatest pressure on Democratic politicians for restricting the flow of unlawful migrants. After all, 70 percent of union families back outlawing the employment of illegals.[39] The AFL-CIO did play an active role in the deliberations of the Select Commission. This participation occurred through two channels: the energetic membership of Jack F. Otero, vice-president of the Brotherhood of Railway and Airline Clerks, on the 16-person body; and formal presentations made by leaders of both the federation and individual unions. Generally speaking, labor favored a package approach to immigration reform. Through Otero and policy papers prepared in the Washington headquarters, it endorsed employer sanctions; an employee identification system such as a counterfeit-proof Social Security card; vigorous border control and interior enforcement of immigration laws; stricter application of existing legislation on wage and working standards; continued Department of Labor certification for employment of temporary H-2 non-immigrant alien workers (the AFL-CIO adamantly opposed revival of the bracero program); and amnesty for illegal aliens residing in the United States based on demonstrated attachment to the community, provided that "the legislation process should not begin until the massive flows of illegal aliens into the United States have been stopped."[40]

Thomas R. Donahue, the AFL-CIO's secretary-treasurer, has endorsed a comprehensive policy that defers amnesty until U.S. authorities regain control of the country's borders. Nevertheless, organized labor has failed either to initiate or put its resources behind a program that entails assertive action at the border. A confluence of factors explain the gap between the union movement's rhetoric and behavior on immigration.

First, illegal immigration is not a major problem for many of the most powerful unions represented on the 35-member Executive Council of the AFL-CIO. Of special importance is the low priority accorded this issue by established industrial unions—the Steelworkers, Communications Workers, CWA, and Auto Workers, for example—whose leaders command notable influence within the labor movement. Unlike the garment trades, food and commercial establishments, hotels, and some types of construction, the industries organized by the "big boys" of labor do not have conditions that favor an influx of illegals.[41]

Second, such prominent liberals as Lane Kirkland (president), Donahue (secretary-treasurer), J.C. Turner (Operating Engineers), Glenn E. Watts (CWA), Sol. C. Chaikin (ILGWU), Murray H. Finley (Amalgamated Garment Workers), and the late Lloyd McBride (Steelworkers), have frequently set the tone of discussion within the AFL-CIO's Executive Council. These men share with many other labor notables compassion for the underdog. While differing on nuances of policy, they generally favor a liberal approach to resolving the illegal immigration problem—an approach that includes broad amnesty provisions. Even if more conservative union leaders, possibly from the building trades, supported a vigorous policy that emphasized control and law enforcement, they would hesitate to speak out lest they be perceived as illiberal, inhumane, or even racist by the Executive Council's opinion leaders.

Third, relatively few people participate in the drafting, evaluation, and approval of the AFL-CIO's position on immigration. The federation's counsel, research department, or legislative department will draft a proposal for the Executive Council, either at the request of a union official such as president Kirkland or because the issue is of salience. The person preparing the resolution will work closely with Jack Otero, labor's recognized expert on immigration policy, and perhaps Peter Allstrom, director of research and communication for the Food and Beverage Trades Department. Once completed, the draft resolution may be submitted for comments to appropriate departments within the AFL-CIO,[42] as well as to such affected unions as the ILGWU, Amalgamated Garment Workers, the Service Employees, Food and Commercial Workers, and the American Federation of Government Employees (the union to which INS personnel belong). After any wrinkles are ironed out, the resolution is assured approval by the Executive Council with little or no debate. This process is strictly a "headquarter's operation"; little or no opportunity is afforded locals and individual members—many of whom endorse a strong stance on curbing the entry of illegals—to take part in policy development. Hence, the views of a small group of union leaders prevail. In all fairness to the leadership, it should be noted that, despite the bulletins and memoranda dispatched to individual unions and state organizations, little support from locals emerged for the bills emphasizing employer sanctions that the AFL-CIO threw its weight behind in the 1970s.

Fourth, because established industrial unions give such low priority to illegal immigration, they tend to defer to their Hispanic leaders—a group that feels entitled to greater recognition and responsibility in labor circles—in formulating a position on the issue. Most of these leaders, who have formed the Labor Council for Latin American Advancement (LCLAA) within the AFL-CIO, champion a sweeping amnesty plan. LCLAA also expresses grave reservations about such enforcement measures as worker identification cards, civil and criminal penalties on employers who knowingly hire illegals, and a greatly increased capability for the Border Patrol.

Fifth, at least 25 percent of the members of the Executive Council are either Jewish (Chaikin and Shanker) or first- or second-generation Americans (for example, Fosco, Gleason, and Sweeney).[43] The same is true for staff members of the federation and individual unions. For them immigration is not an abstraction, but a relevant experience to their family, ethnic group, or religious faith. In the absence of strong pressure from their members to act on the problem, these men are not disposed to lead the fight for rigorous enforcement of U.S. immigration laws.

Sixth, Washington labor officials often have more contacts with other union leaders than with their members, thereby reinforcing the tendency to view a subject like illegal immigration as extremely complex and amenable only to liberal solutions. This perspective is frequently sharpened as unionists interact with liberals within the Democratic Party, the NAACP, and the Roman Catholic Church (Monsignor George Higgins, a Catholic University professor and a key church expert on labor matters, enjoys an extremely close relationship with many key union officers).

Finally, most labor leaders resist a highly restrictive border policy because they subscribe to the thesis that "growth is good" and that additional people will expand the size of the market, thereby boosting productivity and investment. While not carrying this position to its logical extreme—none proposes an open border—they still consider population growth as an important contributor to economic advancement. To them, economic expansion signifies not only greater opportunities for current members, but also a new pool of workers whose recruitment could swell the ranks of the labor movement. Renewed growth might also give momentum to organized labor, whose percentage of an aging work force has declined from a high of 25.5 percent in 1953 to 19.7 percent in 1978.[44]

The AFL-CIO finally went to bat for the Simpson-Mazzoli bill in 1983. This action came only after the successful introduction by Representative August F. Hawkins (D-Calif.) of an amendment to outlaw discrimination on the basis of national origin and nationality in businesses with five or more workers. The previous threshold figure had been 20 employees.

The division or opposition of traditional Republican and Democratic constituencies left the role of advocacy for the Simpson-Mazzoli bill in the hands of individual politicians and an unusual coalition. Included among the proponents were patriotic organizations such as the American Legion and the Veterans of Foreign Wars; environmental groups such as the National Audubon Society, the Environmental Fund, and Zero Population Growth; and representatives of governors and state and local governments, especially those facing monumental outlays for education, housing, health care, and other social services provided to illegals.

The coalition's catalyst and adhesive was the Federation for American Immigration Reform (FAIR), an organization formed in January 1979 on initial pledges of $50,000 that has expanded to 16 staff members supported by direct mail solicitations that brought in $1 million in 1983. FAIR's executive director, Roger L. Conner, has proven an extremely articulate and effective spokesman for immigration reform. In scores of public addresses, interviews, and media presentations, he has emphasized that the "victims" of immigration are the marginal workers with low education, who may not be willing or able to work 60 hours a week. "If the immigrants coming in were competing for jobs with architects, lawyers and engineers, the immigration problem would have been solved a long time ago," he contended. If the only way to get Americans to do the "dirty work" illegal aliens gladly take is to raise the minimum wage, then so be it, Conner argued. The cost will fall on those who want maids, who eat in restaurants—who can afford it, he said, arguing that these people "who had historically served as advocates of the underclasses were so emotionally blocked by rhetoric on immigration they had abandoned the interests of the poor."[45]

FAIR has also emphasized the burden on farmland, water supply, energy, and other natural resources caused by uncontrolled immigration. It pointed out that decisions (or nondecisions) taken now will have a tremendous effect on the size of the U.S. population, which will grow to between 330 and 400 million people within 50 years if current rates of immigration continue. Thus, admission levels to the country should be established in Washington by elected representatives, not by the demands of entering foreigners or by politicians in Mexico City, Manila, Havana, or Port-au-Prince as has been the case in recent years. According to the International Labor Organization, the third world's total workforce will be 600 to 700 million people larger in the year 2000 than it was in 1980. In view of the impossibility of accepting more than a small fraction of the world's poor and given the limitations on future U.S. economic growth, FAIR endorsed the Senate version of the Simpson-Mazzoli bill as a first step toward preserving and enhancing the quality of American life. Conner believes, however, that the United States should regain control of its borders before decreeing a blanket amnesty.

> To charges that FAIR engages in racism, Conner responds that the issue in the modern immigration debate isn't the race or ethnicity of the people, it is the numbers of people who are coming . . . I don't believe we can [absorb the present flow] and meet the needs of minority and disadvantaged Americans for a better standard of living, and I don't think we can protect the natural resource base of this country for future generations at that level of people in the United States.[46]

MEXICO AND ILLEGAL IMMIGRATION

Since the late nineteenth century, Mexican leaders have generally favored immigration to the United States. At first they argued that the workers, upon returning home, brought with them valuable skills and improved techniques. In recent years they have viewed the border as an "escape valve," relieving pressure on a political system that has failed to provide adequate opportunities for people.

Mexico's strategy with respect to immigration reform became apparent during debates over the Carter and Simpson-Mazzoli proposals. To begin with, Mexican authorities self-righteously insisted that legislation in this field was strictly a matter of domestic U.S. politics and, in view of their tradition of nonintervention, they pledged to steer clear of the controversy. They complemented this promise by promptly jumping into the 1977 debate and accusing

U.S. authorities of failing to consult them before promoting a reform plan. This contention, repeated by some scholars on both sides of the border, flew in the face of a record of contacts, some at high levels, between U.S. and Mexican authorities.[47] In reality, when Mexicans speak of "failure to consult," they mean failure to win their blessing of proposed bills. The López Portillo administration even encouraged Chicano groups to speak out against immigration reform.[48] On December 8, 1982, the Mexican Senate unanimously passed a resolution questioning the United States' right to control immigration and expressing

> our alarm and concern for the repercussions which will affect both countries if the Simpson-Mazzoli legislation is passed, because this transcendent matter should not be considered from a unilateral perspective, but rather should be treated from a bilateral and even multilateral perspective, taking into account the far-reaching migratory phenomenon of undocumented workers between our two countries.[49]

The solons who objected most strongly to denying undocumented workers access to such social services as free legal advice and education for their children, proceeded to refer U.S. immigration policies to the Latin American Congress, the World Congress, the Group of Parliamentarians for a New World Order, and its own Foreign Relations Committee.

Opinion leaders in Mexico invariably treat the subject in terms of benefits accruing to the U.S. economy, police brutality against migrants, employers' unwillingness to honor contracts, and the paucity of social benefits conferred upon exploited aliens. The "possible violation of migration laws does not sanction the infringement of labor laws, and even less of human rights," López Portillo proclaimed in his September 1, 1977, state of the nation address.[50]

An announcement by the Ku Klux Klan in 1977 that it would supplement the Border Patrol by organizing vigilante surveillance of the frontier proved a godsend for Mexican journalists. Even though no Klan action took place, a flurry of front page articles warned the Mexican public of the proposed outrage to their compatriots. The president of the minuscule Revolutionary Socialist party even alleged that the Klan's action had the blessing of the government of the United States, where "respect for human rights is nonexistent."[51] Such philippics gloss over the short-term economic advantages to Mexico of immigration, as well as the human-rights issue raised when a country cannot—or will not—provide opportunities for its own people. Also overlooked are the imprisonment, beatings, and extortion suffered by Central Americans and other undocumented immigrants at the hands of Mexican authorities. Massive deportations occurred even as the country's U.N. delegation sought approval of a sweeping report, highly condemnatory of the United States, on the rights of migrant workers throughout the world. Nor is attention directed to the obstacles encountered by U.S. citizens who attempt to obtain employment or purchase property in Mexico.

Moreover, officials in Mexico City criticize estimates that several million Mexican illegals reside in the United States, while embracing figures that are substantially lower. For instance, in 1977 López Portillo alluded to the "several thousand Mexican workers [who] in search of other horizons cross our borders."[52] The National Migration Survey, sponsored by the Mexican Ministry of Labor and conducted from December 1978 to January 1979, tentatively concluded that only 405,467 to 1.2 million Mexicans were working or looking for work in the United States.[53] Mexican politicians and scholars continually emphasize that too little is known about illegal immigration to permit prudent policymaking. The completion of every study gives rise to calls for additional research in what appears to be an effort to postpone addressing the problem as long as possible.

To minimize even more the seriousness of the issue, Mexican officials identify the migration to the United States as "natural," a "part of culture," and "a way of life."[54] Though seldom openly expressed, an element of irredentism informs some comments about migration. A declaration by former Foreign Minister Castañeda carried a hint of this belief: "Mexico cannot constitutionally, politically, juridically, or morally take restrictive, repressive steps to impede the movement of Mexicans into or out of the country, or the entry or departure of Mexicans from United States territory."[55] Similar arguments might be advanced, but are not, in behalf of Poles seeking to enter the Soviet Union, Hungarians crossing into Austria, or Germans moving into Poland. The Mexican government also refers to illegals as *indocumentados* or "undocumented workers"—a euphemism adopted by the Carter administration in 1977 that ignores the criminality of entering a country without a visa or other required papers.

López Portillo, among others, appealed to the "melting pot" ethos to which many Americans subscribe by analogizing the current influx of migrants to the flow of Europeans to the United States at the end of the nineteenth century. Like the European phenomenon, the Mexican migration embraces large numbers of poor Catholics, most of whom are young, unattached males who return home after working in a foreign land for limited periods. Similarly, the Mexicans speak a different language and are products of a different culture. But the geographic distance involved in the earlier movement and the arrival of all aliens by boat enhanced the element of control by limiting the speed and size of the flow. Moreover, world population was then 1.25 billion compared to over 4.6 billion in 1984. The European phenomenon consisted largely of legal immigrants who entered during a strongly expansionist economic period when the country was predominantly rural and the demand was great for miners and factory workers. Recessions would then generate a return to their homeland of Italians thrown out of work. In contrast, a bracero encountering hard times in the United States can anticipate even worse conditions back home because of the linkage of the two economies. Additionally, at the time of the European immigration, the United States had open frontiers and unsettled areas crying for people. Now the nation faces depleting oil and gas supplies, dwindling resources of other vital minerals, farmlands lost to sprawling growth, soil erosion, imperiled groundwater, and threatened timber supplies. "Heavy immigration undercuts the effectiveness of conservation efforts and exacerbates each of these problems."[56] López Portillo should realize that despite the more favorable environment for the European immigration, it aroused such opposition that Congress enacted highly restrictionist legislation in the 1920s.

Lastly, Mexican presidents express a desire to export "products not people." Such a cliché sounds reasonable until one realizes that economic policies pursued in recent years have promoted capital-intensive oil exports while discouraging the production of goods and services that employ relatively more people. Emphasizing Mexico's development instead of immigration reform, a concept also extolled by Hispanic-Americans, is appealing. It proposes to deal with the symptoms of a large illegal-alien population "at its source," while improving the conditions in which millions of poor people live. Too, it avoids the hard choices necessary to change U.S. laws. However, the argument turns out to be an illusion, for development is a slow and uncertain process and cannot be expected to serve as a major restraint on immigration in this century. In fact, economic growth may stimulate rather than slow migration. Ironically, "substantial emigration is now an implicit component of the development strategies of many sending countries. They see this emigration as a means of limiting unemployment, maximizing foreign-currency earnings and providing an outlet for dissidence."[57]

Mexico finds itself in a dilemma with respect to immigration policy. While opposing the Simpson-Mazzoli legislation, it moved in 1983 to impede the accelerating flow of Central American aliens through its own porous southern frontier. This action took the form of tighter rules for issuing visas, increased patrols along the Guatemalan border, and a shift in emphasis by the government's refugee commission from coordinating assistance to more careful monitoring of refugee activities. In implementing the new policy, Mexican officials employed many of the same arguments advanced by restrictionists in the United States. For instance, Interior Minister Manuel Bartlett Díaz warned that the influx of Central Americans, mainly Guatemalans and Salvadorans, had over the past two years "taken jobs from Mexicans" and caused "social pressures because of the excess of demand in all services."[58]

PROSPECTS

Failure by the United States to establish an immigration policy in the early 1980s will complicate bilateral relations and, possibly, increase Mexican influence over this country. In 1983 a baby was born in Mexico every seventeen seconds—214 per hour, 5,137 per day, and 1.88 million in the entire year. This sharp rise means that the average Mexican is under 16 years of age and has yet to enter the job market or, in the case of women, has yet to reach the years when she will bear the most children. As will be seen Chapter 8, not enough jobs are being created in Mexico, and the current flood of illegal immigrants may become a tidal wave as hundreds of thousands of young people are unable to find satisfactory job opportunities at home.

The U.S. political system has responded to, if not resolved, many crucial problems that have confronted it. Unequal treatment of blacks precipitated the antidiscrimination presidential initiatives of the 1940s, *Brown v. the Board of Education Topeka* and other landmark Supreme Court decisions of the 1950s, and the civil rights legislation of the 1960s. The unjust treatment of females produced scores of judicial actions and federal and state statutes designed to advance women's equality. Consumer abuses exposed by Ralph Nader in the 1960s spawned corrective action the following decade. Publicized degradation of the environment led to passage of acts to control emissions into the air, clean up rivers, lakes, and streams, and regulate the transportation and disposal of toxic substances. Yet, the growth in the number of illegal aliens may exacerbate the immigration problem rather than give rise to policies that will resolve it.

In the cases of abuses suffered by blacks, women, and consumers, interest groups—aided by politicians and the mass media—enlarged the power capability of these groups, enabling them to play a greater role in shaping policy. Illegal immigration will also expand the power capability of an already important interest group; namely, Hispanic-Americans and, specifically, Chicanos, who will use their enhanced status to thwart rather than advance curbs on unlawful entries.

Several factors—low educational level, high unemployment, lack of resources, fragmented leadership, low and declining percentage of registered voters and office holders, relative newness in the United States of many of their people, language difficulties, disagreements over goals within its constituency, discrimination, cultural restraints—have prevented the 8.8 million Chicanos from playing the role for Mexico that Jewish and Greek organizations play for Israel and Greece. Radical movements like La Raza Unida and the Brown Berets have emerged, as well as middle-class professional groups like the 100,000-member League of United Latin American Citizens and the Mexican American Legal Defense and Education Fund. But no single individual or organization has gained the national prominence and influence that the late Dr. Martin Luther King and the NAACP brought to blacks.[59] In February 1983 a loosely structured coalition of Hispanic leaders selected Governor Toney Anaya of New Mexico to head a new political lobbying group that hopes to influence candidates for the Democratic Party's 1984 presidential nomination.[60]

Complicating matters is the fact that Mexico's fiercely nationalistic elites often scorned their Chicano cousins as traitors or *pochos*, a term that ridicules their inferior economic and social status. Late in the Echeverría administration, a rapprochement began between Mexican-American groups and Mexican officials. The former wished to reaffirm their cultural origins; the latter were anxious to befriend the second fastest growing U.S. minority. "It finally dawned on us that the position of 16 million [sic] Mexican-Americans will affect Mexico's future in a number of areas," stated a Mexican politician who strongly endorses the mutual courtship. "An anti-Mexican or even neutral Chicano movement could spell disaster for us, but on our side they can be a very important lobby."[61] López Portillo stimulated cultural contacts; welcomed leaders of moderate and radical Chicano organizations to Mexico; and in 1979 established a mixed commission embracing, for Mexico, the ministers of labor and education, and for Mexican-Americans, the Forum of National Hispanic Organizations, an umbrella agency representing 62 Chicano groups.[62] U.S. immigration policy dominates the agenda of meetings held between Mexicans and Mexican-Americans. Indeed, the Chicano groups apparently see activities in Mexico as a means to strengthen their own image and bargaining position in Washington. An example of their success came in early 1980 when Hispanics persuaded President Carter to name Julian Nava as ambassador to Mexico. The son of an immigrant, holder of a Ph.D. from Harvard, and special assistant to the president of California State University, Nava had no diplomatic experience and proved an undistinguished envoy.

Although reluctantly agreeing to accept him as the new ambassador, the Mexican government felt patronized by the appointment.[63] By the time Nava reached Mexico City, López Portillo's relations with Chicanos had cooled, possibly because radical groups embarrassed his administration by issuing truculent communiqués from the Mexican capital. Greater economic mobility, increased political participation, the reconciliation of internal divisions, and the acquisition of skills in coalition building will augment the political power of Chicanos. Decades will pass before they can aspire to the influence wielded by other ethnic groups. Still, their numerical growth and geographic concentration will magnify their role as power brokers in pivotal states, a status enhanced by two mechanisms: single member, winner-take-all districts for selecting members of Congress and the Electoral College for choosing presidents. William Greener, a spokesman for the Republican National Committee, stated that the importance of the Hispanic vote in the 1984 presidential election can be summed up in three words: California, Texas, and Florida. These states with their large Hispanic population

embrace one-third of the electoral vote required to win the presidency.[64] The 1984 national elections combined with the U.S. economic recovery, mounting tensions amoung supporters of Simpson-
Mazzoli over whether to endorse a watered down version of the bill,
and the unlikelihood of another Mariel-type influx of Cubans or Hai-
tians militate against effective immigration reform in the mid-1980s.
A peace accord in Central America that involved the resettling in the
United States of thousands of anti-Sandinista Nicaraguans could alter the outlook.

CONCLUSIONS

Virtually without dissent Mexicans have opposed immigration
reform in the United States. Such reform is viewed as harmful to
their nation's economic well-being and an encroachment upon the
nation's sovereignty. Mexico has used a number of tactics to thwart
changes in the law, not the least of which has been appeals to the
humanitarian sensibilities of the U.S. people, whose immigration
policy has been among the most liberal in history. Its public officials
have also implicitly linked the sale of oil to a flexible border policy.

Agreement in Mexico over what U.S. laws should be is con-
trasted by the disarray in the United States over proper legislation.
Public support for reform, even among Hispanics, is overwhelming—a fact that should be determinative in a democracy. Yet, an ar-
ray of interest groups, whose objectives are lauded by Mexico, have
delayed and diluted legislation—so that the likelihood that the Simpson-Mazzoli bill, even if passed, would stem unlawful entries appears remote. Chicano leaders, encouraged by Mexican politicians,
have even excoriated this modest congressional initiative on the
grounds that it will accentuate civil rights abuses and produce a lat-
ter-day Third Reich.

Keeping open the safety valve may prove inimical to Mexico's
long-term interests because it not only facilitates the exodus of highly
motivated, often skilled young workers, who compete with Chicanos
and blacks for jobs in the U.S. market. It also removes the pressure
from Mexican notables to accomplish the political, economic, and
social reforms needed to generate opportunities in their country. Ultimately, it could provoke a militant backlash against foreign
workers, especially in the sunbelt. In the meantime, the inability or
unwillingness of Washington to stem the influx of illegal workers de-

TABLE 4: Hispanic Population in 15 U.S. States (1980)

Rank	State	Hispanic Population	Hispanic Percentage of State Population	Percentage of U.S. Hispanic Population
1	California	4,543,770	19.2	31.1
2	Texas	2,985,643	21.0	20.4
3	New York	1,659,245	9.5	11.4
4	Florida	857,898	8.8	5.9
5	Illinois	635,525	5.6	4.4
6	New Jersey	491,867	6.7	3.4
7	New Mexico	476,089	36.6	3.3
8	Arizona	440,915	16.2	3.0
9	Colorado	339,300	11.7	2.3
10	Michigan	162,388	1.8	1.1
11	Pennsylvania	154,005	1.3	1.1
12	Massachusetts	141,043	2.5	1.0
13	Connecticut	124,499	4.0	0.9
14	Washington	119,986	2.9	0.8
15	Ohio	119,880	1.1	0.8

Source: Congressional Hispanic Caucus.

167

prives the United States of an important tool with which to influence Mexico's behavior, while sharpening the U.S. demand for such vital imports as Mexican oil. The growth in the numbers and political power of Hispanics works against Washington's exercising a basic element of sovereignty and regaining control of its southern border, which has been compared to "a sieve blasted by buckshot."

NOTES

1. Wayne A. Cornelius, *Mexican Migration to the United States: Causes, Consequences, and U.S. Responses* (Migration and Development Study Group, Center of International Studies; Cambridge, Mass.: M.I.T., 1978), p. 14.

2. Peter H. Smith, *Mexico: The Quest for a U.S. Policy* (New York: Foreign Policy Association, n. d.), p. 22.

3. Paul R. Ehrlich et al., *The Golden Door* (New York: Wideview Books, 1981), p. 207.

4. Smith, *Mexico: The Quest for a U.S. Policy,* p. 23.

5. Ehrlich, *The Golden Door,* pp. 208–209.

6. David S. North, "The Migration Issue in U.S.-Mexican Relations," paper prepared for presentation at the Second Annual Symposium on Mexico-U.S. Economic Relations, Mexico City, May 23–25, 1979, p. 8.

7. North, "The Migration Issue," p. 8.

8. Howard F. Cline, *The United States and Mexico* (Cambridge: Harvard University Press, 1953), p. 393.

9. William V. Shannon, "The Illegal Immigrants," *New York Times,* January 14, 1975, p. A-33.

10. *New York Times,* December 31, 1974, p. A-26 and September 29, 1975, p. A-17.

11. Quoted in Guido Belsasso, "Undocumented Mexican Workers in the U.S.:A Mexican Perspective," in Robert H. McBride (ed.), *Mexico and the United States* (Englewood Cliffs, N.J.: Prentice Hall, 1981), p. 143.

12. Ehrlich, *The Golden Door,* pp. 178–185.

13. Identical bills were introduced in the House by Rodino (H 9531) and in the Senate by Senators Eastland, Kennedy, Bentsen, and DiConcini (S 2252).

14. Quoted in the *New York Times,* November 7, 1978, p. A-22.

15. U.S. Government, Select Commission on Immigration and Refugee Policy, U.S. Immigration Policy and the National Interest, the final report and recommendations of the Select Commission on Immigration and Refugee Policy with supplemental views by Commissioners, March 1, 1981 (Washington: U.S. Government Printing Office, 1981).

16. Quoted in Aaron Segal, "The Half-Open Door," *The Wilson Quarterly* 7, No. 1 (1983): 128.

17. *New York Times,* October 6, 1983, pp. A-1, B-9.

18. *Richmond Times-Dispatch,* November 25, 1978, p. A-2.

19. *New York Times,* September 30, 1982, p. A-20.

20. *Wall Street Journal,* October 7, 1982, p. 31.

21. Rep. Lester L. Wolff (D-NY), quoted in *U.S. News and World Report,* April 25, 1977, p. 35.

22. *New York Times,* November 15, 1983, p. A-17.

23. Results of the poll appeared in Federation for American Immigration Reform, *FAIR/Fact Sheet* 2, No. 7 (February 1981):1.

24. Robert L. Lineberry, *Government in America*, 2d ed. (Boston: Little Brown, 1983), p. 228; *New York Times*, November 15, 1983, p. A-17. The Census Bureau estimated that 3 million Hispanic Americans were registered and 2.5 million voted in 1980; see *New York Times*, October 6, 1983, p. B-9.

25. *New York Times*, August 26, 1982, p. A-28.

26. *New York Times*, August 16, 1982, p. A-12; and August 18, 1982, p. A-7.

27. Quoted in James Fallows, "Immigration: How It's Affecting Us," *Atlantic Monthly* 252, No. 5 (November 1983):105.

28. *New York Times*, August 24, 1982, p. A-19.

29. Institute of Human Relations, *Blueprint for Social Justice* 2, vol. 37 (October 1983):6.

30. National Association for the Advancement of Colored People, "Problems of Immigration & Refugees," testimony presented to the Select Commission on Immigration and Refugee Policy," n.d. (mimeo.), p. 3.

31. Raúl Yzaguirre, president of the National Council of La Raza, made this assertion in the *Washington Post*, November 24, 1983, p. A-27.

32. *Today*, November 25, 1983, p. 5.

33. *Washington Post*, August 8, 1980, p. A-13.

34. Segal, "The Half-Open Door," p. 120.

35. *U.S. News & World Report*, June 2, 1980, p. 21.

36. Federation for American Immigration Reform, "The House Debate: The Simpson-Mazzoli Bill: December 16–18," 1982 (mimeo.), p. 2.

37. *Phoenix Gazette*, September 3, 1982.

38. *Gallup Poll, Gallup Report*, No. 306 (November 1982), p. 15.

39. *New York Times*, November 15, 1983, p. A-17.

40. Summary of Statement of Thomas R. Donahue, Secretary-Treasurer, AFL-CIO, to the Senate Subcommittee on Immigration and Refugee Policy and the House Subcommittee on Immigration and Refugees and International Law in Joint Hearings on the Report of the Select Commission on Immigration and Refugee Policy, Washington, May 5, 1981 (mimeo.), p. 15.

41. These include: low worker skills and modest job entry requirements; little or no need for employees to master the English language; low wages; large number of small, undercapitalized firms in the sector; strong price competition that gives rise to intense cost-cutting pressures; labor-intensive production, decentralized, often remote, location of workplaces (frequently in ghettos); small work units, called "cockroach shops" in the garment industry, located in the Southwest or in major urban centers; a high percentage of employees belonging to minority groups; and weak or non-existent tradition of union organization.

42. Food Trades is the department most likely to be consulted.

43. Angelo Fosco, president of the Laborers, was born in Poland of Italian parents—the kind of background that elicits sympathy for immigrants.

44. U.S. Department of Labor, *Handbook of Labor Statistics* (Washington, D.C.: Government Printing Office, 1980), p. 412.

45. *Washington Post*, November 29, 1983, p. B-7.

46. The views of Conner and his organization appear monthly in FAIR's *Immigration Report*; the above quotation appeared in the October 1982 issue, p. 4.

47. On at least three occasions, U.S. officials discussed the Carter plan with their Mexican counterparts before its introduction. One meeting involved Stuart Eisenstadt, White House counselor for domestic affairs. Interview with Robert A. Pastor, College Park, Maryland, February 1, 1983.

48. *Washington Post*, March 3, 1978, A-16.

49. *Excelsior*, December 9, 1982, p. 1-A.

50. Quoted in Belsasso, "Undocumented Mexican Workers in the U.S.," p. 145.

51. Roberto Jaramillo Flores, quoted in *Excelsior*, October 29, 1977.

52. Quoted in Belsasso, "Undocumented Mexican Workers in the U.S.," p. 145.

53. Belsasso, "Undocumented Mexican Workers in the U.S.," pp. 150–51.

54. Belsasso, "Undocumented Mexican Workers in the U.S.," pp. 155–56.

55. *Excelsior*, June 2, 1979, p. 1-A.

56. Neil Peirce, "The Fearsome Long-Term Implications of 1 Million Immigrants a Year," *Washington Post*, November 15, 1981.

57. Michael S. Teitelbaum, "Immigration: A Popular Answer Is No Answer," *Los Angeles Times*, May 25, 1983, Part II, p. 7.

58. *New York Times*, June 22, 1983, p. A-3.

59. *Wall Street Journal*, June 9, 1982, p. 26.

60. *New York Times*, February 22, 1983, p. A-13.

61. *Washington Post*, March 3, 1978, p. A-16.

62. *Washington Post*, September 26, 1979, p. A-1.

63. *Washington Post*, September 12, 1980, p. A-30.

64. *New York Times*, May 19, 1983, p. A-12.

8

ECONOMIC CRISIS OF 1982
AND PROSPECTS FOR
U.S.-MEXICAN RELATIONS

INTRODUCTION

Long-standing familiarity and dependence often lead to a pro-
liferation of names for the same concept. Just as the nomadic Somalis
have 45 separate words to identify the camel because of the drome-
dary's importance to their lives, many Latin American nations have
adopted synonyms for devaluation, a curse that frequently afflicts
their monies. "Downward adjustment," "depreciation," "technical
correction," "dirty float," and "crawling peg"—these are among the
many entries in the region's economic thesaurus.

Until recently, Mexicans had little experience with the phenomenon of "devaluation," with the exception of Echeverría's action in
1976, deemed by many an aberration. The peso enjoyed the status of
one of the strongest currencies in the third world, and an impressive
surge in oil exports after Echeverría left office offered the prospect of
its becoming even stronger. After a period of retrenchment, López
Portillo backed an ambitious development program designed to
achieve sustained economic growth for his nation. The strategy relied on unprecedented borrowing abroad to finance the expansion of
the oil sector and the creation of a diversified industrial base that
would enable Mexico to attain full employment and a favorable
trade balance. The president also pledged to revitalize the agrarian
sector, long the economy's Achilles' heel, in order to achieve self-sufficiency in grains by 1985.

Economic advancement, it was hoped, would enhance Mexico's
burgeoning influence in the region and strengthen its position with

respect to the United States. López Portillo's strategy proved a disaster, as symbolized by a 600 percent devaluation of the peso by the time the president completed his term. Would the economic crisis of 1982 provide the opportunity for U.S. retribution against Mexico, whose oil-inspired assertiveness had so rankled officials in Washington? Would the United States take advantage of this "time of troubles" to expand its influence over its southern neighbor?

LOST OPPORTUNITY

The oil boom converted Mexico from an ugly stepsister to a dazzling Cinderella of the international petroleum and banking scene, as oil earnings soared from $3 billion to $14 billion in the five years leading to 1980. The black gold and green dollars helped Mexico achieve a key goal of its 1979 Industrial Development Plan: gross domestic product rose by approximately 8 percent each year between 1978 and 1981. This expansion generated vast profits for the private sector and helped create one million new jobs annually.[1] Mexico's growth became the envy of a world floundering in recession. Such glamour, however, diverted attention from the beginnings of "petrolization"—a neologism connoting an overheated economy fueled by oil revenues, growing reliance on foreign creditors to pay for surging food, capital, and luxury imports (which rose from $6 billion in 1977 to $23 billion in 1981), a convulsed agricultural sector, and—above all—outsized budget deficits. Rather than raising taxes, Mexican leaders chose to cover the growing deficits by printing brand new peso notes.

This action spurred inflation, which fell from 20.7 percent in 1977 to 16.2 percent in 1978 only to climb back to 21 percent in 1979. Even with slight monthly adjustments vis-à-vis the dollar, the peso's overvaluation became abundantly clear. A dearer peso discouraged tourism, inhibited the exportation of Mexican manufactures (some of which were relatively labor-intensive), and exacerbated reliance on oil and its derivatives to earn foreign exchange. Hydrocarbons, which generated 16 percent of Mexico's export earnings in 1976, accounted for over 75 percent of these revenues six years later.

Economic bottlenecks intensified the inflation. The transportation system sagged under the pressure of food and industrial imports. For instance, Mexican trains chugged along at an average speed of 12 kilometers an hour in a rail system little improved since Pancho Villa and his troops used it 65 years before. The accident-laden highways, sometimes reminiscent of chariot scenes from *Ben-Hur*, were designed to bear one-fifth of the current load. And the antiquated ports bore testimony to the country's tradition of conducting two-thirds of its trade overland with the United States.[2]

Alarmed by the danger signals on the horizon, López Portillo in May 1979 reorganized his cabinet in what was called "one of the most dramatic political changes since Lázaro Cárdenas threw [former president] Plutarco Elías Calles out of Mexico in 1935."[3] Attracting the greatest attention was the removal of Interior Minister Jesús Reyes Heroles, a gifted political theorist and the driving force behind the 1977 political reform that expanded the role of opposition parties by facilitating their official recognition and enlarging their representation in Congress.[4] More important from an economic perspective was the departure of Ricardo García Sainz, who was generally viewed as an incompetent minister of planning and budget. This post was designed to exercise central control over planning, budgeting, and evaluation of programs—a role similar to that discharged by the Office of Management and Budget in the United States.

As a replacement, the president selected Miguel de la Madrid Hurtado, who had distinguished himself in the central bank, Petróleos Mexicanos, and the finance ministry before becoming deputy finance minister. He enjoyed a reputation as a tough economic conservative and had emerged within the councils of government as the chief spokesman for tight-fisted budgeting policies against the expansionist views of Carlos Tello Macías, who was García Sainz's predecessor until the president discharged him near the end of 1977.[5]

Analysts expected that de la Madrid would squeeze credit to cool down the investment splurge that had occurred since the beginning of 1979. Following the stagnation of the Echeverría years, private investment had revived, and by mid-1978 industry was working close to capacity. The government tightened credit in November 1978 to slow down the economy, but it eased restrictions in early 1979 and demand again outpaced supply. The result was a 7.4 percent increase in prices for the first four months of the year, compared with a 5.9 percent rate in the same period the year before. Meanwhile, the balance-of-payments deficit in the first quarter rose to $615.7 million, twice that of the three months at the beginning of 1978.[6]

Adjectives like "strong," "competent," "bold," and "sophisticated" adorned press reports of de la Madrid's appointment, and it appeared that he would put his nation's finances in order. After all,

López Portillo, whose bureaucratic reforms at the beginning of his administration had reallocated economic responsibilities and created the Ministry of Planning and Budgeting, wanted centralized control over budgetmaking.[7] Instead of deciding at the outset of the budgetary process the size of the pie to be apportioned, past practice had found a host of chefs—cabinet members, heads of quasipublic agencies, governors, and so forth—insisting on the addition of more and more ingredients until the pie grew out of proportion to available resources. At the national bankers convention in Acapulco, de la Madrid echoed the sentiments of Manuel Espinosa Iglesias, president of the prestigious Banco de Comercio Exterior, who said: "We have to put a stop to the inflation before the inflation puts a stop to the economy."[8]

However, the new minister disappointed those who expected him to follow a disciplined economic regimen. The salience of his position pushed him into the political limelight, and the upward trajectory of his career seemed even more assured when, on April 15, 1980, López Portillo unveiled a much-vaunted Global Development Plan. De la Madrid authored this program which, as the first integrated socioeconomic blueprint in the nation's history, attempted to coordinate the nine sectoral plans and 31 state plans cited above. People began mentioning his name in reverential tones. Invitations to social gatherings filled his mailbox. His name began to appear on lists of *presidenciables*, those individuals considered eligible to be "tapped" to succeed López Portillo in 1982.

A technocrat with no constituency, de la Madrid's exercise of limited restraint in 1980 gave way the following year to a preference for saying "sí" rather than "no" to powerful—and potentially helpful—cabinet colleagues, agency heads, governors, and other similarly well-placed politicians. As Table 5 indicates, budget deficits grew along with the minister's presidential aspirations.

Symptoms of petrolization became unmistakable in 1979 as prices rose 30 percent, foreign indebtedness reached $55 billion, traditional exports declined in value, and imports shot up because of a prolonged drought, an overvalued peso, and gross inefficiency in the agricultural sector, whose much-talked-about conversion to self-sufficiency through the Mexican Food System subsequently turned out to be a Potemkin promise. Yet the Iraqi-Iranian War drove oil

TABLE 5: Revenues and Expenditures of Mexico's Public Sector: 1979 to 1981[a] (billions of pesos)

Year	Revenues	Expenditures	Deficit	Percent Deficit
1979	769.3	917.3	148.0	19.2
1980	1,161.4	1,379.5	218.1	18.8
1981	1,544.7[b]	2,108.3	536.6	36.5

[a]Includes financial activities of the federal government, as well as those of 27 quasistate agencies over which centralized budgetary control is exercised.

[b]Preliminary figures.

Source: Banco de México, S.A., *Informe Anual, 1981* (Mexico City: Banco de México, 1982), p. 87.

charges from $12.70 to $26 per barrel during the year. This petroleum income kept the bankers and corporate managers flying in with briefcases bulging with loan applications and investment opportunities, engendering the illusion that petroleum earnings would assure the country's "permanent prosperity." In 1980 alone the external public debt grew by over $4 billion and total foreign investment, most of it U.S., rose from $1.4 billion to $8.2 billion.[9]

THE OIL GLUT

The picture looked relatively promising until a worldwide oil glut developed in the spring of 1981. A confluence of factors—Saudi Arabia's record output of 10.3 million bpd, expanded sales by Mexico, Great Britain, and other non-OPEC producers, energy conservation in the face of unparalleled crude prices, and economic stagnation in industrial nations—generated a 2 to 3 million bpd surfeit.

To meet this challenge, 12 of the 13 OPEC members decided on May 26, 1981, to congeal crude prices at current levels and to cut output by at least 10 percent. Saudi Arabia rebuffed the majority and, in search of a unified pricing formula that would advance long-term economic stability, elected to maintain both its high production and its selling price of $32 per barrel.

The shift from a seller's to a buyer's market stunned López Portillo.[10] After all, he had witnessed the rebirth of his nation's oil sector amid the most favorable conditions that the international petroleum industry had ever enjoyed, and it appeared that the world possessed an unslakable thirst for energy. He and his advisors assumed in spawning development plans that the past was prologue to a future of even higher prices that would steadily rise through 1990 to about $40 per barrel and meet Mexico's financial needs. Such exuberance nurtured arrogance within PEMEX, which sometimes subjected its customers to sudden, even retroactive, price hikes, irregular delivery schedules, and the demand that clients accept a larger percentage of the heavier Maya crude to obtain the more attractive Isthmus variety in their shipments. To make matters worse, the prices of key Mexican commodities such as silver, coffee, and copper also declined.

López Portillo pledged never to "rat on OPEC"—an entity whose pricing policies Mexico had followed closely. Yet on June 3, 1981, PEMEX began dispatching telexes to its buyers around the world, informing them of a $4 per barrel reduction in charges effective June 1. The price of Isthmus would fall from $38.50 to $34.50; that of Maya would drop from $32 to $28. The upshot was that a standard barrel of Mexico's marker crude (a 40/60 blend of Isthmus and Maya) declined from $34.60 to $30.60, effectively undercutting prices established at the recently concluded OPEC meeting.

Market resistance triggered this move. PEMEX's clients groused about the difficulty of persuading their customers to buy high-cost crude because of anemic demand, low utilization of refineries, and soaring interest rates. Companies like Tenneco, Ashland, EXXON, and Shell, which enjoyed alternate sources of supply, claimed to be losing money on the heavier Mexican crude, while buyers in Sweden, the Philippines, Yugoslavia, India, and France also suspended purchases. Thus, Díaz Serrano acted to pacify his near-mutinous clients who were avidly pursuing less expensive supplies.

Undoubtedly, the PEMEX chief had informed López Portillo of the need to adjust prices—seldom does a leaf fall in Mexico without the president's knowledge!—but questions of timing and amount may have remained unanswered. Rather than consulting the economic cabinet, composed of de la Madrid and three other ministers with economic responsibilities, as he had agreed, Díaz Serrano confronted them with a fait accompli. His behavior produced a number of flushed faces around Mexico City, one of the reddest of which belonged to López Portillo himself, who refused to back his close friend, the director-general, on the dubious grounds that he had not purged unreliable buyers from the sales list as promised.

Díaz Serrano resigned three days after slashing the export price, and Julio Rodolfo Moctezuma Cid, a former minister of finance, became the new head of PEMEX. However, Patrimony Minister Oteyza, who by virtue of his post was also chairman of PEMEX, wasted no time in taking charge of petroleum policy following the change of command. In a mid-June address to Congress he characterized Díaz Serrano's decision to lower prices as "hasty," accused the industrialized nations of "basic selfishness" in demanding reductions, and warned that Mexico's clients must face the possibility that a "barrel lost by them today, may be lost forever."[11]

Oteyza hoped to compensate for these losses by tripling exports to Japan to 300,000 bpd. The Japanese government applauded the prospect of closer economic ties, but insisted that ultimate purchase decisions resided with private domestic companies. The $2 price adjustment dampened their enthusiasm for Mexican oil at a time when supplies and storage facilities were already at their limit. Moreover, they privately expressed misgivings over the quality of PEMEX's crude and the monopoly's poor performance in meeting delivery dates.

The Compagnie Française des Pétroles (CFP), a Paris-based corporation, along with other PEMEX clients, had voiced identical concerns about delivery schedules and quality. The $2 increase came on top of these problems, prompting the firm, in keeping with the terms of its contract, to suspend purchases of 100,000 bpd of PEMEX crude during the third quarter of 1981. On July 4, in an act even more abrupt than Díaz Serrano's price proclamation, Oteyza's ministry stated its intention to exclude the French from such economic projects as subway construction, automobile production, and the Mexican nuclear program because the oil had been furnished in the context of a broader cooperative framework.

The French government, a CFP stockholder, pressed for conciliation, foreseeing lucrative opportunities for French firms in Mexico's plans to build 20 nuclear power stations. In addition, President François Mitterrand was striving to enhance French influence in the Caribbean. Following a mid-July meeting with Mexican officials,

CFP agreed to resume its 100,000 bpd imports on August 1, apparently on terms favorable to it.

Why did Oteyza vent his wrath on France, especially when CFP acted legally and other countries had stopped imports? To begin with, he could hardly pummel fellow developing nations like India, Yugoslavia, or the Philippines. Sweden, which had halted purchases in March, was too small to pick on, while the multinational giants— EXXON and Shell, leaders of the flight from Mexico—were too large. Moreover, the Japanese shrewdly avoided a confrontation by neglecting to denominate tankers to pick up cargoes in July. Daily exports, which had exceeded one million barrels during the first quarter of 1981, plunged to no more than half that volume in July. Given this alarming situation, Oteyza attempted to apply as much pressure as possible to a major buyer to convey his government's resolute attitude toward fair-weather friends. France appeared to offer the right-sized target.

The Reagan administration sought to strengthen ties with Mexico following the often tempestuous nature of bilateral relations during the Carter years. Thus, in August 1981 the U.S. Department of Energy gave a dramatic boost to Mexico's export drive when it announced the direct purchase from PEMEX of 109.15 million barrels of oil for the U.S. strategic petroleum reserve with deliveries to be made over the next five years.[12] This accord marked the third time that Mexico had supplied crude to the reserve, created to safeguard the United States against blackmail by OPEC and other exporters. Still, the other transactions had involved private oil companies as intermediaries, whereas the mid-1981 deal sprang from direct negotiations between agencies of the Mexican and U.S. governments.

Washington's action helped turn a full-blown debacle into a mere disaster for Mexico. In a desperate move to regain customers, Oteyza did cancel most of the $2 per barrel increase that he decreed following Díaz Serrano's resignation. Thus, the price for a mixture of Maya and Isthmus ended up at $30.70 per barrel, just 10¢ above the price that had ushered in the chaos. Meanwhile, the Mexican government estimated that the lost exports had cost it $1 billion in an episode facetiously called the "billion dollar dime." For the year, PEMEX earned only $14.6 billion from oil, gas, and petrochemical sales, just two-thirds of the amount projected.[13]

Mexico also demonstrated a lack of diplomatic sensitivity and sophistication in its treatment of the French, whose Socialist chief executive had assiduously courted López Portillo. CFP did resume purchases from PEMEX in August, but these shipments recommenced only after France had undergone its greatest humiliation in Mexico since Napoleon III's troops were forced from the ancient Aztec nation in 1867. Mexico's bludgeoning of France to buy oil placed in question the country's dependability as an ally, particularly during periods of stress.

POLITICS AND HEADACHES

Unfortunately, the economic dislocations of 1981 transpired at the worst possible time to rationalize spending or bring sanity to the budgetary process, for they preceded the final year of the presidential term when spending and corruption reach a crescendo as politicians assure themselves a sybaritic retirement. Activities during the so-called Year of Hidalgo—Father Miguel Hidalgo, who catalyzed Mexico's independence movement, gazes sternly from the country's ten peso coin—have given rise to the doggerel: *Este es el año de Hidalgo: Buey el que no roba algo* (This is the year of Hidalgo; he is a fool who doesn't steal something).[14]

Two international factors further clouded economic conditions: the spot price of Saudi Arabian marker crude fell to less than $30 per barrel and the U.S. prime rate climbed to 17 percent, raising Mexico's interest burden from $5.4 billion in 1980 to $8.2 billion in 1981. As the president explained it, the peso was "taken by assault." Capital flight during the first six weeks of the year may have approached $2.5 billion, double the figure for the whole of 1981.[15]

With the central bank rapidly running out of reserves, the Mexican government allowed the peso to float on February 17, 1982, thereby achieving a 31 percent devaluation. Finance Minister David Ibarra Muñoz promised an emergency economic plan to stabilize the economy. However, the most specific target announced at the time of devaluation—a 3 percent cut in public outlays—lacked credibility because of substantial wage increases and anticipated huge overspending on the budget.[16] López Portillo, who called himself "a devalued president" after the peso's collapse, reorganized the cabinet in late March, placing close associates of de la Madrid in the pivotal economic posts of central bank president, minister of planning and budget, and finance minister. Silva Herzog, who replaced Ibarra Muñoz, lobbied for the imposition of austerity measures only to be checkmated for political reasons discussed below. Ultimately, on April 19, a presidential decree set forth a number of belt-tightening steps, including:[17]

- Reducing the public sector deficit as a proportion of gross domestic product by 3 percent (from an official figure of 11.3 percent in 1981);
- Requiring an 8 percent cut in budgeted federal expenditures, excluding debt service, wages, or municipal and state allocations;
- Increasing prices, tariffs, and other charges to raise an additional $3.25 billion in public revenues;
- Limiting net external borrowing to a maximum of $11 billion in 1982;
- Expanding the total currency in circulation to an amount equal to the increase in the net reserves of the Bank of Mexico;
- Paring the current account deficit by $3 to $4 billion below 1981 levels against original 1982 projections of $15 billion;
- Adjusting domestic interest rates to take into account external rates as well as local exchange rate movements so as to favor peso deposits; and
- Permitting intervention by the Bank of Mexico in the exchange rate to prevent overvaluation of the peso.

Not only was the decree late in coming, but its provisions were largely ignored, except for the central bank's raising reserve requirements for commercial banks to 100 percent. What accounted for the deadlock and drift following a devaluation designed to stimulate the moribund economy?

Put briefly, the PRI resisted economic retrenchment in an election year, especially in view of the difficulties besetting the campaign of de la Madrid, who wound up as the party's nominee. Observers quickly labeled him a "clone" of López Portillo because the two men shared technical, relatively nonpolitical backgrounds. De la Madrid possesses impressive credentials: legal training at Mexico's National Autonomous University, a Harvard master's degree in public administration, a moderate political philosophy, and—as previously mentioned—vast experience in his nation's Byzantine bureaucracy, with emphasis on management, finance, and planning.

Even though he was tapped as PRI's standard bearer in September 1981, an unexpectedly early date,[18] his campaign got off to a slow start. De la Madrid's insistence on having his own men in charge of PRI gave rise to an intraparty dispute that was resolved only when its president, Javier García Paniagua, whom many believed would be Mexico's next chief executive, stepped down in favor of Pedro Ojeda Paullada in mid-October. Formerly labor minister and also a presidential contender, Ojeda Paullada became merely a figurehead as Manuel Bartlett Díaz, a de la Madrid confidant, actually managed the campaign as the party's secretary-general. However, Ojeda's extemporaneous comments sometimes clashed with de la Madrid's and proved embarrassing to the candidate. For instance, the PRI was determined to get as many voters as possible to the polls in the July 4, 1982, balloting. The quest for a large turnout sprang not from fear of the six opposition candidates, none of whom had even a remote chance of winning. Rather, PRI's major opponent was abstentionism, which had shot up from 28.6 percent in López Portillo's election to 50 percent in the 1979 congressional contests (see Table 6). Reversing this trend seemed crucial to dispel the idea of disenchantment with both a political system honeycombed with corruption and a governing party that has converted cooptation from an art form to an exact science. More than a political apparat, it controls federal, state, and municipal governments, runs an escalator to power for the ambitious, flourishes as a patronage trough, and manipulates—through captive unions and pliant campesino organizations—blue-

TABLE 6:   Abstentions in Mexican Elections, 1961 to 1979

Year	Election	Percent Abstentions
1961	Congressional	31.5
1964	Presidential	20.0
1964	Congressional	33.3
1967	Congressional	37.4
1970	Presidential	36.0
1970	Congressional	35.0
1973	Congressional	36.2
1976	Presidential	28.6
1976	Congressional	38.1
1979	Congressional	50.0

Sources: Proceso, June 25, 1979, p. 24 (1961, 1964, 1967, 1970, 1973, and 1976 congressional); *Visión*, July 28, 1979, p. 14 (1979 congressional—estimated); *New York Times*, July 7, 1964, p. 12 (presidential—estimated); *Facts on File*, July 18, 1970, p. 544 (1970 Presidential—estimated); and *Facts on File*, July 10, 1976, p. 498 (1976 presidential).

collar workers and impoverished peasants. As described in Chapter 1, it has also mastered the use of "gifts," "travel expenses," and other euphemisms for payoffs to reporters and columnists to assure favorable coverage of its candidates.[19] Apparently oblivious to PRI's strategy of obtaining a high turnout, Ojeda Paullada told reporters that he was not worried by abstentionism, for it "is the people's tacit acceptance of conditions in Mexico, the system, and the PRI."[20]

In theory, three pillars provide a broad base of support for the PRI: a peasant sector composed of campesinos living on *ejidos*; a popular sector comprised of teachers, managers, bureaucrats, professionals, owners of small businesses, and other middle-class elements; and a labor sector embracing the Confederation of Mexican Workers.

In practice, the party's backing is more limited. For instance, PRI officials in Mexico City and state governors cynically exploit the peasants, who boast the party's largest membership on paper, but have few genuine leaders. In contrast, the well-educated members of the popular sector produce scores of leaders; nonetheless, the middle class is increasingly disenchanted because of the devaluations and inflation. As a result, the 4 million-member CTM stands as the regime's sturdiest guarantor of stability. Traditionally, Confederation leader Fidel Velázquez and his fellow *charros*—or "cowboys" as Mexican labor bosses are called—have trumpeted their assent of government policies and cajoled, wheedled, threatened, and coerced members to muster crowds for campaign rallies. De la Madrid and his campaign advisers looked for them to help assure a robust turnout in the July 4, 1982, election.

Any favors tendered by the CTM's geriatric leaders carry a hefty price tag. While Velázquez lives modestly compared to his colleagues, many union chiefs pursue self-indulgent pleasures that include palatial homes, weekend jet trips to Paris, and bloated U.S. bank accounts. They complement their union salaries with various bribes, payoffs, illicit business ventures, and job selling—activities long condoned by a governing party eager to stay on good terms with its staunchest ally.[21]

Velázquez, who had earlier inveighed against choosing a *técnico* over a *político* as the next president, preferred Ojeda Paullada over de la Madrid as the PRI candidate. To propitiate Velázquez and other *charros* and obtain their support for the former minister of planning and budget, the government granted the country's workers salary increases of up to 30 percent on March 18. This action, which came on the heels of a 34 percent raise in the cost of living granted at the beginning of the year, spurred higher prices and thereby vitiated the stimulative effects of the late February devaluation. In a further act of ingratiation, PRI increased labor's allocation of deputy and senate candidates in the congressional contests also scheduled for July 4.

Labor put its collective shoulder to the wheel, assuring de la Madrid's triumph (75 percent) and abstentionism's loss (28.5 percent) (see Table 7), although middle-class voters "turned out in droves" to back the right-wing National Action Party (PAN).[22] But the salary increase signaled a lack of commitment to a stabilization plan, and capital flight—which had abated after the devaluation—began anew during the weeks before the election. Still, the government failed to take corrective action in July, perhaps reluctant to burden the voters immediately after they had favored the PRI with such a large margin of victory.

Reality intervened in Mexico's economic wonderland in August. At the beginning of the month, the Ministry of Commerce announced sharp price increases in tortillas (100 percent), gasoline (60 percent), and electricity (30 percent). On August 5, 1982, the Ministry of Finance unveiled a two-tier exchange system: a "preferential" rate of 50 pesos to the dollar reserved for crucial imports, interest and principal payments on public and private foreign debt, and other priority transactions; and an "ordinary" rate of 70 pesos to the dollar for exports, tourists entering the country, and payments of interest and principal on foreign currency bank deposits in Mexico.[23] On August 13 Silva Herzog jetted to Washington to inform the U.S. Treasury Department and the Federal Reserve Board that his country, its foreign exchange nearly exhausted, teetered on the brink of bankruptcy. This prospect sent shock waves through the world's banking community because Mexico's default on its staggering foreign debt could have tumbled the international financial structure. "Put simply, the potential impact of Mexico's crisis . . . [was] greater than the collapse of the Penn Square Bank and Drysdale Securities in the U.S., the affair of Banco Ambrosiano in Italy and the problems of AEG-Telefunken in West Germany combined."[24] United States leaders, central bankers in other developed countries, IMF officials, and representatives of private banks began collaborating in a multibillion dollar bailout scheme. Provisions of this program included:

- $1.7 billion guarantee for grain exports to Mexico by the U.S. Commodity Credit Corporation;

TABLE 7: Results of the July 4, 1982, Presidential Election in Mexico

Candidate	Party	Total Votes Received	Percent Votes Cast	Percent Eligible Voters (31,516,370)
Miguel de la Madrid	Institutional Revolutionary Party (PRI)	16,145,254	71.63	51.23
	Authentic Party of the Mexican Revolution (PARM)*	242,187	1.07	0.77
	Popular Socialist Party (PPS)*	360,565	1.60	1.14
Pablo Emilio Madero	National Action Party (PAN)	3,700,045	16.41	11.74
Arnoldo Martínez Verdugo	Unified Socialist Party of Mexico (PSUM)	821,995	3.65	2.61
Ignacio González Góllaz	Mexican Democratic Party (PDM)	433,886	1.93	1.38
Rosario Ibarra de la Piedra	Revolutionary Workers Party (PRT)	416,448	1.85	1.32
Candido Díaz Cerecedo	Socialist Workers Party (PST)	342,005	1.52	1.09
Manuel Moreno Sánchez	Social Democratic Party (PSD)	48,413	0.21	0.15
Others (Unregistered)		28,474	0.13	0.09
Total		22,539,272	100.00	71.52
Invalid Votes		1,053,616		3.34
Abstentions		7,923,482		25.14
Total		31,516,370		100.00

*Also nominated de la Madrid as presidential candidate.
Source: Secretaria técnica, Comisión Federal Electoral, Mexico City, 1982.

184

- \$1 billion prepaid crude sale by PEMEX to the U.S. strategic petroleum reserve;
- \$1.85 billion bridging loan from the Bank of International Settlement in Basel until a support package could be negotiated with the IMF; and
- A fresh line of credit from private bankers who agreed to postpone for 90 days payments on part of Mexico's \$85 billion foreign debt.

While negotiations with the IMF were hanging fire, López Portillo demonstrated his revolutionary credentials on September 1 by nationalizing domestic banks and their assets. He justified this act, which caught all but the president's closest advisors by surprise, on the grounds that the banking community had "betrayed us" by facilitating speculation against the peso, which had lost 75 percent of its value during 1982. "I can affirm that in recent years a group of Mexicans, led, counseled and supported by private banks, have taken more money out of the country than all the empires that have exploited us since the beginning of our history."[25] But it was gross financial mismanagement, not a plot by banking gnomes, that sparked the capital flight. And "this profoundly revolutionary measure" by a lame duck leader elicited memories of Echeverría's land seizures. It appeared designed to loft the plummeting popularity of the chief executive, secure for him a place alongside Cárdenas in his country's pantheon of heroes, and mollify the left. Some 300,000 workers, peasants, and civil servants flocked to Mexico City's central plaza to praise the intrepid action of "the patriotic president." In the opinion of one writer, "López Portillo was looking increasingly like a bullfighter awarded both ears and the tail" because of his undaunted move.[26] Demagoguery reached its zenith when López Portillo began collecting "voluntary" contributions from laborers, campesinos, and government employees to compensate the owners of Mexico's banks[27]—a program in which the military refused to participate.

A common thread joined the nationalization speech to earlier discourses by López Portillo (August 5, 1982, on the dual exchange rate) and Silva Herzog (August 17, 1982, on the financial crisis). They urged patriotic unity and individual sacrifice amid critical conditions, while largely shifting the blame for the economic malaise to forces "beyond our control." An analysis of these speeches finds the uncontrollable forces divided between specific groups and world conditions. The former included: bankers, multinational corporations, bad "denationalized" Mexicans, orthodox technocrats, and pressure groups; the latter embraced the oil glut, fall in petroleum prices, decline in the export price of other Mexican primary products, reduced quantity of petrodollars available to major world banks, attractive interest rates in the United States that draw Mexican capital north of the border, and higher interest rates and more rigorous terms on loans made abroad.[28] As López Portillo sanctimoniously expressed it: "We haven't sinned, neither as a government nor as a country, and we have no reason to engage in acts of contrition."[29]

The IMF's imprimatur was a sine qua non for international bankers to support a stabilization plan. Weeks of negotiations produced an accord on November 10, 1982, whereby the IMF would provide Mexico with a $3.84 billion "extended fund facility" credit, as well as $440 million to $880 million from its compensatory financing facility established to assist countries suffering from declining exports. For its part, Mexico would slash its budget deficit from 16.5 percent of GNP in 1982 to 8.5 percent in 1983 with further cuts contemplated in 1984 (5.5 percent) and 1985 (3.5 percent). Moreover, it would limit foreign borrowing to no more than $5 billion in 1983 and take steps to build up its hard currency reserves to $2 billion. The Mexicans also pledged to modify the foreign exchange controls imposed in August, with a view to moving eventually to a unified exchange rate.

At the urging of the IMF's executive-director and the U.S. secretary of the treasury, 530 private banks supplied Mexico with $5 billion in credit to carry it through 1983. In addition, major foreign banks provided a $433 million bridging loan, required to meet debt obligations falling due at the end of February 1983, until the first payment of $1.7 billion from the large credit was available.

DEALING WITH A PROSTRATE MEXICO

The United States captained the lifeboat that rescued the Mexican economy. While extremists impugned Uncle Sam's motives, the de la Madrid administration recognized Washington's significant contribution and, at least during its first year, rejected the confrontationist style so often exhibited by the preceding regime. Rather than indulge in a fiesta of nationalist outbursts typical of López Portillo's last months in office, President de la Madrid stoically blamed the crisis on Mexico, admonished his country to prepare for even more extensive sacrifices, and adopted a tough stabilization plan without a prolonged conflict with the IMF that would have inflamed public opinion. Although working vigorously with the Contadora Group in behalf of negotiations in Central America, Foreign Minister Sepúlveda lowered his nation's decibel level with respect to the regional conflict. In May 1983 Mexico accepted a reduction in the price of natural gas, caused by an abundant supply in North America, without engaging in the posturing and pouting displayed some five years before. As a result of contracts signed in the summers of 1981 and 1982, the Mexican government defied domestic critics to become the principal foreign supplier to the U.S. strategic petroleum reserve, furnishing slightly over one-third of the 370 million barrels in storage in October 1983. Additionally, in a sharp departure from the xenophobia and ultranationalism of recent years, Mexico announced in mid-1983 a relaxation of foreign investment rules. The "Mexicanization" law would be retained; yet, government officials promised more flexibility in its application and pledged to broaden the number of sectors in which foreigners may hold a majority of the equity. According to one local economist, "allowing more foreign investment is the only way Mexico can get hold of large amounts of money without getting on its knees and begging to the banks."[30]

The economic malaise encouraged some U.S. officials to seek to drive Mexico to its knees. A few spoke of "teaching Mexico a lesson"[31]—possibly by linking food sales to imports of oil and other items. As things turned out, moderate views prevailed. While the United States did obtain oil at a bargain price in August 1982—40 million barrels of Isthmus grade for approximately $1 billion when the official price was $34 per barrel—no attempt was made to humiliate Mexico. After all, kicking a prostrate neighbor might have satisfied in the short-term those irritated by that country's hubris in the late 1970s, but only at a potentially enormous cost to the United States in the long run.

In all likelihood, a humbled Mexico would have repudiated the accord with the IMF, an international agency despised by many nationalists and leftists. Such action would give a fillip to the rate of inflation, which began to slow in 1983, and send even more illegals north of the Rio Grande. Mexico might also have been attracted to a debtor's cartel with Argentina and Brazil (the combined foreign loans of the three superdebtors exceed $200 billion), leading to a default on its international obligations. Debt repudiation would deal a stunning blow to U.S. banks, the nine largest of which had 44 percent of their capital loaned to Mexico in 1981. Failure to meet interest payments on these loans for a year would eliminate over one-third of their annual net profits.[32] Repudiation would also wreak havoc on the international banking and financial system.

Treating Mexico as an international mendicant would invite both the expropriation of foreign firms and even closer relations with OPEC, with which the de la Madrid government has orchestrated its oil production and pricing policy. Above all, a humiliated Mexican regime would be an inviting target for its domestic and foreign foes—a forbidding prospect for the United States in view of the turmoil bedeviling Central America. In fact, former National Security Adviser Brzezinski warned a State Department forum in April 1983 that Mexico could well follow Iran into revolution. Even though a beguiling hypothesis, several elements essential to Ayatollah Khomeini's success in toppling the shah are missing in Mexico: a compelling opposition leader, a support network of revolutionists throughout the country, a revolutionary ideology with which to rally the regime's detractors, and an unreliable army. United States contiguity further militates against an upheaval in Mexico.

The inexactness of the analogy must not blind observers to the Herculean problems confronting Mexico. The world banking community, which has resorted to "exotic financing arrangements and juggled bookkeeping techniques . . . to disguise the non-performing status of many international loans," has heaped praise on the nation's disciplined economic management; for instance, the London-based financial publication *Euromoney* named Silva Herzog its 1983 "Finance Minister of the Year." Such accolades appear as whistling past the graveyard, for they deflect attention from the incredibly high social and political costs of the belt-tightening plan—costs that have further eroded the legitimacy of the PRI and the decrepit political system it manages. A declining GNP, receding wage levels, high unemployment, diminished subsidies, continued inflation, and widespread shortages of consumer and capital goods have impelled centrifugal forces within the governing party, renown for its resilience and cooptive skill. Indeed, traditionally dependable CTM leaders, under pressure from members whose purchasing power has slipped badly since 1981, have publicly taken to task de la Madrid's managerial team for alleged indifference to the plight of working people. The peasantry, long the venerated but neglected stepchild of the Mexican revolution, looks forward to even deeper impoverishment with the termination of the handsomely funded Mexican Food System. Fortunately for the country's elite, the relative disorganization and geographic dispersion of the campesinos makes their protests less threatening than that of their blue-collar counterparts. Still machete-armed peasants grouped in the Pacto Ribereño have blockaded oilfields in Chiapas and Tabasco, depriving PEMEX of hundreds of thousands of barrels of crude oil production. Broad segments of the middle class, which forms the centerpiece of the PRI's popular sector, have demonstrated cynicism that blends into alienation because of the rising prices, foreign exchange controls, financially-imposed curbs on foreign travel, and anemic job prospects for them and their children. In the short run, many middle class Mexicans will complain loudly, while moving into smaller condominiums, evading new taxes such as the one imposed on automobiles, and casting protest votes for the PAN's candidates. In the long run, these same men and women, unless convinced that the PRI offers economic opportunities and an improved quality of life, could convert the PAN into a serious power-contender or forge new, alternative political structures, most likely on the right of the political spectrum.

Overhanging the disenchantment displayed by the PRI's several constituencies is the intraparty strife between politicians and technocrats. Several factors explain the former's declining influence: the importance of managers and planners in an economy with a growing public sector, the size of which expanded with the 1982 bank nationalization; the elevation to the presidency of *técnicos* in 1976 and 1982; López Portillo's support of political reform, which has assured opposition parties 100 seats in the chamber of deputies and a forum for excoriating official policies; and de la Madrid's devotion to "moral renovation," an anti-corruption theme articulated from Chihuahua to Quintana Roo during the 1982 presidential campaign that offends party stalwarts, already upset by political liberalization. De la Madrid's cabinet choices provided indisputable evidence of the technocrats' ascendancy: only two of his 20 appointees boasted a political background; none had ever held elective office. Oil monies facilitated an expansion in government jobs, other forms of patronage, "commissions" for larcenous office-holders, and substantial outlays for education, rural health, social security, and large-scale construction activities. This bonanza masked the *técnico-político* schism, kept traditional *priistas* in the fold, and stirred dreams of a dynamic and affluent Mexico.

The depression and emergence inside and outside the PRI of mordant criticism of government actions revealed the party's fragility. Reports of the demise of Mexico's single party-dominant system are premature. Yet the PRI must change to survive; specifically, it must increase its responsiveness, decentralize decisionmaking, and invite genuine (not merely symbolic) participation by peasants, young people, women, skilled workers, and other groups largely excluded from the party's top councils. Complicating this task is the imperative for de la Madrid to devise a Solomonic compromise between politicians and technocrats within the revolutionary family.

Continued vote manipulation in the 1983 state and local elections in which opposition parties recorded several noteworthy victories indicates that political reform, if undertaken at all, will await the resolution of the economic crisis. De la Madrid seemed more papist than the pope in adhering to the IMF guidelines. His administration added to its hard currency reserves in 1983 thanks to surpluses in trade and current account balances. Nevertheless, this surfeit resulted not from an aggressive export drive, but from a two-tier exchange rate that starved importers of dollars with which they acquire consumer items, capital goods, and inputs for industrial production. The oil sector shared in these cutbacks with the result that PEMEX drilled only 379 new wells in 1983 compared to 499 in 1980. Meanwhile, the lack of funds with which to purchase parts led the state monopoly to cannibalize its drilling fleet, reducing the number of operating rigs from 223 to 185. Failing to make vital capital investments in 1983 and 1984 severely constrained Mexico's ability to earn dollars from hydrocarbon and non-hydrocarbon exports later in the decade.

The enforced austerity accentuated Mexican dependence on the United States. To weather the economic storm without the collapse of their nation's badly strained political institutions, de la Madrid and Silva Herzog continuously looked to Washington for assistance—in the form of guaranteed foodstuffs, prepaid oil shipments to the U.S. strategic petroleum reserve, swaps of dollars for pesos between the Federal Reserve and the Mexican central bank, and good offices with international financial entities.[33]

More than any other recent event, the economic crisis of 1982 demonstrated the symbiotic relationship between the two nations. The well-being of U.S. banks depends upon a healthy Mexico. United States border towns are plunged into a depression if Mexicans cannot afford dollars with which to make purchases. United States firms see their orders, profits, and payrolls shrink when Mexicans lack the wherewithal to buy their goods and services. A sour economy below the Rio Grande is an important "push" factor affecting illegal immigration. And the risk that the violence affecting Central America will spread northward is inversely related to Mexico's stability. The interdependence characterizing bilateral affairs means that attempts by either country to influence the other's behavior will affect the initiator—a fact that argues for negotiation over exhortation and conciliation over confrontation in U.S.-Mexican relations.

NOTES

1. *New York Times*, May 22, 1982, p. 2.
2. Alan Riding, "Mixed Blessing of Mexico's Oil," *New York Times Magazine*, January 11, 1981, p. 25.
3. *Latin America Political Report*, May 25, 1979, p. 157.
4. Javier López Moreno discusses the Federal Law of Political Organization and Electoral Processes in *La reforma política en méxico* (Mexico City: Centro de Documentacíon Política, A.C., 1979), pp. 11–22.
5. *Latin America Economic Report*, May 25, 1979, p. 153.
6. *Latin America Economic Report*, May 25, 1979, p. 153.
7. For an excellent discussion of recent bureaucratic changes, see John J. Bailey, "Presidency, Bureaucracy, and Administrative Reform in Mexico: The Secretariat of Programming and Budget," *Inter-American Economic Affairs* 34, No. 1 (Summer 1980): 27–59.
8. *Latin America Economic Report*, June 1, 1979, p. 164.
9. Riding, "Mixed Blessing of Mexico's Oil," p. 25.
10. This section benefits from material that originally appeared in George W. Grayson, "Oil and Politics in Mexico," *Current History* 80, No. 462 (November 1981): 380ff.
11. *Excelsior*, June 17, 1981, p. 1-A.
12. At the time of the sale, the reserve contained 175 million barrels—with the goal of reaching 750 million barrels, an amount that would satisfy domestic consumption for four-and-a-half months without imports.
13. Frank E. Niering, Jr., "Mexico: The Problems Mount," *Petroleum Economist* 49, No. 7 (July 1982): 276.
14. Susan Kaufman Purcell and John F. H. Purcell, "State and Society in Mexico: Must a Stable Polity be Institutionalized?" *World Politics* 32 (January 1980): 200.
15. *Latin America Weekly Report*, February 26, 1982, p. 1.
16. *Latin America Weekly Report*, February 26, 1982, p. 1.
17. *Bank of London & South America Review* 16 (May 1982): 102.
18. Scholars, diplomats, and journalists alike believed that the laying on of hands would follow the October 22–23 North-South summit in Cancún lest a lame duck status diminish López Portillo's effectiveness at that meeting, which he cochaired. But several considerations explain the early announcement, which came on September 25. First, deteriorating economic conditions favored appointing personnel and making decisions that would span the outgoing and incoming administrations. Second, López Portillo sought to signal Washington and the international financial community that a moderate-to-conservative manager, friendly to pri-

vate business, would assume the reins of government, thereby spiking rumors that a populist politician might be anointed. Third, supporters of competing *gallos*, or presidential hopefuls, were poised to jump the gun in a move to force the incumbent's hand. Finally, the prospect of a serious electoral challenge from a unified left—a threat that never materialized—may have spurred the start of PRI's vaunted juggernaut.

19. For instance, the PRI paid $70 to $100 a day to Mexican reporters covering de la Madrid's campaign; see the *Wall Street Journal*, April 22, 1982, p. 26 and the *New York Times*, May 28, 1982, p. A-2.

20. *Proceso*, December 21, 1981, p. 7.

21. For a description of corruption in what is perhaps Mexico's strongest union, the Oil Workers, see Grayson, *The Politics of Mexican Oil*, Chapter 4.

22. While no scientific study of the 1982 election has been published, it appears that other factors, besides the active participation of organized labor, contributed to the robust turnout: a large field of candidates stirred interest in the race; the introduction of a voter-identification card with a space to be punched by election officials to indicate that the individual had cast a ballot; PRI's technical, systematic approach to mobilizing voters; the enormous outlay of money on advertising by the de la Madrid campaign, which did not flinch from using such government equipment as mobile television units; and fraud. With respect to charges of vote stealing and manipulation leveled by the opposition parties, see *Proceso*, July 12, 1982, pp. 6–10.

23. *Wall Street Journal*, September 15, 1982, p. 36.

24. *Financial Times*, August 20, 1982, p. 10.

25. *Excelsior*, September 2, 1982, p. 1-A.

26. *Latin America Weekly Report*, November 19, 1982, p. 6.

27. *Washington Post*, September 26, 1982, p. A-20.

28. *Excelsior*, August 6, 1982, pp. 1-A, 9-A, 11-A; August 18, 1982, pp. 1-A, 18-A, 30-A; and September 2, 1982, pp. 1-A, 18-A, 20-A, 28-A, 30-A.

29. *Excelsior*, September 2, 1982, p. 28-A.

30. *Wall Street Journal*, June 20, 1983, p. 31.

31. Riding, "Mixed Blessing of Mexico's Oil," p. 59.

32. William R. Cline, "Mexico's Crisis, the World's Peril," *Foreign Policy*, No. 49 (Winter 1982–83): 107.

33. A respected editor argued that the Reagan administration quietly, perhaps even illegally, transferred resources to Mexico in 1982 and 1983; see, "Mexico's Money Miracle: the Sober Truth," *Latin American Times*, No. 54 (October 1983): 9–12.

CONCLUSIONS

Smoke from dozens of sources obscures the view of influence patterns in U.S.-Mexican relations. These include Washington's past exploitation of its neighbor—a legacy reinforced when U.S. troops enter Honduras or Grenada; the readiness of Mexicans to attribute every evil imaginable to the United States, which often serves as a convenient scapegoat when problems arise at home or abroad; the escalating number of contacts on scores of issues between countless individuals and institutions on both sides of the border; the secretive character of decisionmaking below the Rio Grande, where an admission of yielding to Yankee influence is the kiss of death to a promising political career; the fragmented, desultory, and—sometimes—biased nature of news reporting about bilateral affairs; and the unwillingness of Mexicans to publicize the receipt of U.S. assistance lest they appear dependent on the colossus of the North.

These impediments aside, certain generalizations flow from this study concerning attempts by one nation to modify the other's behavior in accord with its own goals. First, deeply rooted suspicion of U.S. hegemonial ambitions finds Mexico on the defensive with regard to most initiatives. As evidenced in the GATT case, the persistent attempt by Washington to shape a policy outcome may prove self-defeating inasmuch as it strengthens the hand of individuals and organized interests in Mexico hostile to that outcome. Mexico gave mere lip service to backing the Caribbean Basin Initiative, and only through a negative action—namely, President Reagan's threatening to stay home—did Washington persuade Mexico to strike Cuba from the Cancún guest list. The sheer number of U.S. officials involved with Mexico makes it likely that, no matter how low-keyed the White House wishes to maintain relations, one or more individuals in government posts will make insensitive statements or engage in activities deemed interventionist in Mexico City. The slightest spark ignites a nationalistic flame. Mexico stimulated greater economic intercourse with other industrialized nations to minimize the extent of the perceived U.S. intervention. Yet so interlocked are the U.S. and Mexican economies that progress toward diversification was, at best, marginal, and dependence on the United States remains the most conspicuous attribute of Mexican foreign policy.

Second, Mexico's emergence as an oil power under López Portillo diminished Uncle Sam's paternalism toward it and reduced U.S. efforts to crudely manipulate Mexican decisionmaking. Not only have attitudes among U.S. elites evolved with respect to proper relations with third world countries, but concern has arisen that obtrusiveness might lead PEMEX to reduce its shipments north of the border at a time when Mexico has become the chief oil exporter to the United States. Although discretion in contacts over energy was helpful, the expansion of Mexican exports to the United States resulted mainly from contiguity and the imperative to earn foreign exchange amid deteriorating economic conditions. Nevertheless, formidable constraints on output, exacerbated by a dollar shortage in the early 1980s, means that PEMEX will supplement not supplant Mideast suppliers in the U.S. market.

Third, even though petroleum enhanced U.S. respect for, and attentiveness to, its neighbor, the lack of knowledge of the United States, hubris, and international considerations prevented Mexican leaders from wielding the oil weapon in a fashion suitable for effecting major changes in U.S. policy. Above all, Mexican presidents have failed to grasp either the limitations under which the U.S. government functions or the essentially improvisional character of its foreign policy responses and concerns. It's important to remember that the ultimate signing of a natural gas agreement in 1979 and the failure to enact the Simpson-Mazzoli bill in 1982 or 1983 sprang principally from domestic political factors in the United States.

Fourth, maladroit leadership, ill-conceived policies, and unprecedented corruption thrust Mexico into an economic crisis that was sharpened by a worldwide recession and declining oil prices. An inability to fulfill the promise of self-sustained growth coupled with incurring an $85 billion foreign debt limited Mexico's ability to exert influence, while enhancing its vulnerability to U.S. pressure—particularly for favorable oil deals and a commitment to belt-tightening austerity as decreed in an IMF-sponsored stabilization plan. Improving management of its assets, generating jobs for the 800,000 men and women who enter the work force each year, and creating opportunities for the 40 percent of the population who live in hardscrabble poverty at the base of an ever more distended social pyramid are preconditions to Mexico's becoming a more influential state. Equally important is the need to reform an ossified political system whose weaknesses were exposed and accentuated by the economic depression. The inability of the PRI to effectuate changes and create a new political equilibrium could lead to a reordering of power relations within Mexico. Such a process, fraught with uncertainty, could deflect attention from projecting influence abroad even as it enkindled greater xenophobia.

Fifth, the crisis, which converted a seller's market into one favoring buyers, appeared to perform a teaching function as Mexico abandoned seeking, in a doctrinaire and (sometimes) high-handed manner, to employ oil pricing and export policy to exert leverage over the United States and other clients. This new pragmatism, symbolized by large shipments to the U.S. strategic petroleum reserve and graceful acceptance of lower natural gas prices, was complemented by closer ties to OPEC. Such coordination, which involved limiting crude exports to prevent a plunge in world prices, helped stabilize the market, thereby earning for the country substantial goodwill among cartel members. In the event of future energy shortages, solidarity with OPEC could assure Mexico a means to assert influence in concert with other oil-endowed nations.

Sixth, lack of consensus at home toward a rigorous border policy has frustrated U.S. efforts to affect Mexico's behavior with respect to illegal immigration. In contrast, Mexicans present a cohesive front against U.S. efforts to control the flow of unlawful workers across their northern frontier. Strongly influenced by ideas of the Enlightenment, North Americans optimistically believe in the existence of solutions for virtually all problems, including unlawful immigration. Yet as Mexican-Americans grow in number, hone their political skills, and enter into coalitions, they will be an increasingly significant interest group sensitive to Mexico's goals and hostile to serious U.S. immigration reform.

Seventh, Mexico has realized greater success in influencing U.S. policy when it has acted in combination with sister republics—notably Venezuela, Colombia, Panama, and other states with democratic institutions—and when its goals coincided with those of U.S. interest groups. For instance, Mexican-encouraged opposition by certain Latin American nations, most recently manifest in the Contadora Group, somewhat restrained U.S. military involvement in Central America, a demarche increasingly unpopular in the region as well as in the United States itself. Of course, neither the opposition of Mexico nor the Contadora Group prevented the landing of U.S. forces in Grenada when the U.S. president deemed his nation's vital interests imperiled. Immigration and Central American policy vividly show the linkages between a nation's foreign and domestic interests, a phenomenon particularly striking in U.S.-Mexican affairs.

Eighth, to the extent that Mexico expands its influence with other nations, it will strengthen its bargaining capability with the United States. Establishing the Joint Oil Facility bolstered its standing with small countries of the Caribbean basin. Yet, in refusing to enter GATT, Mexico forfeited an opportunity to become the representative for less-developed nations in this important international organization, preferring instead to speak out in UNCTAD, the nonaligned movement, SELA, and other relatively impuissant organizations.

Finally, that only Washington could avert bankruptcy in its southern neighbor and cushion the shock of an austerity program revealed that, the oil boom notwithstanding, Mexico had become acutely more dependent on the United States. Self-interest informed Washington's action because of the security threat posed by a prostrate Mexico coupled with the overexposure of U.S. banks. The ties between Mexico and the United States—indeed, between Mexico and international financial institutions—meant that the nation's collapse could tumble the world economic order.

Returning to questions identified in Chapter 1 and alluded to throughout the book, the United States sedulously refrained from treating Mexico as a supplicant state. Taking advantage of its economic distress would be interpreted as an attack on Mexico's sovereignty, an affront to the honor of its president, a means to prevent the pursuit of Mexican interests throughout the region, and an assault on the country's economic viability.

How Mexico emerges from the economic crisis of the early 1980s will bear strongly on its ability to exercise influence. If after, say, two years of hardship it disregards or jettisons the austerity program and reverts to ultranationalistic attacks on the IMF, the United States, the large banks, and everyone else in sight, the country will have shown itself incapable of putting its own house in order despite the benefits accruing from economic recovery in the West. The result could be sharply deteriorating economic conditions and political unrest at home, complemented by a shrill third world foreign policy focused on Central America. The vulnerability of the large banks dictates their forbearance, but Mexico would be regarded as a Spanish-speaking pariah, and the unhealthy situation likely to arise might even give credence to those who see the inexorable march of warfare northward from Central America.

Economic chaos would enlarge the voice of the Mexican right, elements of which look sympathetically to the army, define the Central American conflict in East-West terms, and regard the United States with undisguised enthusiasm. Turmoil below the Rio Grande would also provide ammunition to right-wingers in the United States anxious for the Marines to return to the "Halls of Montezuma." Success by Guatemalan guerrillas would nourish such hawkishness. Alternatively, enduring economic sacrifices, accomplishing political reforms, and battling corruption could transform Mexico into a self-confident nation whose status as a regional, indeed a middle-level, power would be undisputed. The heightened prestige emanating from weathering the severe social and economic storm would enhance its ability to influence U.S. policy toward Central America and could even convince Washington of Mexico's appropriateness for such sensitive missions as mediating regional conflicts.

SELECTED BIBLIOGRAPHY

Alisky, Marvin. *Latin American Media: Guidance and Censorship*. Ames: Iowa State University Press, 1981.

Alvarez, Luis Echeverría. *VI Informe de Gobierno*. Mexico City: Cultura y Ciencia Política, A. C., 1976.

Beals, Carleton. *Porfirio Díaz: Dictator of Mexico*. Westport, Conn.: Greenwood Press, 1971.

Belsasso, Guido. "Undocumented Mexican Workers in the U.S.: A Mexican Perspective," *Mexico and the United States*, ed. Robert H. McBride, pp. 128–57. Englewood Cliffs, N.J.: Prentice Hall, 1981.

Brandenburg, Frank. *The Making of Modern Mexico*. Englewood Cliffs, N.J.: Prentice Hall, 1964.

Cline, Howard F. *The United States and Mexico*. New York: Atheneum, 1965.

Cornelius, Wayne A. *Mexican Migration to the United States: Causes, Consequences, and U.S. Responses*. Migration and Development Study Group, Center of International Studies. Cambridge, Mass.: Massachusetts Institute of Technology, 1978.

Couturier, Edith B. "Mexico," *Latin American Foreign Policies: An Analysis*, ed. Harold Eugene Davis, Larman C. Wilson, et al., pp. 117–35. Baltimore: Johns Hopkins University Press, 1975.

Dam, Kenneth W. *The GATT: Law and International Economic Organization*. Chicago: University of Chicago Press, 1970.

Ehrlich, Paul R., et al. *The Golden Door*. New York: Wideview Books, 1981.

Flawn, Peter T. "A Regional Perspective," *U.S. Policies Toward Mexico: Perceptions and Perspectives*, ed. Richard D. Erb and Stanley R. Ross, pp. 31–39. Washington, D.C.: American Enterprise Institute for Public Policy Research, 1979.

Garner, John Michael. "Outlook for Mexican-U.S. Trade," *Business Mexico*, ed. John H. Christman. Mexico City: American Chamber of Commerce of Mexico, 1980.

Grayson, George W. *Politics of Mexican Oil*. Pittsburgh: University of Pittsburgh Press, 1980.

Green, Mária del Rosario. "Mexico's Economic Dependence," *Mexico-United States Relations*, ed. Susan Kaufman Purcell, pp. 104–14. New York: American Academy of Political Science, 1981.

Hansen, Roger D. *The Politics of Mexican Development*. Baltimore: Johns Hopkins University Press, 1971.

Hellman, Judith Alder. *Mexico in Crisis*. New York: Holmes and Meier, 1978.

Looney, Robert E. *Mexico's Economy: A Policy Analysis with Forecasts to 1990*. Boulder, Colo.: Westview, 1978.

McShane, John F. "Emerging Regional Power: Mexico's Role in the Caribbean Basin," *Latin American Foreign Policies: Global and Regional Dimensions*, ed. Elizabeth G. Ferris and Jennie K. Lincoln. Boulder, Colo.: Westview, 1981.

Meyer, Lorenzo. *Mexico and the United States in the Oil Controversy, 1917–1942*. Austin: University of Texas Press, 1977.

Meyer, Michael C., and Sherman, William L. *The Course of Mexican History*. New York: Oxford University Press, 1979.

————. "Roots and Realities of Mexican Attitudes toward the United States: A Background Paper," *United States Relations with Mexico: Context and Content*, ed. Richard D. Erb and Stanley R. Ross, pp. 29–38. Washington: American Enterprise Institute, 1981.

Moreno, Javier López. *La reforma política en méxico*. Mexico City: Centro de Documentación Política, A. C., 1979.

Muñoz, Heraldo (ed.). *From Dependency to Development: Strategies to Overcome Underdevelopment*. Boulder, Colo.: Westview, 1981.

Ojeda, Mario. "The Negotiating Power of Oil: The Mexican Case," *U.S. Mexican Energy Relationships*, ed. Jerry R. Ladman et al. Lexington, Mass.: Lexington Books, 1981.

Paz, Octavio. "Mexico and the United States: Positions and Counterpositions," *Mexico Today*, ed. Tommie Sue Montgomery. Philadelphia: Institute for Human Study, 1982.

Perkins, Whitney T. *Constraint of Empire: The United States and Caribbean Interventions*. Westport, Conn.: Greenwood, 1981.

Philip, George. *Oil and Politics in Latin America: Nationalist Movements and State Companies*. Cambridge: Cambridge University Press, 1982.

Poitras, Guy. "Mexico's Foreign Policy in an Age of Interdependence," *Latin American Foreign Policies: Global and Regional Dimensions*, ed. Elizabeth G. Ferris and Jennie K. Lincoln. Boulder, Colo.: Westview, 1981.

Powell, Richard J. *The Mexican Petroleum Industry, 1938–1950*. New York: Russell and Russell, 1972.

Rubinstein, Alvin Z. (ed.). *Soviet and Chinese Influence in the Third World*. New York: Praeger, 1975.

Schmitt, Karl M. *Mexico and the United States, 1821–1973: Conflict and Coexistence*. New York: Wiley, 1974.

Smith, Justin H. *The War with Mexico*. 2 vols. Gloucester, Mass.: Peter Smith, 1963.

Smith, Peter H. *Mexico: The Quest for a U.S. Policy*. New York: Foreign Policy Association, n. d.

Stevens, Evelyn P. *Protest and Response in Mexico*. Cambridge, Mass.: MIT Press, 1974.

Townsend, William Cameron. *Lázaro Cárdenas, Mexican Diplomat*. Ann Arbor: George Wahr, 1952.

Velasco, S., Jesús, Agustín. *Impacts of Mexican Oil Policy on Economic and Political Developments*. Lexington, Mass.: Lexington Books, 1983.

Weinert, Richard S. "Foreign Capital in Mexico," *Mexico-United States Relations*, ed. Susan Kaufman Purcell. New York: Academy of Political Science, 1981.

Wesson, Robert. *The United States and Brazil: Limits of Influence*. New York: Praeger, 1981.

Wichtrich, Al R. "Mexican-American Commercial Relations," *Mexico and the United States*, ed. Robert H. McBride. Englewood Cliffs, N.J.: Prentice Hall, 1981.

Wilkins, Mira. *The Emergence of Multinational Enterprise: American Business Abroad from the Colonial Era to 1914*. Cambridge, Mass.: Harvard University Press, 1970.

Zoraida Vázquez, Josefina, and Lorenzo Meyer. *México frente a estados unidos: un ensayo histórico, 1776–1980*. Mexico City. El Colegio de México, 1982.

JOURNAL ARTICLES

Bagley, Bruce Michael. "Mexican Foreign Policy: The Decline of a Regional Power?" *Current History* 82, No. 488 (December 1983): 406–09, 437.

Bailey, John. "Presidency, Bureaucracy, and Administrative Reform in Mexico: The Secretariat of Programming and Budget," *Inter-American Economic Affairs* 34, No. 1 (Summer 1980): 27–59.

Bryan, Anthony T. "Mexico and the Caribbean: New Ventures into the Region," *Caribbean Review* 10, No. 3 (Summer 1981): 4–7.

Cline, William R. "Mexico's Crisis, the World's Peril," *Foreign Policy*, No. 49 (Winter 1982–83): 107–18.

"COPPPAL: An Appreciation of the Regional Political Situation," *Comercio exterior* 28, No. 5 (May 1982): 173–79.

Enders, Thomas O. "A Comprehensive Strategy for the Caribbean Basin," *Caribbean Review* 11, No. 2 (Spring 1982): 10–13.

Fagen, Richard R. "The Realities of U.S.-Mexican Relations," *Foreign Affairs* 55, No. 5 (July 1977): 685–700.

Fallows, James. "Immigration: How It's Affecting Us," *Atlantic Monthly* 252, No. 5 (November 1983): 45–106.

Gordon, David. "Mexico: A Survey," *Economist*, April 22, 1978, pp. 1–34.

Grayson, George W. "The U.S.-Mexican Natural Gas Deal and What We Can Learn from It," *Orbis* 78, No. 454 (February 1980): 53–56, 83.

———. "Oil and Politics in Mexico," *Current History* 80, No. 469 (November 1981): 379–84.

Lowenthal, Abraham F. "The Caribbean," *Wilson Quarterly* 6, No. 2 (Spring 1982): 112–41.

"Mexico's Money Miracle: the Sober Truth," *Latin American Times*, No. 54 (October 1983): 9–12.

Niering, Frank E., Jr. "Mexico: The Problems Mount," *Petroleum Economist* 49, No. 9 (July 1982): 276–77.

Pacheco, Javier A. Matus. "Elementos para evaluar la conveniencia del ingresso de Mexico al GATT," *Comercio exterior* 30, No. 2 (February 1980): 118–22.

Pastor, Robert H. "Sinking in the Caribbean Basin," *Foreign Affairs* 60, No. 4 (Summer 1982): 1038–58.

Purcell, Susan Kaufman. "Mexico-U.S. Relations: Big Initiatives Can Cause Big Problems," *Foreign Affairs* 60, No. 2 (Winter 1981–82): 379–92.

————, and Purcell, John F. H. "State and Society in Mexico: Must a Stable Polity be Institutionalized?" *World Politics* 32, No. 2 (January 1980): 194–227.

Riding, Alan. "Mixed Blessing of Mexico's Oil," *New York Times Magazine* January 11, 1981, pp. 22–25, 56, 58, 59.

Sanderson, Steven E. "Presidential Succession and Political Rationality in Mexico," *World Politics* 35, No. 3 (April 1983): 315–34.

Segal, Aaron. "The Half-Open Door," *Wilson Quarterly* 7, No. 1 (1983): 116–29.

Story, Dale. "Trade Politics in the Third World: A Case Study of the Mexican GATT Decision," *International Organization* 36, No. 4 (Fall 1982): 767–94.

Womack, John, Jr. "The Spoils of the Mexican Revolution," *Foreign Affairs* 48, No. 4 (July 1970): 677–87.

INDEX

Adams, Tom, 113
AFL-CIO, 142, 143, 155
  Executive Council of, 155, 156
  support of Simpson-Mazzoli bill, 158
Africa, Cuban adventurism in, 102
Agency for International Development
  (U.S.), 10
agrarian reform, 38
Agriculture, Department of, 10
Alemán, Miguel, 28, 31, 49
  endorsement of United Nations
    action in Korea, 31
Algeria, and natural gas, 78
aliens, draft of, 27
aliens, illegal
  apprehensions of, 52
  see also immigration, illegal
Allende Gossens, Salvador, 46, 53
Alliance for Production, 59
Alliance for Progress, 30, 113
American Chamber of Commerce in
  Mexico, 126
American Civil Liberties Union, 152
American Federation of Government
  Employees, 156
American Legion, 158
American Petroleum Institute, 65
Anaya, Toney, 164
Anderson, Annelise G., 152
anticommunism of Mexican
  government, 31
Arafat, Yasser, 48
Arbenz Guzman, Jacobo, 31
Argentina, 187
Askew, Reubin, 126, 147
Associated Press, 9
Ayutla, Revolution of, 16
Avila Comacho, Manuel, 26, 27, 28

banks, nationalization of

domestic, 185
Bartlett Díaz, Manuel, 163, 181
Bentsen, Lloyd M., 78
Black Caucus, 154
Bogota Treaty (1948), 30
Border Patrol, U.S., 139, 145, 146,
  147, 150, 160
  upgrading of, 154
border traffic, U.S.-Mexico, 136
bracero program, 141, 155
  coalition to terminate, 142
Brazil, 187
Brazilian Workers' Party, 102
Bridge of Friendship, 1
Brotherhood of Railway and Airline
  Clerks, 155
Brown, Edmund, Jr., 143
Brown Berets, 164
*Brown v. the Board of Education
  Topeka*, 163
Brzezinski, Zbigniew, 81, 188
budget deficits, increasing,
  174–175
Buendia, Manuel, 129

caciques, 20
Calhoun, John C., 15
California Agricultural Relations
  Act, 142
Calles, Plutarco Elías, 23, 28
  173
Canada, 3, 65, 114
  and natural gas, 77, 78–79
Cancun summit, 118
Cárdenas, Lázaro, 24, 25, 32, 37, 173
  Mexicanization efforts of, 29
Caribbean Basin
  and Cuba, 93–118
  Mexico and, 95–97
Caribbean Basin Initiative (CBI), 94,

ABOUT THE AUTHOR

George W. Grayson is John Marshall Professor of Government and Citizenship at the College of William and Mary, where he has taught since 1969.

In addition to this volume, he has written *The Politics of Mexican Oil*, published in 1980 by the University of Pittsburgh Press. He also has published scores of articles in newspapers, magazines, and journals, including *Foreign Policy, Orbis*, and *The Journal of Inter-American Studies and World Affairs*.

Grayson, who serves on the board of editors of *Inter-American Economic Affairs*, and as a contributing editor for the *Handbook of Latin American Studies*, lectures regularly at the National War College and the Foreign Service Institute of the Department of State. He has also appeared frequently on the "MacNeil-Lehrer Newshour."

Grayson has served in the Virginia State Legislature since 1974.